Workshop on the Future of Event Detection (FuturED 2024)

Miami, Florida, USA
15 November 2024

ISBN: 979-8-3313-0846-9

Printed from e-media with permission by:

Curran Associates, Inc.
57 Morehouse Lane
Red Hook, NY 12571

Some format issues inherent in the e-media version may also appear in this print version.

Association for Computational Linguistics
209 N. Eighth Street
Stroudsburg, Pennsylvania 18360

Phone: 1-570-476-8006
Fax: 1-570-476-0860

acl@aclweb.org

Additional copies of this publication are available from:

Curran Associates, Inc.
57 Morehouse Lane
Red Hook, NY 12571 USA
Phone: 845-758-0400
Fax: 845-758-2633
Email: curran@proceedings.com
Web: www.proceedings.com

FuturED 2024

Workshop on the Future of Event Detection

Proceedings of the Workshop

November 15, 2024

Order copies of this and other ACL proceedings from:

Association for Computational Linguistics (ACL)
317 Sidney Baker St. S
Suite 400 - 134
Kerrville, TX 78028
USA
Tel: +1-855-225-1962
acl@aclweb.org

Introduction

Welcome to the 1st Workshop on the Future of Event Detection (FuturED), held as part of the 2024 Conference on Empirical Methods in Natural Language Processing (EMNLP). Our one-day event takes place on November 15, 2024, in a hybrid format, allowing for both virtual and in-person participation in Miami, Florida.

With the exponential growth of digital data, Event Detection (ED) has become a critical challenge in Natural Language Processing and Data Mining, with key applications in areas such as early warning systems, emergency response, situational awareness, public health monitoring, and understanding societal trends. Despite recent advances in Large Language Models (LLMs) and Generative AI, ED remains a challenging problem, especially when applied across diverse domains, low-resource languages, different data modalities, finer granularities, and extensive integrations. FuturED aims to serve as a forum for discussing the latest advancements in ED research and applications, and exploring how this field will evolve over the next twenty years. The workshop emphasizes bringing together researchers from interdisciplinary fields who have approached ED from various angles, both in theory and in practice, to foster a comprehensive vision of ED's future.

We accepted seven papers to the workshop, as well as two EMNLP Findings papers, covering a wide range of topics—from specialized ED methods to broader discussions about the field's progress, from text-only data to multimodal approaches, and from static learning scenarios to dynamic social network data streams. These papers highlight the scope and depth of ongoing research, while also shedding light on the challenges and potential future directions for ED. Along with the oral presentations, FuturED features two keynote talks from Professor Heng Ji of the University of Illinois Urbana-Champaign and Dr. Lise St. Denis of the University of Colorado Boulder. Their talks will address key challenges and innovations in ED while offering a forward-looking perspective on its future, particularly in the era of LLMs and their applications across various domains.

The FuturED Organizing Committee would like to extend our sincere thanks to our keynote speakers for their inspiring talks, the authors for their valuable contributions, and the Program Committee members for their hard work. We are also grateful to the EMNLP 2024 Workshop Chairs for their support. We hope this workshop and the discussions that arise will provide valuable insights for future ED research and pave the way for further advancements in the field.

FuturED 2024 Organizers

Organizing Committee

Program Chairs

Joel Tetreault, Dataminr Inc.
Thien Huu Nguyen, University of Oregon
Hemank Lamba, Dataminr Inc.
Amanda Lee Hughes, Brigham Young University

Program Committee

Program Committee

Milad Alshomary, Leibniz Universität Hannover
Kfir Bar, Reichman University
Philip Blair, Blair Software
Elizabeth Boschee, Information Sciences Institute
Florian Boudin, Nantes University
Allaa Boutaleb, Sorbonne University / RTE France
Susan Windisch Brown, University of Colorado at Boulder
Cody Buntain, University of Maryland
Aoife Cahill, Dataminr
Tommaso Caselli, Rijksuniversiteit Groningen
David Caswell, Reynolds Journalism Institute
Nathanael Chambers, US Naval Academy
Yi-Pei Chen, The University of Tokyo
Jonathan Chen, UC Berkeley
Danilo Croce, University of Roma, Tor Vergata
Akash Dudhwal, The English and Foreign Languages University
Kevin Duh, Johns Hopkins University
Francis Ferraro, University of Maryland, Baltimore County
Mark Finlayson, FIU
Preston Fu, UC Berkeley
Guillermo Garrido, Google
Guillaume Grosjean, Réseau de Transport d'Électricité (RTE)
Sadid A. Hasan, Microsoft
Ruifang He, Tianjin University
Elvis Hsieh, UC Berkeley
I-Hung Hsu, USC Information Sciences Institute
Po Hu, Central China Normal University
Lifu Huang, Virginia Tech
Ruihong Huang, Texas A&M University
Junbo Huang, University of Hamburg
Yangfeng Ji, University of Virginia
Xiaomeng Jin, University of Illinois, Urbana Champaign
Sanjeev Kumar Karn, Siemens
Tracy Holloway King, Adobe Inc.
Udo Kruschwitz, University of Regensburg
Pasquale Lisena, EURECOM
Jian Liu, Beijing Jiaotong University
Stephanie M. Lukin, U.S. Army Research Laboratory
Cynthia Matuszek, UMBC
Margot Mieskes, University of Applied Sciences, Darmstadt
Ben Miller, Emory University
Seyedabolghasem Mirroshandel, Stony Brook University
Teruko Mitamura, Carnegie Mellon University
Roser Morante, UNED
Laurens Müter, Netherlands Police, Utrecht, the Netherlands
Minh Van Nguyen, University of Oregon

Jessica Ouyang, University of Texas at Dallas
Gabriele Pergola, University of Warwick
Jerome Picault, RTE
Thierry Poibeau, LATTICE (CNRS & ENS/PSL)
Youssra Rebboud, EURECOM, sophia antiopolis
Georg Rehm, DFKI
German Rigau, UPV/EHU
Irene Russo, ILC CNR
Ori Shapira, OriginAI
Étienne Simon, University of Oslo
Reece Suchocki, University of Colorado Boulder
Douglas Summers-Stay, U.S. Army Research Laboratory
Sara Tonelli, FBK
Samia Touileb, University of Bergen
Raphael Troncy, EURECOM
Natalia Vanetik, Shamoon College of Engineering
Erik Velldal, University of Oslo
Clare Voss, Army Research Laboratory
Sijia Wang, Virginia Tech
Qi Yan, UBC
An-Zi Yen, National Yang Ming Chiao Tung University
Pengfei Yu, Department of Computer Science, University of Illinois at Urbana-Champaign
Ke Zhang, Dataminr, inc
Hanwen Zheng, Virginia Tech
Lilja Øvrelid, Dept of Informatics, University of Oslo
Gözde Şahin, Koç University

Keynote Talk

Event Detection: Something Olde and Something New

Heng Ji
University of Illinois at Urbana Champaign (UIUC)
2024-11-15 09:15:00 – Room: **Room 1**

Abstract: When the first event detection shared task was launched at the Message Understanding Conference (MUC-5) in 1993, building a system to detect just one event type in one language took a month of development. Thirty years later, we've seen remarkable progress: modern event detection systems can identify over 3,000 event types across hundreds of languages and multiple data modalities—including text, speech, images, and video. These systems now offer much higher accuracy, coverage, and portability, all at a fraction of the original cost, pushing the boundaries of what's possible in areas like disaster management, business analytics, decision support, and beyond. While these advancements are impressive, the exciting potential lies ahead.
In this talk, I will not only revisit the key techniques that have driven event detection forward but also explore what the next decades could hold in the era of large language models (LLMs). I will propose several PhD dissertation-worthy research directions that could shape the future of event detection, such as never-ending event knowledge base construction, event-based LLM knowledge updating, corpus-level complex event detection and analysis, multimodal event detection and knowledge integration, and emerging applications in situation understanding, hypothesis generation, simulation, and predictive analytics.

Bio: Heng Ji is a professor at Siebel School of Computing and Data Science, and an affiliated faculty member at Electrical and Computer Engineering Department, Coordinated Science Laboratory, and Carl R. Woese Institute for Genomic Biology of University of Illinois Urbana-Champaign. She is an Amazon Scholar. She is the Founding Director of Amazon-Illinois Center on AI for Interactive Conversational Experiences (AICE). She received her B.A. and M. A. in Computational Linguistics from Tsinghua University, and her M.S. and Ph.D. in Computer Science from New York University. Her research interests focus on Natural Language Processing, especially on Multimedia Multilingual Information Extraction, Knowledge-enhanced Large Language Models and Vision-Language Models, and AI for Science. The awards she received include Outstanding Paper Award at ACL2024, two Outstanding Paper Awards at NAACL2024, "Young Scientist" by the World Laureates Association in 2023 and 2024, "Young Scientist" and a member of the Global Future Council on the Future of Computing by the World Economic Forum in 2016 and 2017, "Women Leaders of Conversational AI" (Class of 2023) by Project Voice, "AI's 10 to Watch" Award by IEEE Intelligent Systems in 2013, NSF CAREER award in 2009, "Best of ICDM2013" paper award, "Best of SDM2013" paper award, ACL2020 Best Demo Paper Award, NAACL2021 Best Demo Paper Award, Google Research Award in 2009 and 2014, IBM Watson Faculty Award in 2012 and 2014 and Bosch Research Award in2014-2018. She was invited to testify to the U.S. House Cybersecurity, Data Analytics, & IT Committee as an AI expert in 2023. She was invited by the Secretary of the U.S. Air Force and AFRL to join Air Force Data Analytics Expert Panel to inform the Air Force Strategy 2030, and invited to speak at the Federal Information Integrity R&D Interagency Working Group (IIRD IWG) briefing in 2023. She is the lead of many multi-institution projects and tasks, including the U.S. ARL projects on information fusion and knowledge networks construction, DARPA ECOLE MIRACLE team, DARPA KAIROS RESIN team and DARPA DEFT Tinker Bell team. She has coordinated the NIST TAC Knowledge Base Population task 2010-2020. She served as the associate editor for IEEE/ACM Transaction on Audio, Speech, and Language Processing, and the Program Committee Co-Chair of many conferences including NAACL-HLT2018 and AACL-IJCNLP2022. She was elected as the North American Chapter of the Association for Computational Linguistics (NAACL) secretary 2020-2023. Her research has been widely supported by the U.S. government agencies (DARPA, NSF, DoE, ARL, IARPA, AFRL, DHS) and industry (Amazon, Google, Bosch, IBM, Disney).

Keynote Talk

Detecting pivotal shifts during complex wildfires: hazards, incident response, community impacts and community response

Lise St. Dennis
University of Colorado Boulder
2024-11-15 14:15:00 – Room: **Room 2**

Abstract: The impacts of wildfires are intensifying in the United States due to a combination of a warming climate, policies and practices contributing to a long-term buildup of fuels on the landscape and housing practices that continue to put more people in harm's way. Teasing apart and making sense of these contributing factors poses numerous challenges for researchers, land managers, and incident management organizations struggling to assess both our current situation and viable paths forward. Recent advances in natural language and data synthesis techniques are a critical component of making sense of this critical moment in time. In this talk I will present current research as part of the CU Earth Lab Wildfire Research Team and collaboration with the USDA Forest Service Wildfire Risk Management Science Team, Human Dimensions Lab to make progress in some of the most critical areas.

Bio: Lise is a research scientist at Earth Lab responsible for the Global Social Sensing Project, a research initiative to develop datasets Earth scale related to the societal impact and societal disruption of natural hazard events for use in Earth Sciences, natural hazards research, and for real-time response applications. Lise has a multidisciplinary background in computer science, data science, human-centered design, crisis informatics, emergency response, and natural hazards research. She holds degrees in Computer Science, Human-centered computing and brings over a decade of industry software design and development experience to her academic research role. Her doctoral research focused on the challenges of integrating social media into formal emergency response and as part of this research participated in over forty emergency response activations with the Virtual Operational Support Team (VOST) community. Her current research extends that knowledge into the Earth Analytics domain, finding new methods for capturing information related to emergency response and societal impacts at scale for use in Earth sciences and natural hazards research. Related work includes development of the ICS-209-PLUS dataset: a geospatial, research grade dataset combining daily snapshots of incident response, hazard characteristics and societal impacts. Design of a neural net classifier for organizing social media for emergency response and natural hazards research. In her free time, Lise loves using her art and design skills, spending time with family and hiking in Boulder County open space with her dogs. She is still an active member of the VOST community and co-lead for the PNWVOST Team.

Table of Contents

Program

Friday, November 15, 2024

09:15 - 09:00 *Opening Remarks*

09:15 - 10:00 *Keynote by Heng Ji: Event Detection: Something Olde and Something New*

10:00 - 10:30 *Session 1*

DEGREE^2: Efficient Extraction of Multiple Events Using Language Models
Philip Blair and Kfir Bar

An Incremental Clustering Baseline for Event Detection on Twitter
Marjolaine Ray, Qi Wang, Frédérique Mélanie-Becquet, Thierry Poibeau and Béatrice Mazoyer

10:30 - 11:00 *Coffee Break*

11:00 - 12:20 *Session 2*

BERTrend: Neural Topic Modeling for Emerging Trends Detection
Allaa Boutaleb, Jerome Picault and Guillaume Grosjean

MUMOSA, Interactive Dashboard for MUlti-MOdal Situation Awareness
Stephanie M. Lukin, Shawn Bowser, Reece Suchocki, Douglas Summers-Stay, Francis Ferraro, Cynthia Matuszek and Clare Voss

A Comprehensive Survey on Document-Level Information Extraction
Hanwen Zheng, Sijia Wang and Lifu Huang

Generative Approaches to Event Extraction: Survey and Outlook
Étienne Simon, Helene Olsen, Huiling You, Samia Touileb, Lilja Øvrelid and Erik Velldal

12:20 - 14:15 *Lunch Break*

14:15 - 15:00 *Keynote by Lise Ann St. Denis: Detecting pivotal shifts during complex wildfires: hazards, incident response, community impacts and community response*

Friday, November 15, 2024 (continued)

15:00 - 15:30 *Session 3*

When and Where Did it Happen? An Encoder-Decoder Model to Identify Scenario Context
Enrique Simon, Robert Vacareanu, Salena Torres Ashton, Adarsh Pyarelal, Clayton T. Morrison and Mihai Surdeanu

Reasoning and Tools for Human-Level Forecasting
Elvis Hsieh, Preston Fu and Jonathan Chen

16:00 - 15:30 *Break*

16:00 - 16:20 *Session 4*

Grounding Partially-Defined Events in Multimodal Data
Kate Sanders, Reno Kriz, David Etter, Hannah Recknor, Alexander Martin, Cameron Carpenter, Jingyang Lin and Benjamin Van Durme

16:20 - 17:00 *Panel*

17:00 - 17:15 *Concluding Remarks*

BERTrend: Neural Topic Modeling for Emerging Trends Detection

Allaa Boutaleb
Sorbonne University | RTE France
mohamed_allaa_eddine.boutaleb@etu.sorbonne-universite.fr

Jérôme Picault
RTE France
jerome.picault@rte-france.com

Guillaume Grosjean
RTE France
guillaume.grosjean@rte-france.com

Abstract

Detecting and tracking emerging trends and weak signals in large, evolving text corpora is vital for applications such as monitoring scientific literature, managing brand reputation, surveilling critical infrastructure and more generally to any kind of text-based event detection. Existing solutions often fail to capture the nuanced context or dynamically track evolving patterns over time. BERTrend, a novel method, addresses these limitations using neural topic modeling in an online setting. It introduces a new metric to quantify topic popularity over time by considering both the number of documents and update frequency. This metric classifies topics as noise, weak, or strong signals, flagging emerging, rapidly growing topics for further investigation. Experimentation on two large real-world datasets demonstrates BERTrend's ability to accurately detect and track meaningful weak signals while filtering out noise, offering a comprehensive solution for monitoring emerging trends in large-scale, evolving text corpora. The method can also be used for retrospective analysis of past events. In addition, the use of Large Language Models together with BERTrend offers efficient means for the interpretability of trends of events.

1 Introduction

The concept of weak signals, introduced by Ansoff (1975), refers to early indicators of emerging trends that can have significant implications across various domains. These include events like shifts in public opinion in social trends, early disruptive technologies in innovation, changes in activist groups and public sentiment in politics, and potential disease outbreaks in healthcare. Monitoring and analyzing weak signals offers valuable insights for organizations, researchers, and decision-makers, aiding in informed decision-making.

Key data sources for identifying these trends include large text corpora such as news, social media, research and technology journals or reports. The challenges are: distinguishing meaningful weak signals from irrelevant noise, dealing with context ambiguity, and tracking the extended period over which weak signals may gain significance.

With advances in NLP and AI, researchers have developed various techniques to detect weak signals across different fields,including statistics-based methods, graph theory, machine learning, semantic-based approaches, and expert knowledge. However, most solutions fall short in fully addressing the challenge of detecting emerging trends (Rousseau et al., 2021), either by relying solely on keyword-based analysis, which misses contextual nuances, or by being static and unable to dynamically track evolving weak signals.

In this work, we introduce BERTrend, a novel framework for detecting and monitoring emerging trends and weak signals in large, evolving text corpora. BERTrend leverages neural topic modeling, specifically BERTopic, in an online learning setting to identify and track topic evolution over time. Its key contribution lies in dynamically classifying topics as noise, weak signals, or strong signals based on their popularity trends. The proposed metric quantifies topic popularity over time by considering both the number of documents within the topic and its update frequency, incorporating an exponentially growing decay if no updates occur for an extended period. By combining neural topic modeling with a dynamic popularity metric and adaptive classification thresholds, BERTrend provides a comprehensive solution for detecting and monitoring emerging trends in large-scale, evolving text corpora. We discuss the qualitative results on two comprehensive datasets, including the overall evolution of trends and specific case studies. Combined with Large Language Models (LLMs), the method an efficient way of interpreting the detected trends of events through various dimensions indicating how they evolve over time.

Proceedings of the Workshop on the Future of Event Detection (FuturED), pages 1–17
November 15, 2024

2 Background

Among past works about weak signals detection, many are *keyword-based*. Thus, portfolio maps, pioneered by Yoon (2012), involves constructing keyword emergence maps (KEM) and keyword issue maps (KIM) based on two key metrics: degree of visibility (DoV) that quantifies the frequency of a keyword within a document set; and degree of diffusion (DoD) that measures the document frequency of each keyword. Weak signals are identified as keywords with low frequency but high growth potential. Numerous studies, such as Park and Cho (2017), Donnelly et al. (2019), Lee and Park (2018), Roh and Choi (2020), Yoo and Won (2018), Griol-Barres et al. (2020), have extended and refined this approach with multi-word analysis, signal transformation analysis, and domain-specific applications. However KEMs and KIMs present two major drawbacks: by focusing on keywords only, they can miss the context surrounding a weak signal ; and the output is a single snapshot, which does not gives clear clues of evolution over time.

Topic modeling has emerged as a promising approach for weak signal detection, particularly in large textual datasets. Unlike general topic evolution or drift analysis, which focus on tracking changes in established topics over time, our task aims to identify early indicators of emerging trends. It emphasizes the temporal behavior and growth of small, nascent topics rather than specific content changes within established ones. Thus, Krigsholm and Riekkinen (2019) and Kim et al. (2019) apply text mining and Latent Dirichlet Allocation (LDA) (Blei et al., 2003), to identify future signals in the domain of land administration and policy research databases. Maitre et al. (2019) integrates LDA and Word2Vec to detect weak signals in weakly structured data. El Akrouchi et al. (2021) introduce furthermore two functions for deep filtering: Weakness, which measures the significance, similarity, and evolution of topics using coherence, closeness centrality, and autocorrelation metrics; and Potential Warning, which further filters the terms of the previously filtered topics to identify potential weak signals.

While traditional topic modeling methods like LDA have been useful for weak signal detection, they have notable limitations: it heavily relies on pre-set topic numbers and fails to benefit from the sophisticated, contextual embeddings provided by modern pre-trained models, resulting in less nuanced analysis. Additionally, it operates on a static basis, overlooking the crucial temporal dynamics of weak signals. RollingLDA (Rieger et al., 2021, 2022) uses a rolling window for the identification of gradual topic shifts comparing topic distributions across consecutive windows, RollingLDA can detect changes in the prominence of topics over time. The fixed number of topics is a drawback. It is rather used for long-term evolution monitoring rather than detecting weak signals; interpretability of shifts is limited to keyword comparison.

In contrast, our approach leverages dynamic, high-quality contextual embeddings from pre-trained models. Our embedding-based technique provides a richer, more adaptive analysis that does not require preset topic counts. This shift from static, keyword-based methods to dynamic, embedding-based analysis allows for a more granular and accurate tracking of the evolution and significance of weak signals over time.

3 BERTrend

In this section, we describe BERTrend (Figure 1), a method for identifying and tracking weak signals in large, evolving text corpora. It focuses on identifying emerging signals at a given moment, rather than tracking long-term topic evolution. It leverages the power of BERTopic (Grootendorst, 2022), a state-of-the-art topic model, and wraps it in an online learning framework. In this setting, new data arrives on a regular basis, allowing BERTrend to capture the dynamic evolution of topics over time. The method employs a set of metrics to characterize these topics as noise, weak signals, or strong signals based on their popularity trends. By combining the strengths of neural topic modeling with a dynamic, incremental learning approach, BERTrend enables the real-time monitoring and analysis of emerging trends and weak signals in vast, continuously growing text datasets.

BERTopic leverages pre-trained large embedding models to generate high-quality contextual embeddings of documents, enabling the discovery of meaningful and coherent topics. It utilizes HDBSCAN (McInnes et al., 2017), a hierarchical density-based clustering algorithm, which is robust to outliers and does not require the number of topics to be specified in advance, allowing the model to automatically determine the optimal number of topics based on the inherent structure of the data.

One of the key advantages of BERTopic is its

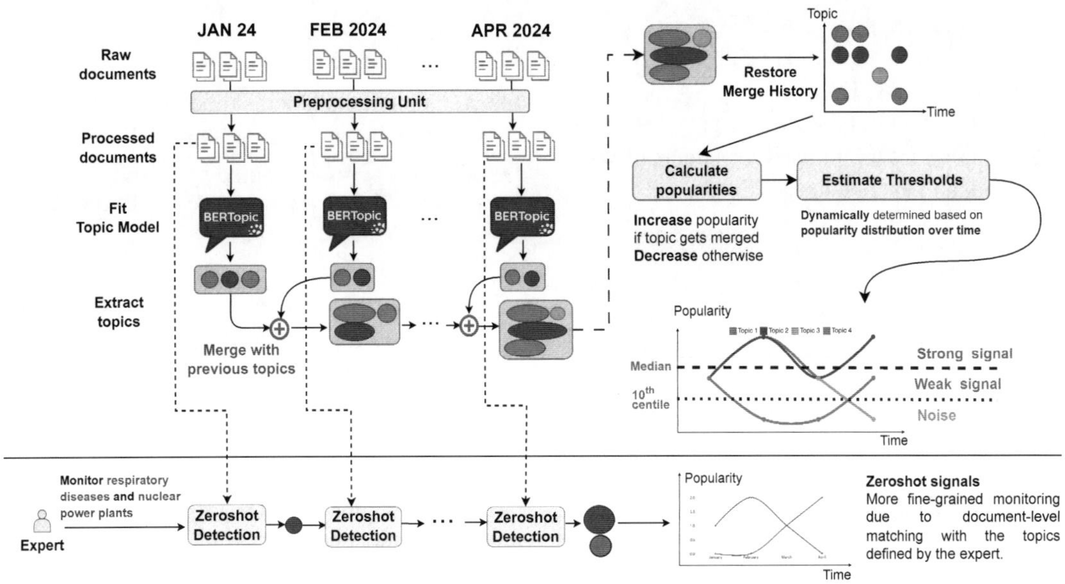

Figure 1: The BERTrend Framework processes data in time-sliced batches, undergoing preprocessing that includes unicode normalization and paragraph segmentation for very long documents. It applies a BERTopic model to extract topics for each batch, which are merged with prior batches using a similarity threshold to form a cumulative topic set. This data helps track topic popularity over time, identifying strong and weak signals based on dynamically chosen thresholds. Additionally, the framework includes a zero-shot detection feature for targeted topic monitoring, providing more fine-grained results due to document-level matching with topics defined by the expert.

ability to simulate online learning through model merging. Different BERTopic models can be fitted on documents from non-overlapping time periods and then merged together based on the pairwise cosine similarity between topics of consecutive models, enabling a form of dynamic topic modeling in an online learning setting.

3.1 Data Preprocessing and Time-based Document Slicing

To accommodate the maximum token lengths recommended by pretrained embedding models and avoid input truncation, lengthy documents are segmented into paragraphs. Each paragraph is treated as an individual document, with a mapping to its original long document source. This ensures accurate calculation of a topic's popularity over time by considering the original number of documents rather than the inflated number of paragraphs.We filter out documents that don't contain at least 100 Latin characters. This threshold was determined by analyzing the corpus of NYT and arXiv after splitting by paragraphs. Documents below this threshold often represent noise (e.g., article endings, incomplete sentences, social media references).

After preprocessing, the entire text corpus D, consisting of N documents, is divided into document slices based on a selected time granularity (e.g., daily, weekly, monthly). A document slice D_t is defined as a subset of documents from D that fall within a specific time interval $[t, t + \Delta t)$, where $t \in \{t_1, t_2, \ldots, t_M\}$, Δt is the chosen time granularity, and M is the total number of document slices. This slicing is crucial for analyzing the temporal dynamics of topics within the corpus.

3.2 Topic Extraction using BERTopic

For each document slice D_t, BERTopic extracts a set of topics $\mathcal{T}_t = \{\tau_t^1, \tau_t^2, \ldots, \tau_t^{K_t}\}$, where K_t is the number of topics in D_t. The process involves:

1. *Document Embedding*: Each document $d \in D_t$ is transformed into a dense vector $\mathbf{e}_d \in \mathbb{R}^h$ using a pre-trained sentence transformer model (Reimers and Gurevych, 2019), where h is the embedding dimension. A topic τ_t^j is described as a set of words $W_{\tau_t^j} = \{w_t^{j,1}, w_t^{j,2}, \ldots, w_t^{j,M_j}\}$, where M_j is the number of words representing the topic.

2. *Dimensionality Reduction*: The embeddings are reduced to a lower-dimensional space using UMAP (McInnes et al., 2018), resulting in reduced embeddings $\mathbf{e}'_d \in \mathbb{R}^r$, where $r < h$.

3. *Document Clustering*: The reduced embed-

dings are clustered using HDBSCAN (McInnes et al., 2017), to group semantically similar documents into clusters. Each cluster $\mathcal{C}_t^j \in \mathcal{C}_t$ is associated with a centroid embedding $\mathbf{c}_t^j \in \mathbb{R}^r$. These clusters represent preliminary groupings of documents that will later be labeled as topics.

4. *Cluster Labeling*: BERTopic assigns labels to clusters to form topics using class-based TF-IDF (c-TF-IDF), considering the frequency and specificity of words within each cluster. Various methods, including LLMs, KeyBERT, and Maximal Marginal Relevance (MMR), can be used to refine the representation of topics. In our work, we maintained the default c-TF-IDF representation without employing additional refinement methods. After labeling, each cluster ($\mathcal{C}_t^j$) becomes a topic (τ_t^j).

Algorithm 1: BERTrend Algorithm

Input: Text corpus D, retrospective window size W, time granularity G, similarity threshold τ, decay factor λ
Output: Topics $\mathcal{T}$, popularity p, signal categories S

1 Initialize $\mathcal{T} = \emptyset, p = \emptyset, S = \emptyset$;
2 $t_{\text{now}} = $ current time;
3 $t_{\text{start}} = t_{\text{now}} - W$;
4 time slices = slice data$(D, t_{\text{start}}, t_{\text{now}}, G)$;
5 **for** $D_t \in$ *time slices* **do**
6     $\mathcal{T}_t = \text{BERTopic}(D_t)$;
7   **for** $\tau_t^j \in \mathcal{T}_t$ **do**
8         $\text{sim}_{\text{max}} = \max_{\tau_t^k \in \mathcal{T}} \text{Similarity}_{cos}(\mathbf{c}_t^j, \mathbf{c}_t^k)$;
9   **if** $sim_{max} \geq \tau$ **then**
10             $k^* = \arg\max_k \text{Similarity}_{cos}(\mathbf{c}_t^j, \mathbf{c}_t^k)$;
11             $D_t^{k^*} = D_t^{k^*} \cup D_t^j$;
12             $p_t^{k^*} = p_{t-1}^{k^*} + |D_t^j|$;
13   **else**
14             $\mathcal{T} = \mathcal{T} \cup \{\tau_t^j\}$;
15             $p_t^j = |D_t^j|$;
16   **for** $\tau_t^k \in \mathcal{T}$ **do**
17   **if** $\tau_t^k \notin \mathcal{T}_t$ **then**
18             $p_t^k = p_{t-1}^k \cdot e^{-\lambda \Delta t^2}$;
19     $\mathbf{P}_{\text{all}} = \bigcup_{\tau^k \in \mathcal{T}} \{p_j^k \mid j \in [t - W + 1, t]\}$;
20     $\mathbf{P}_{\text{all}} = \text{sort}(\mathbf{P}_{\text{all}})$;
21     $P_{10} = \mathbf{P}_{\text{all}}[\lfloor 0.1 \cdot |\mathbf{P}_{\text{all}}| \rfloor]$;
22     $P_{50} = \mathbf{P}_{\text{all}}[\lfloor 0.5 \cdot |\mathbf{P}_{\text{all}}| \rfloor]$;
23   **for** $\tau_t^k \in \mathcal{T}$ **do**
24   **if** $p_t^k < P_{10}$ **then**
25             $S_t^k = $ "noise";
26   **else**
27   **if** $P_{10} \leq p_t^k \leq P_{50}$ **then**
28   **if** $slope(\{p_j^k \mid j \in [t - W + 1, t]\}) > 0$ **then**
29                     $S_t^k = $ "weak";
30   **else**
31                     $S_t^k = $ "noise";
32   **else**
33                 $S_t^k = $ "strong";

3.3 Topic Merging

BERTrend merges topics across document slices to capture their evolution. The topic merging process is formalized in Algorithm 1 (lines 10-12). For each time-based document slice D_{t+1}, the extracted topics $\mathcal{T}_{t+1}$ are compared with the topics from the previous slice $\mathcal{T}_t$ as follows:

1. *Similarity Calculation*: Compute the cosine similarity between each topic embedding $\mathbf{c}_{(t+1)}^j \in \mathcal{T}_{t+1}$ and all topic embeddings $\mathbf{c}_t^k \in \mathcal{T}_t$.
2. *Topic Matching*: If the maximum similarity between $\mathbf{c}_{(t+1)}^j$ and any $\mathbf{c}_t^k$ exceeds a threshold α (e.g., $\alpha = 0.7$), merge the topics and add the documents associated with $\tau_{(t+1)}^j$ to τ_t^k.
3. *New Topic Creation*: If the maximum similarity is below α, consider $\tau_{(t+1)}^j$ as a new topic and add it to $\mathcal{T}_t$.

To maintain topic embedding stability, the embedding of the first occurrence of a topic is retained, preventing drift and over-generalization.

3.4 Popularity Estimation

BERTrend estimates topic popularity over time and classifies them into signal categories based on popularity dynamics. The popularity of topic τ_t^k for document slice D_t is denoted as p_t^k and calculated as follows:

1. *Initial Popularity*: For a new topic τ_t^k of document slice D_t, its initial popularity is set to the number of associated documents: $p_t^k = |D_t^k|$, where D_t^k is the set of documents associated with τ_t^k at time t.
2. *Popularity Update*: For subsequent document slices $D_{t'}$ ($t' > t$):
   - If τ_t^k is merged with a topic in $\mathcal{T}_{t'}$, its popularity is incremented by the number of new documents: $p_{t'}^k = p_{t'-1}^k + |D_{t'}^k|$.
   - If τ_t^k is not merged with any topic in $\mathcal{T}_{t'}$, its popularity decays exponentially: $p_{t'}^k = p_{t'-1}^k \cdot e^{-\lambda \Delta t^2}$, where λ is a constant decay factor (e.g., $\lambda = 0.01$) and Δt is the number of days since τ^k last received an update.

3.5 Trend Classification

To classify topics into signal categories, BERTrend calculates percentiles of popularity values over a rolling window of size W. For each document slice D_t, two empirical thresholds - the 10th percentile (P_{10}) and the 50th percentile (P_{50}) of popularity values within the window $[t - W, t]$ - are computed. Trend classification is performed based on the topic's popularity p_t^k and its recent popularity trend:

- If $p_t^k < P_{10}$, τ_t^k is classified as a "noise" signal.
- If $P_{10} \leq p_t^k \leq P_{50}$:
  - If the topic's popularity has been increasing over the past few days, as determined by a positive slope of the linear regression line fitted to the topic's popularity values within the window $[t - W, t]$, τ_t^k is classified as a "weak" signal.
  - If the topic's popularity has been decreasing, as determined by a negative slope of the linear regression line, τ_t^k is classified as a "noise" signal, as it likely represents a previously popular topic that is losing relevance.
- If $p_t^k > P_{50}$, τ_t^k is classified as a "strong" signal.

BERTrend combines popularity trends with thresholds to identify emerging trends, distinguishing them from declining popular topics. This helps filter out fading "weak signals" that are actually strong but declining trends.

Using percentiles calculated dynamically over a sliding window offers several advantages:

1. *Adaptability to datasets*: The retrospective parameter allows the method to adapt to the input data's velocity and production frequency.
2. *Forget gate mechanism*: The sliding window avoids the influence of outdated signals on current threshold calculations.
3. *Robustness to outliers*: Calculating thresholds based on the popularity distribution reduces sensitivity to outlier popularities and prevents thresholds from approaching zero when many signals have faded away.

3.6 Targeted Zero-shot Topic Monitoring

BERTrend includes an optional zero-shot detection feature that allows domain experts to define a set of topics $\mathcal{Z} = \{z_1, z_2, \ldots, z_L\}$, each represented by a textual description. The embeddings of these topics and the documents in each slice D_t are calculated using the same embedding model. For each document $d \in D_t$, the cosine similarity between its embedding $\mathbf{e}_d$ and the embedding of each defined topic z_l is computed. Documents with a similarity score above a predefined low threshold β (typically 0.4-0.6) for any of the defined topics are considered relevant and included in the corresponding topic's document set $D_t^{z_l}$. The low threshold accounts for the presumed vagueness and generality of the expert-defined topics, as they have incomplete knowledge that would be supplemented by new emerging information. Finally, the popularity and trend classification for the zero-shot topics are performed in the same manner as for the automatically extracted topics, using the document sets $D_t^{z_l}$ instead of D_t^k.

4 Experimental Setup

4.1 Datasets

We selected two diverse datasets for our evaluation: the arXiv dataset, comprising scientific paper abstracts from the computer science category (cs.*) (Cornell-University, 2023), and the New York Times (NYT) news dataset (Tumanov, 2023). Our choice aligns with recommendations from Rousseau et al. (2021) and Yoon (2012), who advocate for the use of scientific articles and news sources in weak signal detection due to their rich, evolving content. The arXiv dataset spans from January 2017 to December 2023, encompassing 367,248 abstracts, while the NYT dataset covers the period from January 2019 to January 2023, including 184,811 articles. These corpora offer a wealth of interpretable topics, facilitating qualitative analysis and interpretation. Moreover, the NYT dataset has been previously employed in weak signal detection research (El Akrouchi et al., 2021), further substantiating its relevance to our study. These datasets were chosen for their diverse content and potential to contain topics that could be considered weak signals, such as early warnings about the COVID-19 pandemic.

4.2 Algorithm parameters

In our experiments, we used the BERTopic framework with carefully selected hyperparameters to optimize weak signal detection performance. We chose the "all-mpnet-base-v2" [1] sentence transformer for document embedding because of its strong performance on various natural language understanding tasks (Reimers and Gurevych, 2019).

In the UMAP dimensionality reduction step, the number of components is set to 5 (default value), and the number of neighbors to 15, which allows UMAP to balance local and global structure in the data, as lower values focus more on local structure while higher values emphasize broader patterns (McInnes et al., 2018). In the HDBSCAN clustering step, we set the minimum cluster size to 2, the smallest possible value, to detect fine-grained

[1] `https://huggingface.co/sentence-transformers/all-mpnet-base-v2`

clusters. The minimum sample size was set to 1, the smallest possible value, to reduce the likelihood of points being declared as noise, as the high number of clusters obtained reduces the need for conservative clustering (McInnes et al., 2017).

Topics were represented by top unigrams and bigrams based on their c-TF-IDF scores. To determine the optimal minimum similarity threshold for merging topics across time slices, we conducted an ablation study varying the threshold from 0.5 to 0.95. We observed that lower thresholds (0.5-0.6) led to overly broad signals and unstable behavior, characterized by a phenomenon we term "threshold collapse." In this scenario, the disproportionate merging of topics results in a few dominant signals that skew the distribution of popularity values. Consequently, the dynamically determined classification thresholds (Q1 and Q3) become volatile, potentially shifting dramatically between consecutive timestamps. This instability compromises the reliability of signal categorization.

Conversely, higher thresholds (0.8-0.95) resulted in an overabundance of micro-signals, hindering the detection of meaningful trends. A threshold of 0.7 was found to provide a balanced approach, ensuring coherence and consistency of detected topics while allowing for semantic evolution without inducing threshold instability.

We also investigated the effect of the retrospective window size, varying it from 2 to 30 days. We found that its impact on BERTrend's performance was minimal when using an appropriate merge similarity threshold. The choice of window size primarily depends on the desired amount of historical data to incorporate in threshold calculations, with larger windows providing more stable, but potentially less responsive, threshold determinations.

For the granularity of the time slices, we chose 2 and 7 days for the NYT News and arXiv datasets respectively, based on our analysis of topic evolution rates in these datasets. This selection accommodates the rapidly evolving nature of news compared to the slower pace of research papers, while maintaining a balance between signal detection sensitivity and computational efficiency.

It is important to note that these parameter choices have been fine-tuned based on the characteristics of the datasets used in this study. For datasets with significantly different topic evolution dynamics and update frequencies, these parameters may require adjustment to achieve optimal performance.

In the zero-shot example (subsection 5.4), we used a lower similarity threshold of 0.45 for merging topics to accommodate the vague and incomplete nature of the user-defined topics, allowing for a more flexible merging process. This approach maximizes the recall in detecting potentially relevant documents of weak signals.

5 Results

Quantitative results about weak signal analysis are very challenging to obtain due to the lack of established metrics and methodology as detailed in section 9.3. Therefore, as in many past works in this research area (e.g. (El Akrouchi et al., 2021), we focus on a qualitative analysis, including retrospective analysis of known outcomes, to highlight its effectiveness and potential applications.

5.1 Overall results

Figure 2 illustrates the evolution of signal type counts and topic counts in the NYT News dataset and the arXiv cs.* papers dataset We observe striking differences in the signal type distributions between these datasets, which can be attributed to the very nature of their respective domains.

In the NYT News dataset, the number of weak signals remains relatively stable over time, with a manageable quantity of 10 to 20 signals every 2 days. This is well-suited for real-time monitoring and trend detection in fast-paced news cycles, where emerging signals quickly evolve into hot topics of discussion. The occasional spikes in strong signals likely correspond to major events or trending news stories that capture significant attention.

Conversely, the arXiv cs.* papers dataset exhibits a consistently higher number of weak signals, reflecting the diverse range of emerging research topics in the computer science domain. The number of strong signals is comparatively lower, as only a subset of novel ideas and approaches eventually gain traction and become widely adopted. This aligns with the nature of scientific research, where numerous proposals emerge, but only a few ultimately make a significant impact.

Interestingly, while the number of topics per time slice in the NYT News dataset fluctuates but remains overall stable, the arXiv cs.* papers dataset shows an increasing trend in the number of topics detected per 7-day interval. This can be attributed to the exponential growth of research papers in recent years, leading to a more diverse and rapidly

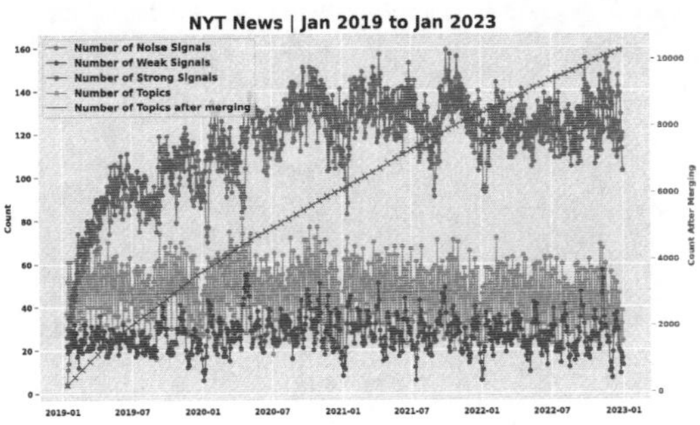

(a) NYT News dataset

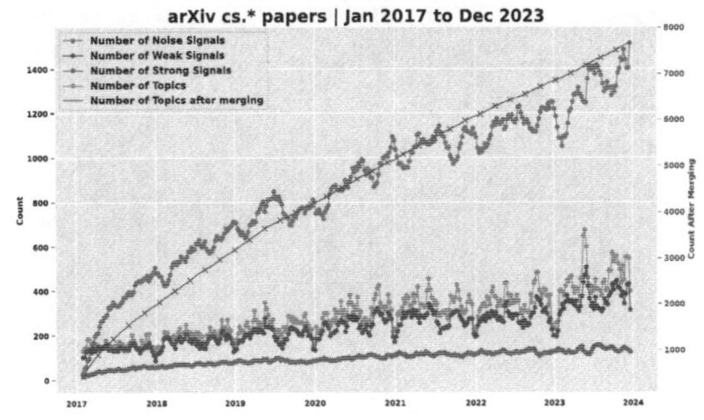

(b) arXiv cs.* dataset

Figure 2: Evolution of Signal Types and Topic Counts in the NYT News and arXiv cs.* Datasets

evolving research landscape. The total number of topics after merging (blue line) steadily increases over time in both datasets, reflecting the accumulation of new topics as the datasets grow.

5.2 Case study

In this section, we conduct a qualitative analysis of the results. We focus on a subset of illustrative topics and zoom into key periods to observe their behavior more closely. The examples are selected for their ease for interpretation.

Figure 3a focuses on the period from 01/2020 to 02/2020, when news media began reporting on the COVID-19 outbreak. We observe the appearance of a new topic (blue signal), due to its dissimilarity with pre-existing topics. Initially, the blue signal is classified as weak because of the low number of articles discussing it. Shortly after, it gains traction, transitioning from a weak to a strong signal within a matter of days, as evidenced by its exponential rise in popularity on the log-scaled y-axis. Concurrently, other strong signals during this period include topics related to the impeachment trial of President Trump (orange signal) and the Taal Volcano eruption (Philippines) in Jan 2020 (green signal), while a topic discussing American football teams (red signal) is classified as noise.

In Figure 3b, we showcase the evolution of three selected topics from the arXiv cs.* papers dataset from 06/2017 to 10/2019. The blue signal, representing attention models, was initially a weak signal before June 2017, as attention methods were being used in conjunction with recurrent networks. However, the introduction of the transformer architecture (Vaswani et al., 2017) in June 2017 marked a turning point, after which the topic quickly gained traction, transitioning into a strong signal and eventually becoming a mega-trend. This rise of transformers largely replaced RNNs (Rumelhart et al., 1986) and LSTMs (Hochreiter and Schmidhuber, 1997) (green signal) in NLP tasks, leading to a decline in the popularity of the green signal. In contrast, papers related to computer vision, especially those mentioning ImageNet (Deng et al., 2009), a widely-used dataset in computer vision, were classified as strong signals in June 2017 and continued to exhibit growth. This analysis demonstrates our method's ability to identify potentially impactful research topics early on, track their evolution, and capture the dynamics between related topics.

5.3 Impact of zero-shot Topic Modeling

Figure 4 illustrates the impact of incorporating zero-shot topic modeling in the BERTrend algorithm. In this approach, an expert defines a general topic of interest, and each document from a slice is compared against this topic using embedding similarity. Documents that surpass a certain similarity threshold are captured, allowing for targeted weak signal detection. This method enables experts to focus on specific topics of interest while offering higher precision and sensitivity in weak signal detection. By performing document-level comparisons using embeddings, the zero-shot approach minimizes the risk of missing relevant documents during the topic modeling pipeline.

In the provided example, we chose the generic zero-shot topic `"Diseases, Outbreaks, Illnesses, Viruses,"` to detect the COVID-19 signal, simulating a scenario where an expert has a general idea of what to monitor but lacks precise knowledge of an impending outbreak. Remarkably, the zero-shot method identified the earliest article in the dataset mentioning the coronavirus pandemic on January 6th, 2020, referring to it as a "pneumonia-like mysterious virus" along-

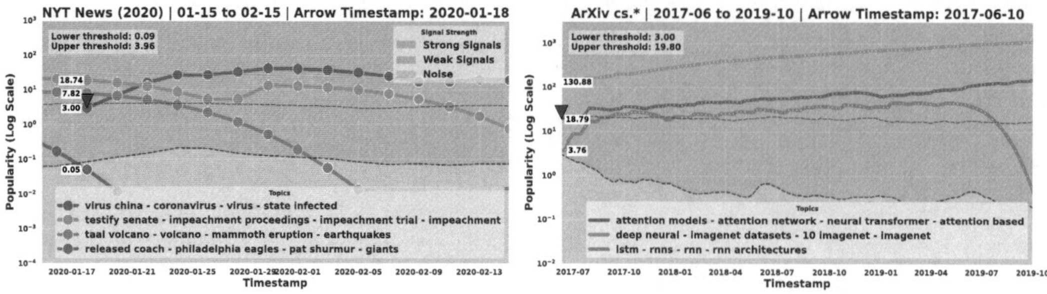

(a) NYT News dataset

(b) arXiv cs.* papers

Figure 3: Log-scaled popularity of selected topics from (a) the NYT News dataset and (b) arXiv cs.* papers.

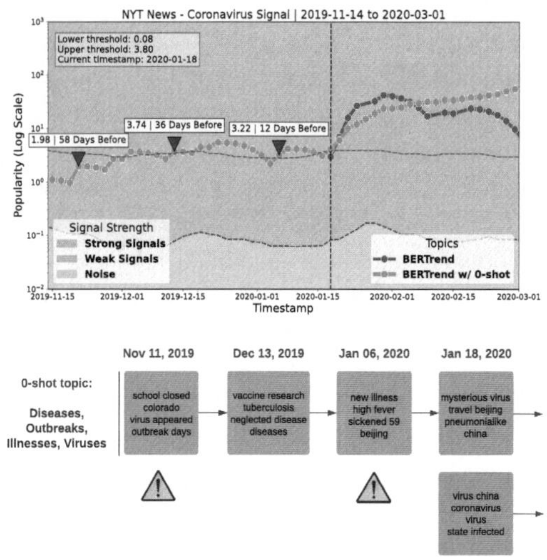

Figure 4: Comparison of COVID-19 Signal Detection with and without zero-shot Topic Modeling

side "coronavirus". This detection occurred 12 days before the automatic BERTrend usage without zero-shot. Furthermore, the zero-shot approach captured potential weak signals even earlier, such as a November 2019 article reporting school closures in Colorado due to a virus outbreak. While these signals may or may not be directly related to the pandemic, they demonstrate the method's ability to identify potentially relevant events. The consistency of the signal's growth is also notable. The automatically detected signal (blue) by BERTrend starts to decrease and becomes less stable around March 2020, not due to a loss in popularity, but because other signals discussing slightly different aspects of the pandemic begin to emerge.

6 Interpretation of trends with LLMs

Topic modeling methods often output topics as sets of keywords, which can be difficult to interpret and may not fully capture the semantic meaning of the topic (Rijcken et al., 2023; Rüdiger et al., 2022).

LLMs can be leveraged to enhance the interpretation of signals detected by BERTrend and of their evolution over time. Although this field of topic analysis through LLMs is new, it is quite promising (Kirilenko and Stepchenkova, 2024).

In this work, we go several steps further by using LLMs not only for having human-readable descriptions of topics, but also useful insights about their evolution between two timestamps, such a summary of the key developments of the event signal since previous timestamp, as well as novelty about the signal w.r.t. previous time period. In addition, we use the LLM to obtain an in-depth analysis of the signal, including: (1) impact, i.e. potential effects of this signal on various sectors, industries, and societal aspects, with both short-term and long-term implications; (2) evolution scenarios - both optimistic and pessimistic scenarios; (3) potential interactions /conflicts with other current trends; (4) drivers and inhibitors (factors/barriers related to the development of the signal. The associated prompt templates are provided in section A.2.

In the example of Figure 5, we use the GPT-4o model [2] with a temperature of 0.1 to generate insightful summaries and highlight new information at each timestamp for a weak signal related to the new Bluetongue viral disease (Catarrhal fever) affecting ruminants that appeared in France in July 2024. This example was selected for its recency to ensure it lies beyond the LLM's training data, minimizing the risk of analysis bias from the model's

[2] https://platform.openai.com/docs/models/gpt-4o

Figure 5: Enhancing Signal Interpretation and Analysis using LLMs

pre-existing knowledge..

By emphasizing new information at each timestamp through a multi-faceted description, the LLM helps to pinpoint key developments and changes within the topic. It provides a comprehensive summary of the signal's evolution, which can then be reintroduced to the LLM for further analysis, assessing its potential impact and possible outcomes.

7 Conclusion

In this paper, we introduced BERTrend, a novel framework for detecting and monitoring weak signals in large, evolving text corpora. BERTrend models the trends of topics over time and classifies them as weak signals, strong signals, or noise based on their popularity metric. The classification is performed using empirically chosen thresholds based on the distribution of topic popularities over a sliding window. The other contributions of this work include: (1) an extensive evaluation on two real-world datasets that demonstrate the effectiveness of our approach; (2) proposals to leverage LLMs to enhance the interpretation of topic evolution.

We are currently exploring LLM-generated evolving knowledge graphs as a structured method for interpreting signals. These graphs monitor topic evolution by tracking the appearance and disappearance of entities and relationships. Future work will involve exploring new datasets, integrating live data, and developing metrics to compare weak signal detection methods.

8 Software availability

In order to foster collaboration and advancement in weak signal detection, the code of BERTrend (and associated tools for visualization and LLM-based interpretation) has been open-sourced. It is available at the following URL:
`https://github.com/rte-france/BERTrend`.

9 Limitations

9.1 Hyperparameter Sensitivity

BERTrend's performance is sensitive to various hyperparameters, including BERTopic parameters, merge threshold, granularity, and retrospective period. We chose BERTopic hyperparameters to produce the most fine-grained topics since larger topics will hinder the early detection process, and weak signals will get lost as the documents that should form them are assigned either to noise topics or other large, more generalized topics. To mitigate the variability of topic embeddings due to the small number of documents per topic, we selected a low merge threshold (0.6-0.7). Granularity depends on the amount of data available per time unit and the frequency of new documents. The retrospective period affects the influence of past signals on current thresholds; we found that a period of a week to a month doesn't change thresholds significantly, but bigger changes can affect classification results. Empirically fixed thresholds (10th percentile and median) balance precision and recall.

9.2 Distinguishing Between Weak Signals and Noise

There remains the challenge of distinguishing between what's considered a weak signal and what's considered noise. Relying on temporal popularity fluctuations alone isn't ideal, as both weak and noise signals behave very similarly. There's also the issue of characterizing what would be a "weak signal," since that changes from one person to another, one domain to another, etc. This is why we added the zero-shot detection to help an expert guide the detection process. We envision exploring the effect of using named entity recognition for better filtering in future work.

9.3 Evaluation Challenges

Evaluating the effectiveness of our weak signal detection method is challenging due to many factors:

- the subjective nature of what constitutes a weak signal, since it depends on the context, the domain, and the specific goals of the analysis, making it difficult to raise a consensus even among domain experts.
- the lack of ground truth data: unlike many other natural language processing tasks, there are no widely accepted benchmark datasets or ground truth annotations specifically designed for evaluating weak signal detection. This lack of standardized benchmarks hinders the ability to objectively compare different approaches and quantify their performance.
- dynamics over time: weak signals are often transient and can grow or dissipate over time. This dynamic nature complicates the evaluation process, as the ground truth itself may change, requiring continuous monitoring and updating of the evaluation data.

To the best of our knowledge, there are currently no established metrics for comparing weak signal detection performance within large volumes of data. Traditional metrics used in evaluating topic models, such as topic coherence topic diversity, and perplexity, are not suitable for assessing weak signal detection. These metrics measure the quality and interpretability of topics over time, but they cannot determine whether a detected signal is truly a weak signal of emerging importance. Given this context, comparing BERTrend with dynamic topic models or other embedding techniques (as described in Balepur et al. (2023), Churchill and Singh (2022), Rudolph and Blei (2018), Yao et al. (2018), Meng et al. (2020), or Xu et al. (2023)) using these metrics would not provide meaningful insights into the nature of the weak signals detected. These methods and their evaluation metrics are designed for different objectives, primarily assessing topic quality and evolution over extended periods of time.

Comparing BERTrend with existing keyword-based approaches (e.g., Park and Cho (2017); Donnelly et al. (2019); Griol-Barres et al. (2020)) is not feasible due to fundamental differences in methodology and output: (1) These methods primarily use Degree of Visibility and Degree of Diffusion metrics on keyword emergence maps and keyword issue maps. Their output is a set of words indicating the presence of a weak signal, whereas BERTrend produces topic sequences over time. (2) BERTrend's dynamic, embedding-based approach captures contextual nuances that keyword-based methods often miss. As noted by Rousseau et al. (2021), "the use of a single keyword may lead to a loss of objectivity" and "the lack of relations and context over the keywords limit the information."

To address the evaluation challenge, our future work will center on a large-scale user study involving domain experts. These experts will review BERTrend's outputs at specific time instants, identifying potential weak signals in their fields.

References

H Igor Ansoff. 1975. Managing strategic surprise by response to weak signals. *California management review*, 18(2):21–33.

Nishant Balepur, Shivam Agarwal, Karthik Venkat Ramanan, Susik Yoon, Diyi Yang, and Jiawei Han. 2023. DynaMiTE: Discovering explosive topic evolutions with user guidance. In *Findings of the Association for Computational Linguistics: ACL 2023*, pages 194–217, Toronto, Canada. Association for Computational Linguistics.

David M. Blei, Andrew Y. Ng, and Michael I. Jordan. 2003. Latent dirichlet allocation. *Journal of Machine Learning Research*, 3:993–1022.

Rob Churchill and Lisa Singh. 2022. Dynamic topic-noise models fornbsp;social media. In *Advances in Knowledge Discovery and Data Mining: 26th Pacific-Asia Conference, PAKDD 2022, Chengdu, China, May 16–19, 2022, Proceedings, Part II*, page 429–443, Berlin, Heidelberg. Springer-Verlag.

Cornell-University. 2023. arxiv dataset. Accessed: 2024-06-14.

Jia Deng, Wei Dong, Richard Socher, Li-Jia Li, Kai Li, and Li Fei-Fei. 2009. Imagenet: A large-scale hierarchical image database. In *2009 IEEE conference on computer vision and pattern recognition*, pages 248–255. Ieee.

Hayoung Kim Donnelly, Yoonsun Han, Juyoung Song, and Tae Min Song. 2019. Application of social big data to identify trends of school bullying forms in south korea. *International journal of environmental research and public health*, 16(14):2596.

Manal El Akrouchi, Houda Benbrahim, and Ismail Kassou. 2021. End-to-end lda-based automatic weak signal detection in web news. *Knowledge-Based Systems*, 212:106650.

Israel Griol-Barres, Sergio Milla, Antonio Cebrián, Huaan Fan, and Jose Millet. 2020. Detecting weak signals of the future: A system implementation based on text mining and natural language processing. *Sustainability*, 12(19):7848.

Maarten Grootendorst. 2022. Bertopic: Neural topic modeling with a class-based tf-idf procedure. *arXiv preprint arXiv:2203.05794*.

Sepp Hochreiter and Jürgen Schmidhuber. 1997. Long short-term memory. *Neural computation*, 9(8):1735–1780.

Hyunuk Kim, Sang-Jin Ahn, and Woo-Sung Jung. 2019. Horizon scanning in policy research database with a probabilistic topic model. *Technological Forecasting and Social Change*, 146:588–594.

Andrei Kirilenko and Svetlana Stepchenkova. 2024. Automated topic analysis with large language models. In *Information and Communication Technologies in Tourism 2024*, pages 29–34, Cham. Springer Nature Switzerland.

Pauliina Krigsholm and Kirsikka Riekkinen. 2019. Applying text mining for identifying future signals of land administration.

Young-Joo Lee and Ji-Young Park. 2018. Identification of future signal based on the quantitative and qualitative text mining: a case study on ethical issues in artificial intelligence. *Quality & Quantity*, 52(2):653–667.

Julien Maitre, Michel Menard, Guillaume Chiron, and Alain Bouju. 2019. Détection de signaux faibles dans des masses de données faiblement structurées. *Recherche d'Information, Document et Web Sémantique*, 3(1).

Leland McInnes, John Healy, Steve Astels, et al. 2017. hdbscan: Hierarchical density based clustering. *J. Open Source Softw.*, 2(11):205.

Leland McInnes, John Healy, and James Melville. 2018. Umap: Uniform manifold approximation and projection for dimension reduction. *arXiv preprint arXiv:1802.03426*.

Yu Meng, Jiaxin Huang, Guangyuan Wang, Zihan Wang, Chao Zhang, Yu Zhang, and Jiawei Han. 2020. Discriminative topic mining via category-name guided text embedding. In *Proceedings of The Web Conference 2020*, WWW '20, page 2121–2132, New York, NY, USA. Association for Computing Machinery.

Chankook Park and Seunghyun Cho. 2017. Future sign detection in smart grids through text mining. *Energy Procedia*, 128:79–85.

Nils Reimers and Iryna Gurevych. 2019. Sentence-bert: Sentence embeddings using siamese bert-networks. *arXiv preprint arXiv:1908.10084*.

Jonas Rieger, Carsten Jentsch, and Jörg Rahnenführer. 2021. RollingLDA: An update algorithm of Latent Dirichlet Allocation to construct consistent time series from textual data. In *Findings of the Association for Computational Linguistics: EMNLP 2021*, pages 2337–2347, Punta Cana, Dominican Republic. Association for Computational Linguistics.

Jonas Rieger, Kai-Robin Lange, Jonathan Flossdorf, and Carsten Jentsch. 2022. Dynamic change detection in topics based on rolling ldas. In *Proceedings of Text2Story - Fifth Workshop on Narrative Extraction From Texts held in conjunction with the 44th European Conference on Information Retrieval (ECIR 2022), Stavanger, Norway, April 10, 2022*, volume 3117 of *CEUR Workshop Proceedings*, pages 5–13. CEUR-WS.org.

Emil Rijcken, Floortje Scheepers, Kalliopi Zervanou, Marco Spruit, Pablo Mosteiro, and Uzay Kaymak. 2023. Towards interpreting topic models with chatgpt. In *The 20th World Congress of the International Fuzzy Systems Association*.

Seungkook Roh and Jae Young Choi. 2020. Exploring signals for a nuclear future using social big data. *Sustainability*, 12(14):5563.

Pauline Rousseau, Daniel Camara, and Dimitris Kotzinos. 2021. Weak signal detection and identification in large data sets: a review of methods and applications.

Matthias Rüdiger, David Antons, Amol M Joshi, and Torsten-Oliver Salge. 2022. Topic modeling revisited: New evidence on algorithm performance and quality metrics. *Plos one*, 17(4):e0266325.

Maja Rudolph and David Blei. 2018. Dynamic embeddings for language evolution. In *Proceedings of the 2018 World Wide Web Conference*, WWW '18, page 1003–1011, Republic and Canton of Geneva, CHE. International World Wide Web Conferences Steering Committee.

David E Rumelhart, Geoffrey E Hinton, and Ronald J Williams. 1986. Learning internal representations by error propagation, parallel distributed processing, explorations in the microstructure of cognition, ed. de rumelhart and j. mcclelland. vol. 1. 1986. *Biometrika*, 71:599–607.

Alexander Tumanov. 2023. New york times articles dataset. Accessed: 2024-06-14.

Ashish Vaswani, Noam Shazeer, Niki Parmar, Jakob Uszkoreit, Llion Jones, Aidan N Gomez, Łukasz Kaiser, and Illia Polosukhin. 2017. Attention is all you need. *Advances in neural information processing systems*, 30.

Weijie Xu, Wenxiang Hu, Fanyou Wu, and Srinivasan H. Sengamedu. 2023. Detime: Diffusion-enhanced topic modeling using encoder-decoder based llm. *ArXiv*, abs/2310.15296.

Zijun Yao, Yifan Sun, Weicong Ding, Nikhil Rao, and Hui Xiong. 2018. Dynamic word embeddings for evolving semantic discovery. In *Proceedings of the Eleventh ACM International Conference on Web Search and Data Mining*, WSDM '18, page 673–681, New York, NY, USA. Association for Computing Machinery.

Sun Hi Yoo and DongKyu Won. 2018. Simulation of weak signals of nanotechnology innovation in complex system. *Sustainability*, 10(2):486.

Janghyeok Yoon. 2012. Detecting weak signals for long-term business opportunities using text mining of web news. *Expert Systems with Applications*, 39(16):12543–12550.

A Software

A.1 Some screenshots

We present in this section some screenshots (Figures 6–12) of our prototype which utilizes BERTrend to explore trends and categorize them into different types of signals, as well as using a LLM to interpret and analyze certain signals. The UI is built using Streamlit[3], and all the visualizations are done using the Plotly library[4].

A.2 Prompt examples for topic evolution analysis

This section gives some examples of the prompts we are using with a LLM (GPT-4o) to obtain detailed insights of topic evolution between two timestamps.

A.2.1 Prompt for evolving topic summary at a given timestamp

```
As an expert analyst specializing in trend analysis
and strategic foresight, your task is to provide a
comprehensive evolution summary of Topic
{topic_number}. Use only the information provided
below:

{content_summary}

Structure your analysis as follows:

For the first timestamp:

## [Concise yet impactful title capturing the
essence of the topic at this point]
### Date: [Relevant date or time frame]
### Key Developments
- [Bullet point summarizing a major development
or trend]
- [Additional bullet points as needed]

### Analysis
[2-3 sentences providing deeper insights into the
developments, their potential implications, and
their significance in the broader context of the
topic's evolution]

For all subsequent timestamps:

## [Concise yet impactful title capturing the
essence of the topic at this point]
### Date: [Relevant date or time frame]
### Key Developments
- [Bullet point summarizing a major development
or trend]
- [Additional bullet points as needed]

### Analysis
[2-3 sentences providing deeper insights into the
developments, their potential implications, and
their significance in the broader context of the
topic's evolution]

### What's New
[1-2 sentences highlighting how this period differs
from the previous one, focusing on new elements or
significant changes]

Provide your analysis using only this format, based
solely on the information given. Do not include any
```

[3]https://streamlit.io/

[4]https://plotly.com/

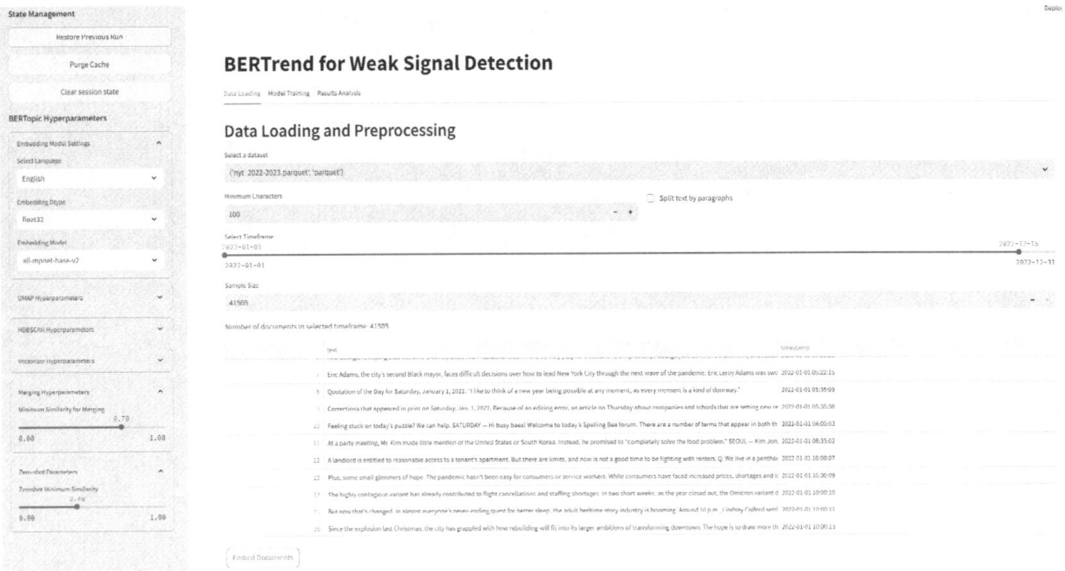

Figure 6: The BERTrend main interface allows users to configure various hyperparameters, including those for BERTopic components and merging thresholds. Users can load and filter data, split text into paragraphs, select specific timeframes, and randomly sample the data. The interface also facilitates the embedding of documents for further analysis.

```
additional summary or overview sections beyond what
is specified in this structure.
```

A.2.2 Prompt for signal analysis

```
As an elite strategic foresight analyst with
extensive expertise across multiple domains and
industries, your task is to conduct a comprehensive
evaluation of a potential signal derived from the
following topic summary:

{summary_from_first_prompt}

Leverage your knowledge and analytical skills to
provide an in-depth analysis of this signal's
potential impact and evolution:

1. Potential Impact Analysis:
   - Examine the potential effects of this signal
   on various sectors, industries, and societal
   aspects.
   - Consider both short-term and long-term
   implications.
   - Analyze possible ripple effects and
   second-order consequences.

2. Evolution Scenarios:
   - Describe potential ways this signal could
   develop or manifest in the future.
   - Consider various factors that could influence
   its trajectory.
   - Explore both optimistic and pessimistic
   scenarios.

3. Interconnections and Synergies:
   - Identify how this signal might interact with
   other current trends or emerging phenomena.
   - Discuss potential synergies or conflicts with
   existing systems or paradigms.

4. Drivers and Inhibitors:
   - Analyze factors that could accelerate or amplify
   this signal.
   - Examine potential barriers or resistances that
   might hinder its development.

Your analysis should be thorough and nuanced, going
beyond surface-level observations. Draw upon your
expertise to provide insights that capture the
complexity and potential significance of this signal.
Don't hesitate to make well-reasoned predictions
about its potential trajectory and impact.

Focus on providing a clear, insightful, and
actionable analysis that can inform strategic
decision-making and future planning.
```

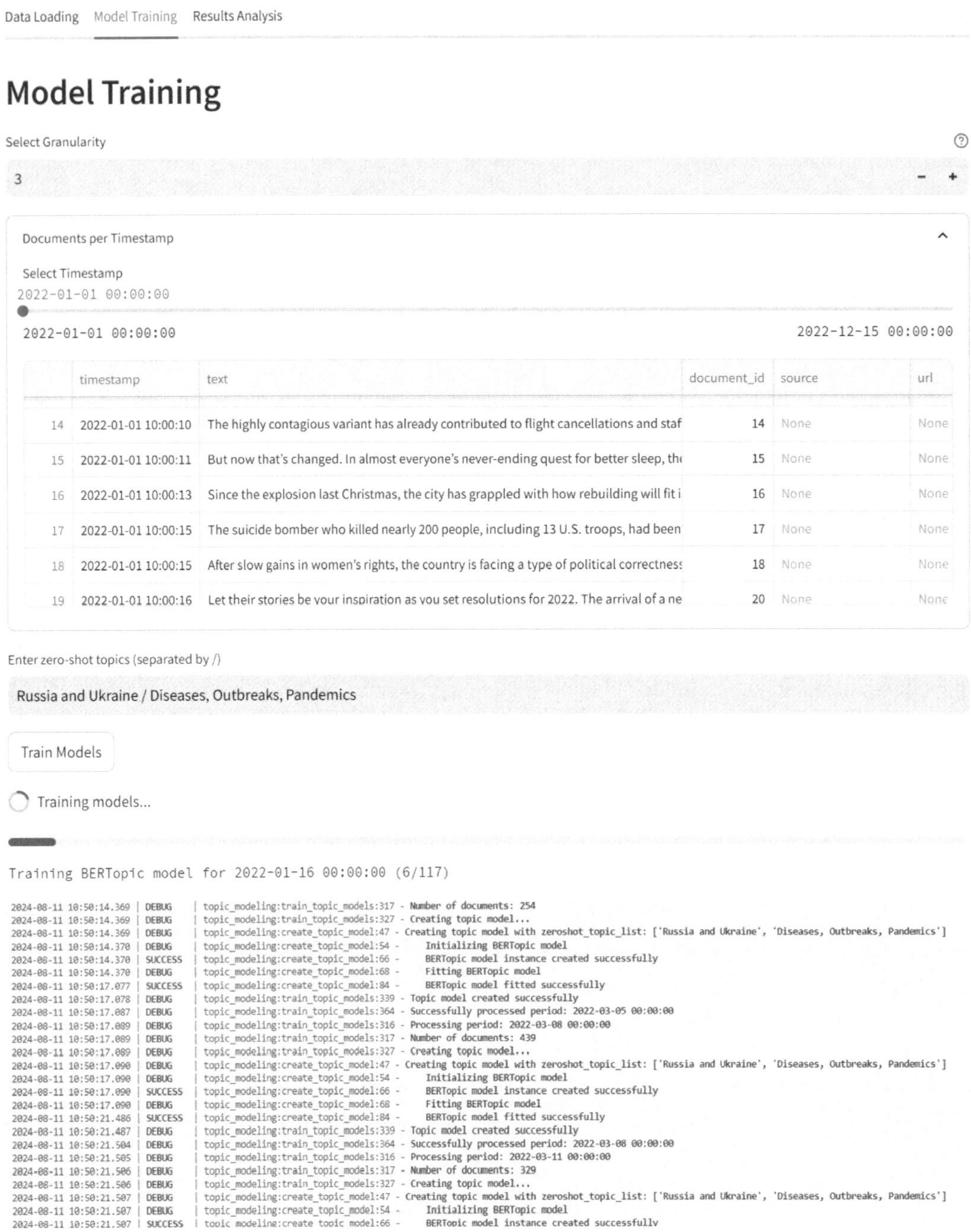

Figure 7: The model training interface enables the creation and merging of multiple BERTopic models based on the selected granularity and merging thresholds. Users can also define zero-shot topics for detection at each timestamp, providing a flexible approach to model training.

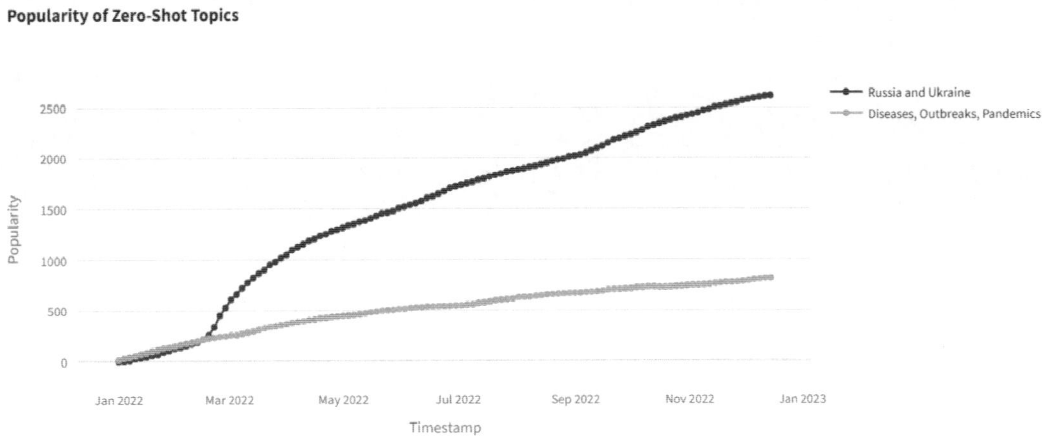

	Topic	Timestamp	Representation	Representative_Docs
111	Russia and Ukraine	2022-11-30	ukraine russia vladimir vladimir putin putin	The complaints not only are misguided but alsc
112	Russia and Ukraine	2022-12-03	ukraine russia moscow ukrainian kyiv wa	Ukraine's president called for legislation to pre
113	Russia and Ukraine	2022-12-06	ukraine russia drones war ukraine military b	The cat-and-mouse experience of Proton, a Swi
114	Russia and Ukraine	2022-12-09	ukraine russia country iran war ukraine n	U.S. officials say Moscow had been pushing for
115	Russia and Ukraine	2022-12-12	ukraine russia kyiv drones war air defens	Moscow said that Washington's plans to supply
116	Russia and Ukraine	2022-12-15	ukraine russia war putin strategy russian	Leaked emails detail how Russia's biggest state
117	Diseases, Outbreaks, Pandemics	2022-01-01	pandemic coronavirus omicron cancellations	The highly contagious variant has already cont
118	Diseases, Outbreaks, Pandemics	2022-01-04	new coronavirus omicron covid pandemic	How do we mourn everything we've lost to Co··

Figure 8: The results page showcases zero-shot topics, allowing experts to visually inspect them with ease. A searchable dataframe accompanies the visualization, enabling users to explore documents related to defined zero-shot topics across various timestamps.

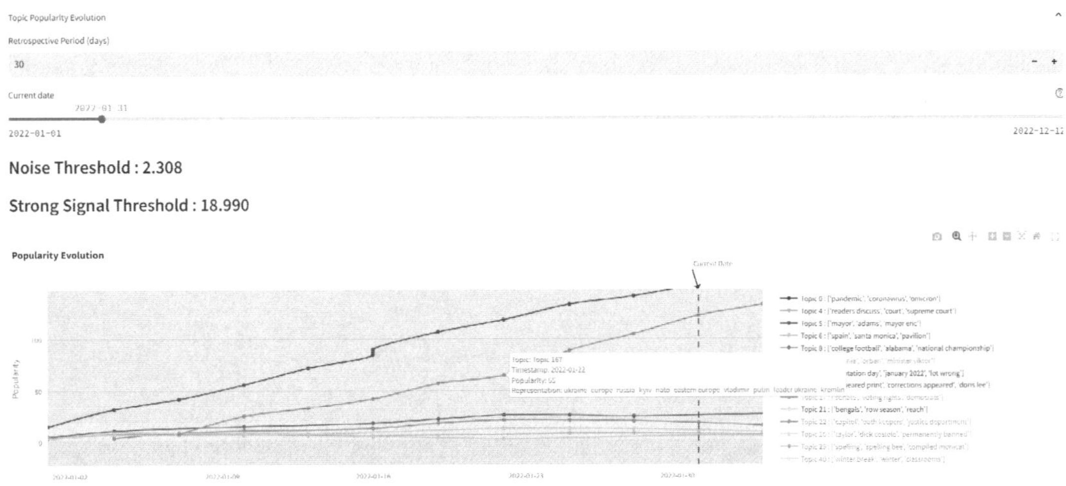

Figure 9: The core functionality of BERTrend: users can define a retrospective period and select specific dates to investigate historical data, determining what was classified as noise, weak signals, or strong signals during that timeframe.

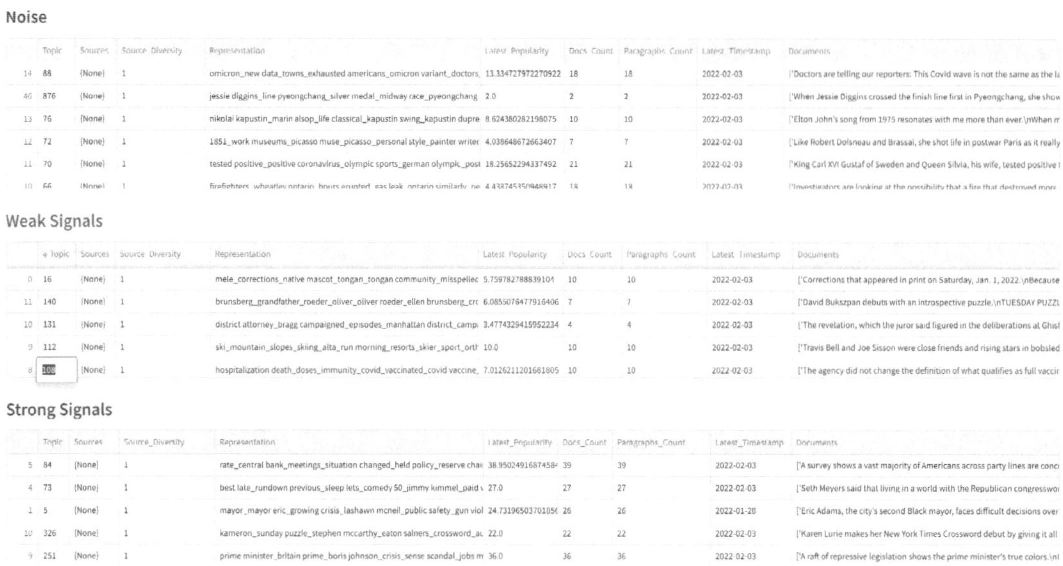

Figure 10: For each selected date, corresponding dataframes classify topics based on their popularity, categorizing them as noise, weak signals, or strong signals. Users can easily retrieve and further analyze a topic by its identifier, as demonstrated with topic number 108.

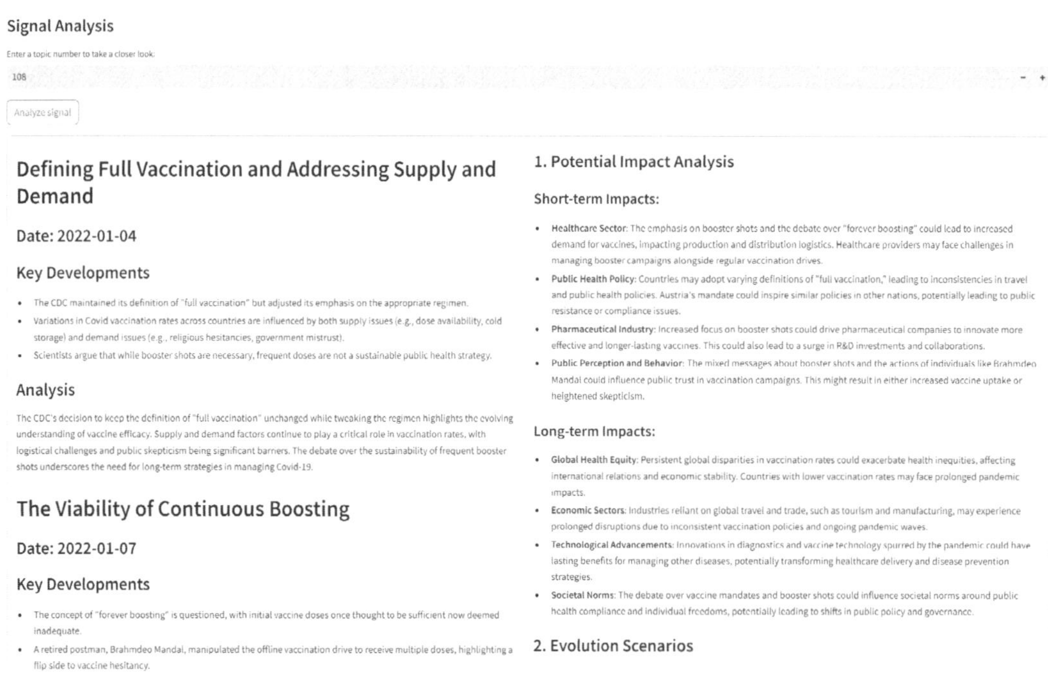

Figure 11: Upon selecting a topic identifier, an LLM generates a comprehensive analysis of the topic's evolution and its various aspects, presented in a detailed report for further examination.

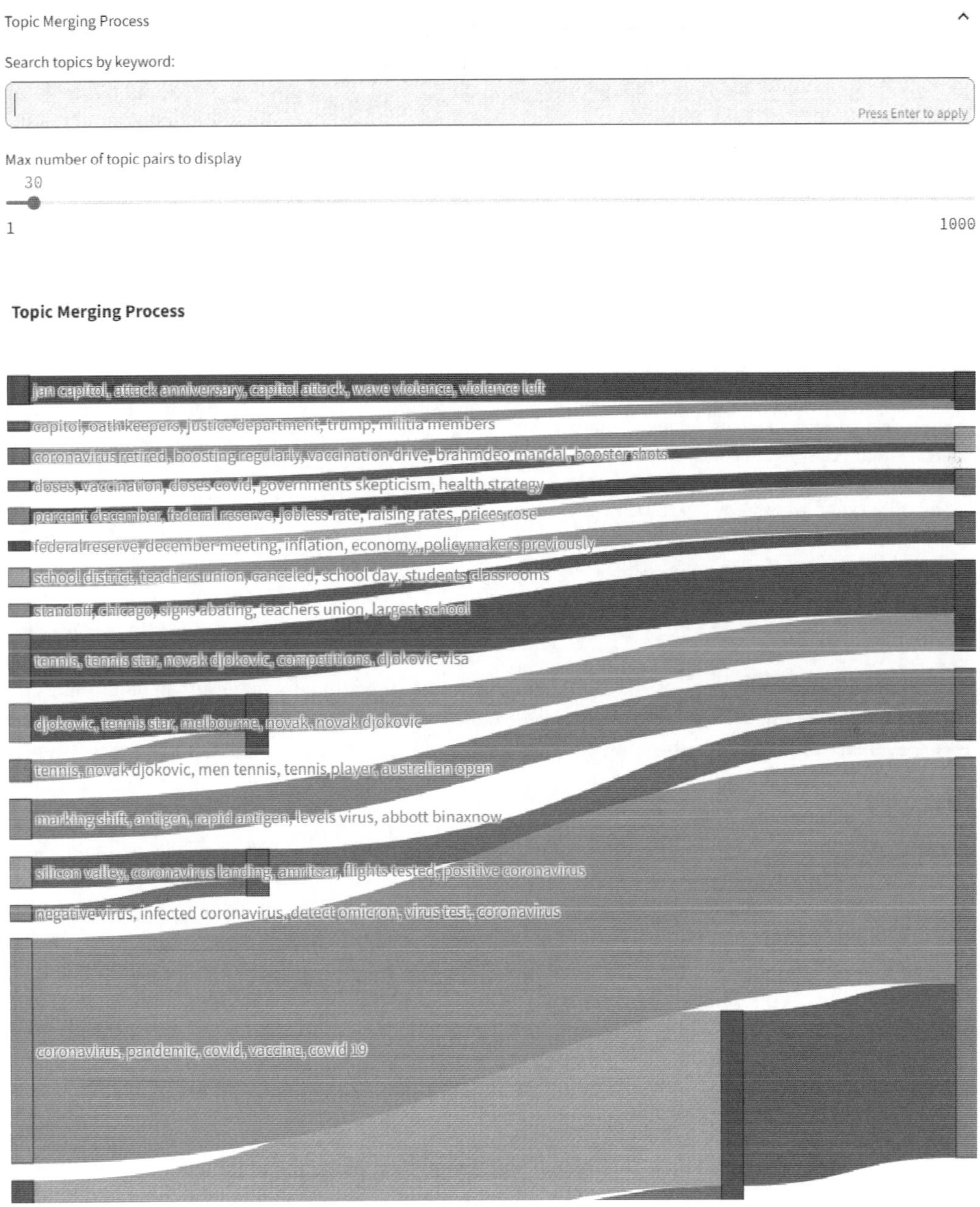

Figure 12: The topic merging process is visualized using a Sankey Diagram, providing a clear and intuitive representation of how topics were combined over time.

An Incremental Clustering Baseline for Event Detection on Twitter

Marjolaine Ray[1], Qi Wang[1], Frédérique Mélanie-Becquet[1], Thierry Poibeau[1], Béatrice Mazoyer[2]

[1]Lattice (CNRS & École normale supérieure-PSL & U. Sorbonne nouvelle), Paris, France
[2]médialab, Sciences Po, Paris, France
Correspondence: beatrice.mazoyer@sciencespo.fr

Abstract

Event detection in text streams is a crucial task for the analysis of online media and social networks. One of the current challenges in this field is establishing a performance standard while maintaining an acceptable level of computational complexity. In our study, we use an incremental clustering algorithm combined with recent advancements in sentence embeddings. Our objective is to compare our findings with previous studies, specifically those by Cao et al. (2024) and Mazoyer et al. (2020). Our results demonstrate significant improvements and could serve as a relevant baseline for future research in this area.

1 Introduction

With the development of social media, the ability to recognize events in streams of short texts—particularly tweets—has become increasingly important. This process, called event recognition, involves identifying significant occurrences within large volumes of data, posing various challenges. A key component of this task is defining a clear and operational concept of what qualifies as an event. In this paper, we will use a working definition of event, as proposed by McMinn et al. (2013). The authors propose in fact a double definition: "**Definition 1**: An event is a **significant** thing that happens at some specific time and place". This needs to be completed by the definition of what 'significant' means, so they add: "**Definition 2**: Something is significant if it may be discussed in the media. For example you may read a news article or watch a news report about it". Because this definition has been used to build other corpora, it can be considered functional. As a result, corpora created with this definition should be comparable, with different annotators likely producing similar outcomes.

One of the main challenges in event recognition is then being able to cluster different texts that refer to the same event. This difficulty arises from the wide range of expressions used to describe similar events. Different sources and users may refer to the same event using different expressions, making it essential for recognition systems to account for synonymy, paraphrasing, and other linguistic variations. Moreover, the temporal dimension is also a critical parameter in event recognition. The timing of events and the sequence in which they are reported can significantly impact the interpretation and relevance of the information extracted. Another challenge in event detection on social networks is the sheer volume of messages posted on these platforms: an effective algorithm must be capable of processing millions of tweets within a reasonable time frame. Many studies propose computationally intensive methodologies that are impractical for many real-world applications. Therefore, research in this field needs to establish baselines on publicly accessible datasets that are both performant and time-efficient.

The primary objective of this paper is thus to establish a performance standard for event detection while maintaining an acceptable level of computational complexity. Our approach involves the use of an incremental clustering algorithm enhanced by recent advancements in sentence embeddings. Specifically, we build upon the incremental clustering algorithm introduced by Mazoyer et al. (2020) in their dataset publication. While effective at the time, their approach relied on lexical descriptions that may now be outdated due to the development of new word embedding techniques, particularly those stemming from recent large language models based on the transformer architecture (Vaswani et al., 2017). In our study, we utilize Sentence-BERT (Reimers and Gurevych, 2019), a model that is especially noteworthy for its ability to encode entire sentences from individual word encodings.

The structure of the paper is as follows: First, we will review recent work in the domain. Next,

Proceedings of the Workshop on the Future of Event Detection (FuturED), pages 18–24
November 15, 2024 ©2024 Association for Computational Linguistics

we will detail our method and experiments. Finally, we will present and discuss our results, concluding with a broader discussion. We conduct experiments on two large public Twitter datasets to demonstrate the state of the art performance, efficiency, and robustness of this method (note that our code is publicly accessible[1]). We then aim to compare our results with previous studies in the field, specifically those by Cao et al. (2024) and Mazoyer et al. (2020). By leveraging these advanced sentence embeddings, we demonstrate that our implementation surpasses more recent and complex approaches in both time-efficiency and the quality of detected events. These short-text representations provide a sophisticated understanding of language and context, allowing for more accurate and nuanced event recognition.

2 Related Work

Hasan et al. (2018) conducted a comprehensive review of event detection techniques on Twitter. Like these authors, we identify three main categories of methods: 'term-interestingness-based' approaches, topic modeling, and incremental clustering. However, we expand upon their typology by adding a fourth category: graph-based approaches.

"Term-Interestingness-Based" Approaches. These methods involve monitoring terms that are probably associated with an event, often identified by a sudden increase in the frequency of certain terms. Typically, they return the top trending events on Twitter. These approaches generally do not allow the detection of low-bursty events.

Topic Modelling. Topic models are widely used techniques derived from Latent Dirichlet Allocation (LDA) (Blei et al., 2003) to uncover the thematic structure within a collection of textual documents. Several works have been interested in adapting this method to make topics evolve over time, and to adapt to the short format of tweets by restricting the number of topics associated with a document. Likhitha et al. (2019) propose a survey of topic modeling methods adapted to short texts.

Incremental Clustering. This family of methods derives from the Topic Detection and Tracking (TDT) initiative (Allan et al., 1998), aimed at identifying and following events in a stream of broadcast news stories. The task of detecting new events (First Story Detection) involves representing documents as vectors in a semantic space. Each new document is compared to existing ones (or to a set of past documents within a time-window) and if its similarity to the closest document (or centroid) falls below a defined threshold, it is identified as a new story. This methodology was then adapted to event detection on Twitter (Petrovic et al., 2010; McMinn and Jose, 2015) with tf-idf (Sparck Jones, 1972) as a vector representation of tweets. More recent works (Mazoyer et al., 2020; Qiu et al., 2021; Pradhan et al., 2024) use BERT (Devlin et al., 2019) or Sentence Transformers (Reimers and Gurevych, 2019) to produce a vector representation of tweets.

Graph-Based Approaches. These methods (Peng et al., 2022; Ren et al., 2022; Cao et al., 2024) leverage the semantic structure of social media, using anchors such as hashtags, user mentions, hyperlinks and named entities. They construct message graphs that include all candidate messages, linking those that share common attributes. The event detection task is then framed as a graph-partitioning problem.

3 Methodology

When working with social media data, one needs to consider both the textual similarity of the documents and their temporal proximity to avoid grouping together tweets posted at significantly different times. Since the number of events is not known in advance, the chosen algorithm does not require the number of events given a priori. Following the method by Mazoyer et al. (2020), we use an incremental clustering algorithm derived from the Topic Detection and Tracking (Allan et al., 1998) initiative.

Algorithm. This mini-batch First Story Detection (FSD) algorithm works as follows: documents are vectorized (we develop embedding methods in the subsequent section), sorted chronologically, and processed in batches of b documents. Each new batch is compared to a window of w previous documents in terms of cosine distance. For each batch document, if the distance to its nearest neighbor is smaller than a threshold t, it joins the same cluster as its nearest neighbor. Otherwise, the document joins a new cluster. The procedure is detailed in Algorithm 1, where δ denotes the cosine distance.

Short-Text Embeddings. In the work published by Mazoyer et al. (2020), the best performing

[1] https://github.com/medialab/twitter-incremental-clustering/

Algorithm 1: "mini-batch" FSD

input: threshold t, window size w, batch size b, corpus $C = \{d_0 \dots d_{n-1}\}$ of n documents in chronological order

output : a list T of cluster ids for each document

```
T ← [] ; i ← 0; j ← 0;
while i < n − b do
    batch = {d_i, ... d_{i+b−1}};
    do in parallel
        for document d in batch do
            if T is empty then
                cluster_id(d) ← j;
                j ← j + 1;
            else
                d_nearest ← nearest neighbor of d in T;
                if δ(d, d_nearest) < t then
                    cluster_id(d) ← cluster_id(d_nearest);
                else
                    cluster_id(d) ← j;
                    j ← j + 1;
            if |T| ≥ w;
            then
                remove first document from T
            add d to T;
    i ← i + b;
```

embedding method is a tf-idf score where the *df* (document-frequency) is computed over the entire tweet dataset (millions of tweets). Over the past five years, numerous models have emerged, particularly large language models (LLMs), which are especially suited for this task as they encode both linguistic and world knowledge, making them highly effective in capturing the nuances and complexities of event detection. We use Sentence Transformers, also known as SBERT (Reimers and Gurevych, 2019), a BERT/RoBERTa (Devlin et al., 2019; Liu et al., 2019) fine-tuning architecture using Siamese networks. This model ensures that the resulting sentence embeddings are both semantically meaningful and comparable, using cosine distance.

Time Complexity. The time complexity of the FSD algorithm is $O(nw)$ (with n the number of documents in the collection and w the number of documents in the time window), since each document in the corpus is compared only with the last w documents in chronological order. In practice, when using the "mini-batch" FSD, computation time is inversely proportional to batch size, as illustrated in Figure 1.

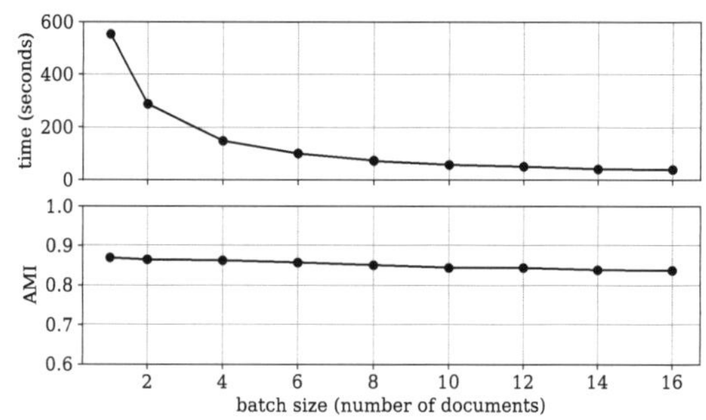

Figure 1: Evolution of execution time and adjusted mutual information (AMI) of the "mini-batch" FSD algorithm depending on batch size b on the entire Event2012 corpus (68,841 documents).

4 Experiments

Baselines. We compare our results (**FSD-SBERT**) with HISEvent[2] (**HE**), the most recent paper on event detection: Cao et al.'s (2024) work on the partition of a graphical neural network representation of tweets using structural entropy minimization. We also evaluate the performance improvement achieved by using Sentence Transformers in

[2]https://github.com/SELGroup/HISEvent

comparison to the tf-idf vectors used in (**TW**)[3] by Mazoyer et al. (2020).

Datasets. We conducted experiments using two extensive, publicly accessible tweets datasets: Event2012 (McMinn et al., 2013) and Event2018 (Mazoyer et al., 2020). The Event2012 dataset contains 150,000 English tweet IDs related to 506 distinct events over a four-week period. In contrast, Event2018 comprises 96,000 French tweet IDs corresponding to 257 unique events, all posted within a span of 23 days. For a fair comparison with baseline methods, we limit our analysis to the subset of the dataset used by Cao et al. (2024). Indeed, these authors downloaded the tweets recently after many were deleted. Their dataset, therefore, contains 68,841 tweets related to 503 events for Event2012 and 64,516 tweets related to 257 events for Event2018. We do not use the distinction adopted by Cao et al. (2024) between open-set (day-by-day detection) and closed-set (detection across the entire corpus), as we argue that events should be allowed to span multiple consecutive days. Therefore, we only evaluate our method on the complete corpus.

Short-Text Embeddings. We use Sentence Transformers (SBERT) models pre-trained on English and French corpora to compute vectors from tweets. Specifically, we use **all-mpnet-base-v2**[4] for the English dataset and **Sentence-CamemBERT-Large**[5] (Martin et al., 2020) for the French dataset.

Parameters. The mini-batch FSD algorithm takes three input parameters: the cosine distance threshold (t), the time-window size (w) and the batch-size (b). Consistently with Mazoyer et al. (2020), we set w to the average number of documents per day in each dataset, and the batch size to 8 documents. The threshold t depends on the type of text-embedding. It was optimized using grid-search and set to 0.5 for English and 0.55 for French.

Evaluation Metrics. We use the scikit-learn (Pedregosa et al., 2011) implementation of adjusted mutual information (AMI) (Vinh et al., 2009) and adjusted rand index (ARI) (Rand, 1971), which are widely employed in event detection evaluation (Cao et al., 2024).

dataset		FSD-SBERT	HE	TW
2012	**ARI**	**0.63**	0.50	0.39
	AMI	**0.86**	0.81	0.82
2018	**ARI**	**0.55**	0.44	0.25
	AMI	**0.81**	0.66	0.72

Table 1: ARI and AMI scores on two datasets: Event2012 (in English) and Event2018 (in French).

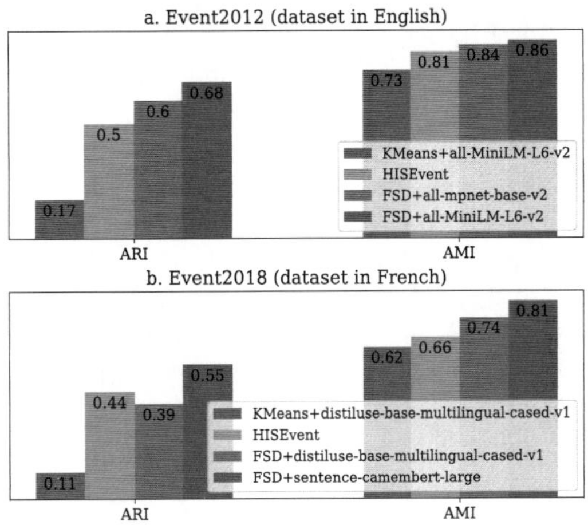

Figure 2: ARI and AMI scores with different SBERT models and different clustering algorithms. All FSD tests ran with $b = 8$ and $t = 0.55$.

5 Results and Discussion

Performance. Table 1 compares the performance of our method (**FSD-SBERT**) with **HE** and **TW**. We observe that Mazoyer et al.'s (2020) mini-batch FSD algorithm combined with Sentence Transformers pre-trained on large text corpora consistently outperforms the baselines on both datasets. The comparison between HISEvent (HE) and twembeddings (TW) seems to indicate that the mini-batch First Story Detection algorithm, even used with a simple tf-idf representation of tweets, is still a strong baseline, since its performance is comparable (and even superior on the French dataset) to HISEvent when using AMI as the indicator, though it is inferior when evaluated with ARI.

It is important to note that Cao et al. (2024) also use Sentence Transformers as a baseline in their article, with a different clustering algorithm (K-means). Their results are represented as the first

[3] https://github.com/ina-foss/twembeddings

[4] https://huggingface.co/sentence-transformers/all-mpnet-base-v2

[5] https://huggingface.co/dangvantuan/sentence-camembert-large

column in Figure 2, with the exact SBERT models they have used ("all-MiniLM-L6-v2"[6] for English and "distiluse-base-multilingual-cased-v1"[7] for French). Our experiments show that the type of SBERT model has an effect on performance: as shown on Figure 2 b, the "multilingual" model is less efficient for French than the language-specific "CamemBERT" model. Nevertheless, regardless of the model used, the FSD algorithm (see the last two columns) is much more efficient than the K-means for both datasets. This gap is explained by the fact that the FSD algorithm is able to take into account the temporality of tweets (by applying a sliding time window when searching for nearest neighbors) unlike the K-means. Moreover, FSD seems to be robust to changes in SBERT models without the need to adapt the parameters: on Figure 2, when using FSD, the same threshold $t = 0.55$ is used for all SBERT models. This common threshold explains the small difference between the values in Table 1 and Figure 2 for the all-mpnet-base-v2 model, since the threshold is set to 0.5 in Table 1 and to 0.55 in Figure 2.

Time efficiency. Increasing the batch size is a way to increase the computation speed with minimal loss in clustering performance: as shown in Figure 1, doubling the batch size only decreases the performance (measured by AMI) by 0.5%. This is why our experiments were all run with a batch size (b) set to 8 documents. With these parameters, our algorithm processes the Event2012 corpus, consisting of 68,841 documents (with a window size w of 2,368 documents), in 72 seconds. In contrast, HISEvent requires 1 hour and 45 minutes to process a block of 8,722 documents, and over 5 days to handle the entire corpus.

The experiments shown on Figure 1 were run on a notebook PC with 32GB of RAM and and 8 2.4GHz CPUs. Note that these tests do not take into account the encoding of the tweets using Sentence Transformers, since we computed the embeddings only once on a GPU server and then stored them to be re-used for further experiments on a notebook computer without GPU. It took 65 seconds using a NVIDIA RTX A4500 GPU to encode the Event2012 corpus, and 240 seconds to encode the Event2018 corpus.

[6]https://huggingface.co/sentence-transformers/all-MiniLM-L6-v2

[7]https://huggingface.co/sentence-transformers/distiluse-base-multilingual-cased-v1

Resources. We observed that executing HISEvent on the entire Event2012 dataset required substantial memory resources, exceeding 62 GB of RAM. In contrast, FSD operates with significantly lower memory requirements (less than 32GB of RAM).

Limitations. Twitter has been an invaluable resource for research on social media and real-time data streams. However, this is no longer possible due to the platform's API restrictions. Nevertheless, we believe this study remains relevant, as other data streams and social networks continue to produce valuable data, and event recognition continues to be a crucial task.

Another limitation related to the mini-batch FSD algorithm is the need to pre-determine the hyperparameter t. However, the consistency of the results with the same t value across several SBERT models (see Figure 2) suggests that this threshold $(t = 0.55)$ could be appliced to other Sentence Transformers models pre-trained on corpora in different languages.

Finally, a potential improvement for this method would be to better account for the nested nature of events in public discourse: for instance, a major political event might consist of numerous smaller sub-events, such as speeches, protests, and negotiations (for example the Yellow Vest protest in France lasted several months, with protests every week, discussions with the government, thousands of declarations, actors and reactions (Wagner-Egger et al., 2022). Each of these sub-events can be reported separately (or not) in different messages. This layered structure would ideally necessitate more sophisticated models capable of capturing and integrating these various components to provide a coherent and comprehensive understanding of the overall event.

6 Conclusion

In this study, we aimed to investigate the performance of incremental clustering combined with Sentence Transformers models for automatically detecting events in a stream of tweets. Our results demonstrated that applying the mini-batch FSD algorithm to SBERT representations significantly improves event detection performance on Twitter. We suggest that future research in this area should adopt this straightforward approach as a baseline for deploying more complex algorithms.

Acknowledgements

This work was funded in part by the Agence Nationale de la Recherche, as part of the ANR Medialex Project (AAPG 2021). Thierry Poibeau is also funded by the "Investissements d'avenir" program, reference ANR-19-P3IA-0001 (PRAIRIE 3IA Institute).

References

James Allan, Jaime Carbonell, George Doddington, Jonathan Yamron, and Yiming Yang. 1998. *Topic detection and tracking pilot study final report.* Carnegie Mellon University.

David M Blei, Andrew Y Ng, and Michael I Jordan. 2003. Latent dirichlet allocation. *Journal of machine Learning research*, 3(Jan):993–1022.

Yuwei Cao, Hao Peng, Zhengtao Yu, and Philip S. Yu. 2024. Hierarchical and incremental structural entropy minimization for unsupervised social event detection. *Proceedings of the AAAI Conference on Artificial Intelligence*, 38(8):8255–8264. Number: 8.

Jacob Devlin, Ming-Wei Chang, Kenton Lee, and Kristina Toutanova. 2019. Bert: Pre-training of deep bidirectional transformers for language understanding. In *Proceedings of the 2019 Conference of the North American Chapter of the Association for Computational Linguistics: Human Language Technologies, Volume 1 (Long and Short Papers)*, pages 4171–4186.

Mahmud Hasan, Mehmet A Orgun, and Rolf Schwitter. 2018. A survey on real-time event detection from the twitter data stream. *Journal of Information Science*, 44(4):443–463.

S Likhitha, BS Harish, and HM Keerthi Kumar. 2019. A detailed survey on topic modeling for document and short text data. *International Journal of Computer Applications*, 178(39):1–9.

Yinhan Liu, Myle Ott, Naman Goyal, Jingfei Du, Mandar Joshi, Danqi Chen, Omer Levy, Mike Lewis, Luke Zettlemoyer, and Veselin Stoyanov. 2019. Roberta: A robustly optimized bert pretraining approach. *arXiv preprint arXiv:1907.11692*.

Louis Martin, Benjamin Muller, Pedro Javier Ortiz Suárez, Yoann Dupont, Laurent Romary, Éric Villemonte de la Clergerie, Djamé Seddah, and Benoît Sagot. 2020. Camembert: a tasty french language model. *Proceedings of the 58th Annual Meeting of the Association for Computational Linguistics*.

Béatrice Mazoyer, Julia Cagé, Nicolas Hervé, and Céline Hudelot. 2020. A french corpus for event detection on twitter. In *Proceedings of the Twelfth Language Resources and Evaluation Conference*, page 6220. European Language Resources Association (ELRA).

Andrew J McMinn and Joemon M Jose. 2015. Realtime entity-based event detection for twitter. In *Experimental IR Meets Multilinguality, Multimodality, and Interaction: 6th International Conference of the CLEF Association, CLEF'15, Toulouse, France, September 8-11, 2015, Proceedings 6*, pages 65–77. Springer.

Andrew J. McMinn, Yashar Moshfeghi, and Joemon M. Jose. 2013. Building a large-scale corpus for evaluating event detection on twitter. In *Proceedings of the 22nd ACM international conference on Information & Knowledge Management*, pages 409–418. ACM Press.

Fabian Pedregosa, Gael Varoquaux, Alexandre Gramfort, Vincent Michel, B. Thirion, O. Grisel, M. Blondel, P. Prettenhofer, R. Weiss, V. Dubourg, J. Vanderplas, A. Passos, D. Cournapeau, M. Brucher, M. Perrot, and E. Duchesnay. 2011. Scikit-learn: Machine learning in Python. *Journal of Machine Learning Research*, 12:2825–2830.

Hao Peng, Ruitong Zhang, Shaoning Li, Yuwei Cao, Shirui Pan, and S Yu Philip. 2022. Reinforced, incremental and cross-lingual event detection from social messages. *IEEE Transactions on Pattern Analysis and Machine Intelligence*, 45(1):980–998.

Sasa Petrovic, Miles Osborne, and Victor Lavrenko. 2010. Streaming first story detection with application to twitter. In *Human Language Technologies: The 2010 Annual Conference of the North American Chapter of the Association for Computational Linguistics (HLT'10)*, pages 181–189. Association for Computational Linguistics.

Abhaya Kumar Pradhan, Hrushikesha Mohanty, and Rajendra Prasad Lal. 2024. EDTBERT: Event detection and tracking in twitter using graph clustering and pretrained language model. *Procedia Computer Science*, 233:481–491.

Xingfa Qiu, Qiaosha Zou, and C. J. Richard Shi. 2021. Single-pass on-line event detection in twitter streams. In *2021 13th International Conference on Machine Learning and Computing*, pages 522–529. ACM.

William M Rand. 1971. Objective criteria for the evaluation of clustering methods. *Journal of the American Statistical association*, 66(336):846–850.

Nils Reimers and Iryna Gurevych. 2019. Sentence-bert: Sentence embeddings using siamese bert-networks. In *Proceedings of the 2019 Conference on Empirical Methods in Natural Language Processing*.

Jiaqian Ren, Lei Jiang, Hao Peng, Yuwei Cao, Jia Wu, Philip S Yu, and Lifang He. 2022. From known to unknown: Quality-aware self-improving graph neural network for open set social event detection. In *Proceedings of the 31st ACM International Conference on Information & Knowledge Management*, pages 1696–1705.

Karen Sparck Jones. 1972. A statistical interpretation of term specificity and its application in retrieval. *Journal of documentation*, 28(1):11–21.

Ashish Vaswani, Noam Shazeer, Niki Parmar, Jakob Uszkoreit, Llion Jones, Aidan N Gomez, Łukasz Kaiser, and Illia Polosukhin. 2017. Attention is all you need. *Advances in neural information processing systems*, 30.

Nguyen Xuan Vinh, Julien Epps, and James Bailey. 2009. Information theoretic measures for clusterings comparison: is a correction for chance necessary? In *Proceedings of the 26th annual international conference on machine learning*, pages 1073–1080.

Pascal Wagner-Egger, Pascal Adam-Troian, Laurent Cordonier, Florian Cafiero, and Gérald Bronner. 2022. The Yellow Vests in France: Psychosocial Determinants and Consequences of the Adherence to a Social Movement in a Representative Sample of the Population. *International review of social psychology*, 35(1).

DEGREE^2: Efficient Extraction of Multiple Events Using Language Models

Philip Blair[1,2] and **Kfir Bar**[1]

[1]Babel Street, Reston, VA, USA*
[2]Blair Software, Amsterdam, The Netherlands
{pblair,kbar}@babelstreet.com

Abstract

Language models (LMs) show exceptional promise in the area of few-shot event extraction, but they suffer from certain limitations. In particular, DEGREE (Hsu et al., 2022) is an LM-based event extraction model that has recently been supplanted by other large language model-based state-of-the-art systems, but it suffers from an inability to cope with multiple events in the same region of an input document. In this work, we present a simple method for extending this system with the ability to gracefully handle different densities of events within documents, thereby rendering it competitive with the state-of-the-art once more, and additionally explore a novel evaluation metric that can be used to qualitatively compare the outputs of different event extraction systems. Finally, we show that our extension allows models to break apart documents into less small pieces during processing without sacrificing accuracy.

```
John met with Alice and then Steve.
[...template...]
Event trigger is met.
John and Alice met at some place.
```

(a) Sample ACE2005 `Contact:Meet` completed prompt from DEGREE.

```
John met with Alice and then Steve.
[...template...]
<EVENTSEP>Event trigger is met.
John and Alice met at some place.
<EVENTSEP>Event trigger is met.
John and Steve met at some place.
```

(b) Our version of the equivalent completed prompt.

Figure 1: Fine-tuning prompts used in our work compared to DEGREE (Hsu et al., 2022). Text in **blue** denotes the input text to perform the event detection on. `[...template...]` represents the input template (Section 3), with the following text being the expected generation of the Large Language Model (LLM). Text in violet denotes the trigger phrase, teal the event participants, and magenta the event location. Finally, orange text denotes special tokens added to the model vocabulary. At inference time, the LLM generates text after the input source portion.

1 Introduction

In the domain of information extraction (IE), event extraction is a task consisting of identifying specific occurrences of things which happen involving participants (LDC, 2005). This task poses a number of unique challenges for information extraction systems, as proper detection of events typically requires an in-depth understanding of the semantics of input sentences, as opposed to simple lexical information. For example, the sentence "John went to San Antonio" denotes a `Movement:Transport`-type event, whereas the sentence "The first point went to San Antonio" does not.

The bulk of the literature on event extraction descends from the original ACE2005 information extraction dataset published by the Linguistic Data Consortium (LDC, 2005). Notably, this decomposes the event extraction task into two subtasks: *event detection* (also known as *trigger extraction*) and *argument extraction*. For example, in the sentence "John met with Alice", "met" is the *trigger* (the phrase which clearly expresses the occurrence of the event), while "John" and "Alice" are the *arguments* of the event. Arguments can have a number of different event-specific types, such as meeting participants, locations, and relevant actors (e.g. the victim of a crime).

Supervised machine learning is a natural choice for modeling this problem, but the drawback of these approaches is that such training generally requires a large quantity of annotated data due to the need to understand the semantic nuances of text when performing this task. Anecdotally, this can be prohibitive in a number of real-world ap-

*Research conducted at Babel Street.

Proceedings of the Workshop on the Future of Event Detection (FuturED), pages 25–31
November 15, 2024 ©2024 Association for Computational Linguistics

plications of event extraction systems, due to the fact that downstream users often (a) require a diverse set of event types and (b) these event types are many times unique to their use case (preventing useful sharing of annotated datasets between different users).

With the advent of powerful language models and Large Language Models (LLMs) (Brown et al., 2020; OpenAI, 2024), a number of novel low-resource and zero-shot methods have been developed which leverage these models' abilities to be fine-tuned to new tasks with relatively little data. One such model, known as DEGREE (Hsu et al., 2022), was until recently considered the state of the art in few-shot event extraction until being supplanted by the EE-LCE (Yu et al., 2024) model. While this would suggest a superior method for fine-tuning LLMs for event extraction, we find that this performance gap can be explained away by controlling for a specific limitation of the DEGREE model: its inability to extract more than one event from the same region of text.

In summary, our contributions are as follows:

1. We present a simple extension of the DEGREE event extraction system which allows it to extract multiple events from the same piece of text.

2. We demonstrate that this extension makes DEGREE competitive with the state-of-the-art generative event extraction model.

3. We describe a novel E2E event extraction evaluation metric which can be used to qualitatively compare model performance irrespective of whether they handle multiple events.

2 Related Work

The bulk of research into event extraction focuses on high-resource scenarios, with models based on traditional supervised machine learning techniques. Examples of this include techniques based on decision trees (Ahn, 2006), support vector machines (Hong et al., 2011), convolutional neural networks (Nguyen and Grishman, 2015), recurrent neural networks (Nguyen et al., 2016), and graph convolutional neural networks (Nguyen and Grishman, 2018). Broadly speaking, all of these approaches are based on the idea of training a machine learning algorithm from scratch to recognize event triggers and arguments using features which are either hand-crafted or, in the case of the neural network-based algorithms, automatically learned.

More recent approaches to event extraction leverage language models. The basic idea of these techniques is to leverage the natural language modeling capacity of pretrained language models in order to reduce training data requirements via posing event extraction as a text-based natural language generation task. Consequently, these techniques focus more on few-shot and zero-shot learning scenarios. The state-of-the-art in this space is EE-LCE (Yu et al., 2024), which is an extension of InstructUIE (Wang et al., 2023). These `flan-t5-xxl`-based (Chung et al., 2022) models are trained via a multi-task learning algorithm designed to cover a large number of information extraction tasks. Their results slightly beat out the previous state-of-the-art, known as DEGREE (Hsu et al., 2022), which is the inspiration for our work.

For a more detailed history of event extraction datasets and systems, see Lai (2022).

3 Methodology

Before describing our extension to the model, we first provide a brief overview of the design of DEGREE (Hsu et al., 2022). The system frames the event extraction task in terms of a natural language generation task, with the generated text being rigidly structured in order to be machine-parsable. Consider the sentence, "John met with Alice." DEGREE might query this input for `Contact:Meet` events with the following input:

```
John met with Alice.
contact event, meet sub-type
The event is related people meeting.
Similar triggers such as meet, met.
The event's trigger word is <Trigger>.
some people met at somewhere.
```

The final two lines serve as a "prototype" template that should appear in the output. In this instance, we expect the fine-tuned model to produce the following completion:

```
Event trigger is met.
John and Alice met somewhere.
```

For inputs where no event is found, the completion `Event trigger is <Trigger>` is generated.

DEGREE is trained by fine-tuning a base LLM to complete patterns such as the above. Once trained, the LLM is able to extract not only the event types which it was trained on, but also, to

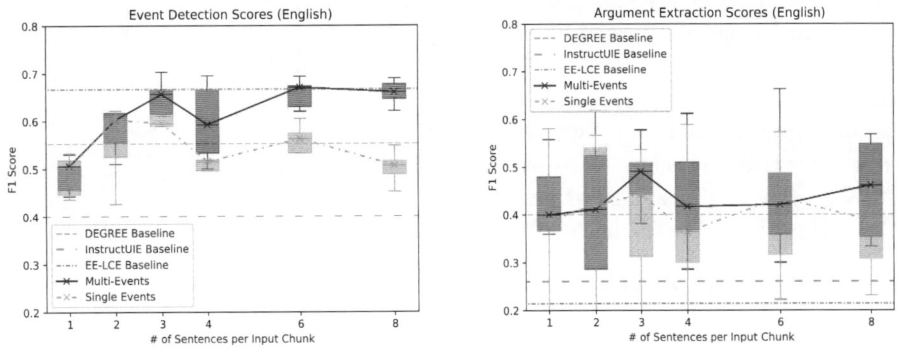

Figure 2: ACE2005 MUC-style (Chinchor and Sundheim, 1993) F1 scores for different system configurations. Horizontal lines represent the median scores of baseline systems. The box plots represent all of the scores from the events and arguments related to the five event types we analyze (Section 3), with the lines in the center of each box denoting the median score. The detailed scores can be found in Appendix B

some extent, new event types in a zero-shot fashion. These completions are easily parsable into structured formats, and the generated strings can be searched for in the original input in order to function as a text annotation algorithm.

As shown above, DEGREE is able to extract zero or one events from a given piece of text. How can entire documents then be handled? DEGREE addresses this by chunking input documents into pieces consisting of three sentences[1]. All of a document's chunks are processed separately (once per event type) in order to perform event extraction across the full input.

One remaining limitation is the handling of multiple events of the same type in the same chunk. DEGREE does not address this situation, so we propose an update to the fine-tuning template structure which allows this type of scenario to be handled. Our proposed template is shown in Figure 1b. The key modification is the introduction of the <EVENTSEP> special token, which separates each event in the output. While a rather minor change, we show below that this is enough to close the gap between DEGREE and the state of the art.

4 Experimental Results

We evaluate our system on a variety of configurations using the ACE2005 dataset (LDC, 2005)'s English data. To determine sentence boundaries, we use the Babel Street Analytics text analysis framework.

Our models are based on `t5-large` (Raffel et al., 2020), as we empirically found this to be a better choice than DEGREE's base model of BART (Lewis et al., 2020). For different numbers of sentences used to chunk apart input documents, we train two versions of each model: one with multi-events turned off (i.e. the same algorithm as DEGREE, with our base model and template, limited to a single event per chunk), and one with multiple events per input chunk. Additional training details can be found in Appendix A.

Additionally, we compare against three baselines: DEGREE, InstructUIE (Wang et al., 2023), and EE-LCE (Yu et al., 2024). For DEGREE and InstructUIE, we use the models published by the authors. For EE-LCE, we use the provided training code to create a model.

To focus on the most pertinent subset of the dataset, we limit our analysis to the five event types with the highest support in the test data: Conflict:Attack, Contact:Meet, Movement:Transport, Personnel:End-Position, and Transaction:Transfer-Ownership. Finally, since we feel that it is more representative of performance on argument extraction, we opt to use a MUC-style (Chinchor and Sundheim, 1993) formula for calculating F1. This is identical to the traditional formula, except partial matches are counted as 50% correct (rather than completely incorrect).

When interpreting the data in Figure 2, we find that extending DEGREE to support multiple events causes two changes in the behavior of the model. First, the event detection performance becomes very similar to the state-of-the-art EE-LCE system, despite being based on a model with 750MM pa-

[1]This choice of three was not explained in DEGREE's paper, but our results in Section 4 agree with this choice.

rameters (in contrast to EE-LCE's 11B). Second, model is able to process more sentences at once without sacrificing accuracy. Because DEGREE requires num_chunks×num_event_types invocations in order to process a document broken apart into num_chunks pieces, this means that we can effectively halve (or more) the number of model invocations required to process a document.

5 Relaxed F1: Co-Arity-Invariant Comparison of Event Extraction Algorithms

Our exploration into the impact of this single-event limitation of DEGREE on its comparative performance led us to consider whether there was a way to compare the *qualitative* performance of these algorithms in a mathematical way. For example, suppose that there is a dataset where each sentence contains one Conflict:Attack event, and we run algorithms A and B on chunks of two sentences. Algorithm A is limited to zero or one outputs per sentence, but it detects an attack event in each pair of sentences. In contrast, algorithm B can output an arbitrary number of events, and it detects both attack events in each pair.

Which is better? In an absolute sense, algorithm B outperforms, since we calculate precision and recall metrics with respect to the number of events contained in the document. For certain applications, however, we may be more interested in knowing which of the two qualitatively performs better. In a certain sense, these algorithms are equivalent, since *within the scope of its limitations*, A and B both extract attack events as much as is possible.

To address this shortcoming, we present a new metric for event detection, which we call *relaxed F1 scores*. The formula for this score is derived from the partial-match-aware MUC formulae (Chinchor and Sundheim, 1993) and defined by the following formula for "relaxed" recall:

$$R^{\text{relaxed}} = \frac{\text{correct} + (0.5 \times \text{partial}) - \text{extra}}{\text{possible} - \text{impossible}}$$

In this equation, "correct" and "partial" denote the number of correctly-extracted, partially-extracted (extractions of the correct type but only a partial overlap with the correct location) events or arguments, "possible" the number of events or arguments in the gold annotation. "impossible" denotes the number of events greater than one in each chunk (i.e. for a chunk with five events, "impossible" would be four). Finally, the "extra" term is needed for algorithms which *can* extract multiple events, in order to make the result comparable with ones which cannot. For these algorithms, "extra" denotes the number of correct (or weighted partial) predictions which were made that would have been impossible if multiple events could not be extracted. In sum, this means that, effectively, for each chunk of text produced during processing, the calculation of relaxed recall becomes binary.

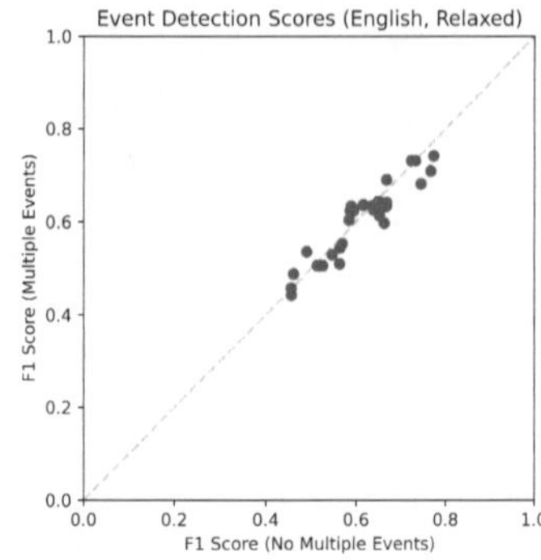

Figure 3: ACE2005 relaxed F1 scores across all system configurations. For further details, see Appendix B.

From this relaxed recall value, relaxed F1 is computed by using the standard formula alongside the standard precision P:

$$F_1^{\text{relaxed}} = \frac{2 \times P \times R^{\text{relaxed}}}{P + R^{\text{relaxed}}}$$

We use this metric to determine whether our multiple event extraction extension qualitatively decreases the event detection performance of DEGREE, with the results shown in Figure 3. This graph shoes a roughly linear correlation between the two values, meaning that our extension does not meaningfully degrade DEGREE's qualitative performance.

6 Discussion

We demonstrate that a simple extension to DEGREE is sufficient to close the gap between it and state-of-the-art systems. This suggests that different generative approaches to event extraction are potentially much more competitive with one another than previously thought.

Furthermore, we present an F1-style event detection metric which can give some insight into the qualitative performance of these algorithms.

We hope that this motivates further research into ways of analyzing these systems' performance in more fine-grained detail. Future work could include a metric that allows for assessing argument extraction performance without depending on event detection accuracy.

7 Limitations

The systems described in this paper are trained on annotated event datasets. While they have some capacity to generalize to new event types in a zero-shot fashion, users should be cautious when using them with event types not found in the training data, as they may produce unexpected predictions.

The analysis presented here focuses on the English-language ACE2005 data. Some of the conclusions presented here may not hold for certain other languages, and the systems described here may not function correctly on non-English input text.

References

David Ahn. 2006. The stages of event extraction. In *Proceedings of the Workshop on Annotating and Reasoning about Time and Events*, pages 1–8, Sydney, Australia. Association for Computational Linguistics.

Tom Brown, Benjamin Mann, Nick Ryder, Melanie Subbiah, Jared D Kaplan, Prafulla Dhariwal, Arvind Neelakantan, Pranav Shyam, Girish Sastry, Amanda Askell, Sandhini Agarwal, Ariel Herbert-Voss, Gretchen Krueger, Tom Henighan, Rewon Child, Aditya Ramesh, Daniel Ziegler, Jeffrey Wu, Clemens Winter, Chris Hesse, Mark Chen, Eric Sigler, Mateusz Litwin, Scott Gray, Benjamin Chess, Jack Clark, Christopher Berner, Sam McCandlish, Alec Radford, Ilya Sutskever, and Dario Amodei. 2020. Language models are few-shot learners. In *Advances in Neural Information Processing Systems*, volume 33, pages 1877–1901. Curran Associates, Inc.

Nancy Chinchor and Beth Sundheim. 1993. MUC-5 evaluation metrics. In *Fifth Message Understanding Conference (MUC-5): Proceedings of a Conference Held in Baltimore, Maryland, August 25-27, 1993*.

Hyung Won Chung, Le Hou, Shayne Longpre, Barret Zoph, Yi Tay, William Fedus, Yunxuan Li, Xuezhi Wang, Mostafa Dehghani, Siddhartha Brahma, Albert Webson, Shixiang Shane Gu, Zhuyun Dai, Mirac Suzgun, Xinyun Chen, Aakanksha Chowdhery, Alex Castro-Ros, Marie Pellat, Kevin Robinson, Dasha Valter, Sharan Narang, Gaurav Mishra, Adams Yu, Vincent Zhao, Yanping Huang, Andrew Dai, Hongkun Yu, Slav Petrov, Ed H. Chi, Jeff Dean, Jacob Devlin, Adam Roberts, Denny Zhou, Quoc V. Le, and Jason Wei. 2022. Scaling instruction-finetuned language models. *Preprint*, arXiv:2210.11416.

Yu Hong, Jianfeng Zhang, Bin Ma, Jianmin Yao, Guodong Zhou, and Qiaoming Zhu. 2011. Using cross-entity inference to improve event extraction. In *Proceedings of the 49th Annual Meeting of the Association for Computational Linguistics: Human Language Technologies*, pages 1127–1136, Portland, Oregon, USA. Association for Computational Linguistics.

I-Hung Hsu, Kuan-Hao Huang, Elizabeth Boschee, Scott Miller, Prem Natarajan, Kai-Wei Chang, and Nanyun Peng. 2022. DEGREE: A data-efficient generation-based event extraction model. In *Proceedings of the 2022 Conference of the North American Chapter of the Association for Computational Linguistics: Human Language Technologies*, pages 1890–1908, Seattle, United States. Association for Computational Linguistics.

Viet Dac Lai. 2022. Event extraction: A survey. *Preprint*, arXiv:2210.03419.

LDC. 2005. ACE (automatic content extraction) English annotation guidelines for events. `https://www.ldc.upenn.edu/sites/www.ldc.upenn.edu/files/english-events-guidelines-v5.4.3.pdf`.

Mike Lewis, Yinhan Liu, Naman Goyal, Marjan Ghazvininejad, Abdelrahman Mohamed, Omer Levy, Veselin Stoyanov, and Luke Zettlemoyer. 2020. BART: Denoising sequence-to-sequence pre-training for natural language generation, translation, and comprehension. In *Proceedings of the 58th Annual Meeting of the Association for Computational Linguistics*, pages 7871–7880, Online. Association for Computational Linguistics.

Thien Nguyen and Ralph Grishman. 2018. Graph convolutional networks with argument-aware pooling for event detection. *Proceedings of the AAAI Conference on Artificial Intelligence*, 32(1).

Thien Huu Nguyen, Kyunghyun Cho, and Ralph Grishman. 2016. Joint event extraction via recurrent neural networks. In *Proceedings of the 2016 Conference of the North American Chapter of the Association for Computational Linguistics: Human Language Technologies*, pages 300–309, San Diego, California. Association for Computational Linguistics.

Thien Huu Nguyen and Ralph Grishman. 2015. Event detection and domain adaptation with convolutional neural networks. In *Proceedings of the 53rd Annual Meeting of the Association for Computational Linguistics and the 7th International Joint Conference on Natural Language Processing (Volume 2: Short Papers)*, pages 365–371, Beijing, China. Association for Computational Linguistics.

OpenAI. 2024. GPT-4 technical report. *Preprint*, arXiv:2303.08774.

Colin Raffel, Noam Shazeer, Adam Roberts, Katherine Lee, Sharan Narang, Michael Matena, Yanqi Zhou, Wei Li, and Peter J. Liu. 2020. Exploring the limits of transfer learning with a unified text-to-text transformer. *Journal of Machine Learning Research*, 21(140):1–67.

Noam Shazeer and Mitchell Stern. 2018. Adafactor: Adaptive learning rates with sublinear memory cost. *Preprint*, arXiv:1804.04235.

Xiao Wang, Weikang Zhou, Can Zu, Han Xia, Tianze Chen, Yuansen Zhang, Rui Zheng, Junjie Ye, Qi Zhang, Tao Gui, et al. 2023. Instructuie: Multi-task instruction tuning for unified information extraction. *arXiv preprint arXiv:2304.08085*.

Yanhua Yu, Yuanlong Wang, Yunshan Ma, Jie Li, Kangkang Lu, Zhiyong Huang, and Tat Seng Chua. 2024. Ee-lce: An event extraction framework based on llm-generated cot explanation. In *Knowledge Science, Engineering and Management*, pages 28–40, Singapore. Springer Nature Singapore.

A Training Details

Our models were trained on Google Cloud Vertex AI `a2-highgpu-1g` machines, equipped with NVIDIA A100 GPUs. We train using the Adafactor (Shazeer and Stern, 2018) optimizer, configured with a learning rate of 10^{-4} and a weight decay of 10^{-5}. Each model is trained for 10 epochs (with the best model selected using the ACE2005 dev set), and a batch size of 8 is used.

The total compute cost for running all of the training experiments was USD$559.81 for the experiments.

B Detailed Results

The scores shown in Figures 2 and 3 can be found in Tables 1 and 2, respectively. In the latter table, we highlight the best scoring run for each number of sentences used to chunk the document, as relaxed scores from runs with different sentence-breaking rules cannot be directly compared.

Model	# Sentences	Multi-Events Enabled	Event Detection	Argument Extraction
InstructUIE	1	N/A	0.441 ± 0.076	0.266 ± 0.158
EE-LCE	1	N/A	0.602 ± 0.111	0.234 ± 0.112
DEGREE (BART)	3	N/A	0.617 ± 0.089	0.377 ± 0.115
DEGREE (T5)	**1**	**Yes**	0.488 ± 0.033	0.402 ± 0.112
DEGREE (T5)	1	No	0.487 ± 0.039	0.396 ± 0.109
DEGREE (T5)	**2**	**Yes**	0.581 ± 0.042	0.398 ± 0.170
DEGREE (T5)	2	No	0.557 ± 0.073	0.391 ± 0.158
DEGREE (T5)	**3**	**Yes**	0.650 ± 0.034	**0.463 ± 0.135**
DEGREE (T5)	3	No	0.585 ± 0.040	0.403 ± 0.122
DEGREE (T5)	**4**	**Yes**	0.597 ± 0.074	0.415 ± 0.153
DEGREE (T5)	4	No	0.506 ± 0.072	0.361 ± 0.143
DEGREE (T5)	**6**	**Yes**	0.657 ± 0.028	0.421 ± 0.159
DEGREE (T5)	6	No	0.548 ± 0.047	0.389 ± 0.149
DEGREE (T5)	**8**	**Yes**	**0.658 ± 0.024**	0.420 ± 0.149
DEGREE (T5)	8	No	0.502 ± 0.031	0.348 ± 0.127

Table 1: Mean and sample standard deviations of the MUC-Style F1 scores for the five event types we analyze. Our configurations and the best scores are in bold.

Model	# Sentences	Multi-Events Enabled	Event Detection
InstructUIE	1	N/A	0.457 ± 0.074
EE-LCE	1	N/A	**0.615 ± 0.110**
DEGREE (BART)	3	N/A	0.650 ± 0.068
DEGREE (T5)	**1**	**Yes**	0.488 ± 0.033
DEGREE (T5)	1	No	0.499 ± 0.037
DEGREE (T5)	**2**	**Yes**	0.574 ± 0.052
DEGREE (T5)	2	No	**0.598 ± 0.078**
DEGREE (T5)	**3**	**Yes**	0.655 ± 0.038
DEGREE (T5)	3	No	**0.658 ± 0.047**
DEGREE (T5)	**4**	**Yes**	0.593 ± 0.083
DEGREE (T5)	4	No	**0.596 ± 0.094**
DEGREE (T5)	**6**	**Yes**	0.667 ± 0.046
DEGREE (T5)	6	No	**0.672 ± 0.057**
DEGREE (T5)	**8**	**Yes**	0.648 ± 0.032
DEGREE (T5)	8	No	**0.653 ± 0.060**

Table 2: Mean and sample standard deviations of the relaxed F1 scores for the five event types we analyze. Our configurations and the best scores (for each value of "# Sentences") is in bold.

MUMOSA, Interactive Dashboard for MUlti-MOdal Situation Awareness

Stephanie M. Lukin[1], Shawn Bowser[1], Reece Suchocki[1], Douglas Summers-Stay[1], Jeffrey Micher[1], Cynthia Matuszek[2], Francis Ferraro[2], Clare R. Voss[1]
[1]DEVCOM Army Research Laboratory, Adelphi MD, USA
[2]University of Maryland, Baltimore County, MD, USA
Correspondence: stephanie.m.lukin.civ@army.mil

Abstract

Information extraction has led the way for event detection from text for many years. Recent advances in neural models, such as Large Language Models (LLMs) and Vision-Language Models (VLMs), have enabled the integration of multiple modalities, providing richer sources of information about events. Concurrently, the development of schema graphs and 3D reconstruction methods has enhanced our ability to visualize and annotate complex events. Building on these innovations, we introduce the MUMOSA (MUlti-MOdal Situation Awareness) interactive dashboard that brings these diverse resources together. MUMOSA aims to provide a comprehensive platform for *event situational awareness*, offering users a powerful tool for understanding and analyzing complex scenarios across modalities.

1 Introduction

After a significant incident or crisis, how do *investigators* determine and assess what happened when in order to produce a report with clear evidence from the sequence of events in detailing lessons learned? How do communities prepare their *responders* to handle similarly complex, critical situations that may come their way in the future? Some crisis response procedures are well-established for specific situations, e.g., an initial fire suppression response to a wildfire[1], so responders can be consistently trained in advance and investigators know what to look for afterwards. But other times, the crisis is so sudden and unexpected that established lines of communication struggle to convey up-to-date information. Following these unforeseen circumstances, both groups, investigators and responders, have a shared need to understand the various types of information about events in the evidence collected and analyzed for post-crisis reports.

The field of information extraction (IE) within computational linguistics has led the way since the late 1980's applying symbolic, then statistical, and most recently neural methods to natural language texts to identify the types of essential elements of information needed for such reports, including entities, relations, and events (Grishman, 2019). Most recently, with neural models such as LLMs and VLMs that can bring together multiple modalities to provide additional sources of information about events, there is now the opportunity to leverage various combinations of multimodal event information to support investigators in combing through text and photographic evidence for report writing and to train responders in preparing to handle such information in the future. Furthermore, the recent development of schema graphs with access to over 3K event types (Zhan et al., 2023) and 3D reconstruction methods for scenario simulation from as little as 24 images, e.g., Kerbl et al. (2023), users can now have hands-on access to interfaces to visualize and annotate complex events online, as they learn from available evidence and documentation what has happened over the course of those events.

In this paper, we introduce our approach to bringing together these various resources in an interactive, MUlti-MOdal Situation Awareness (MUMOSA) dashboard for complex event understanding, ultimately in support of users' real-time event *situational awareness* (SA) and decision-making during a crisis. For a specific role, such as a first responder onsite or incident coordinator at an emergency operations center, the specifics of their SA will be determined by tasks and decisions for their job. However in all cases, their SA will entail "the perception of the elements in the environment within a volume of time and space, the comprehension of their meaning and the projection of their status in the near future." (Endsley, 1995, 2015)[2]

[1]https://www.fs.usda.gov/Internet/FSE_DOCUMENTS/fsm9_039213.pdf

[2]Perception, comprehension, and projection have been

Proceedings of the Workshop on the Future of Event Detection (FuturED), pages 32–47
November 15, 2024 ©2024 Association for Computational Linguistics

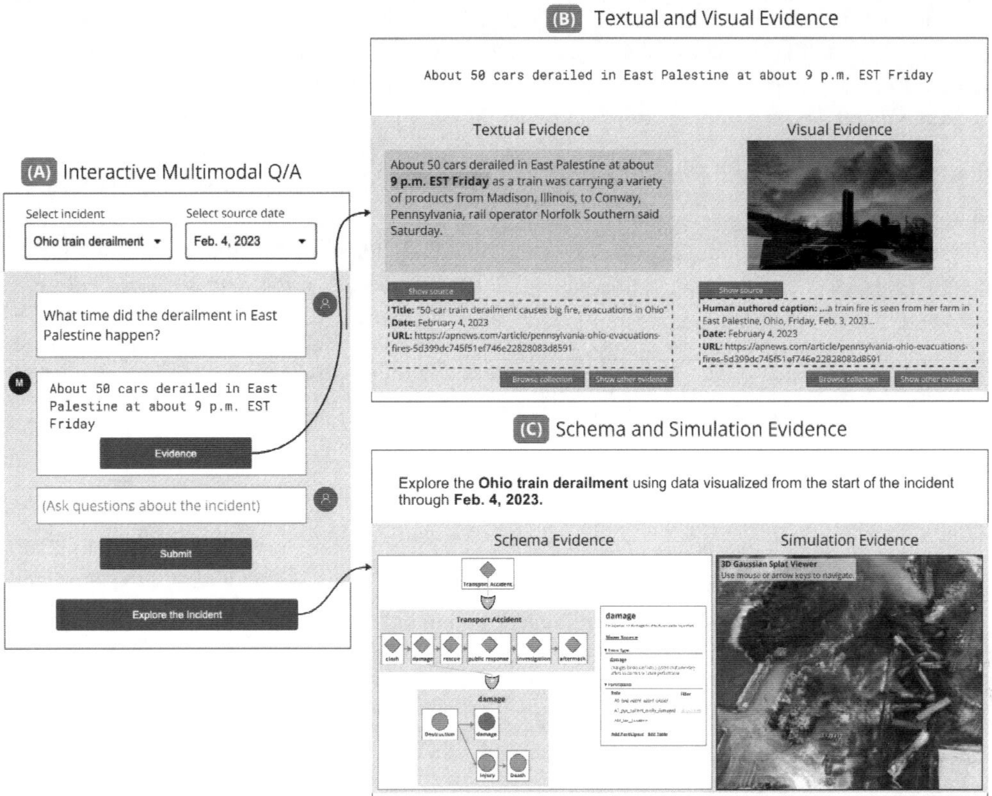

Figure 1: Users engage with the MUMOSA dashboard through (**A**) Interactive Multi-Modal Q/A, selecting the incident with source date and entering questions or directed requests in natural language. They may then choose to examine the source data for the system response via panels in (**B**) Textual and Visual Evidence, or continue engaging the dashboard via Q/A. The selected incident can also be explored in its entirety across events via panels in (**C**) Schemas and Simulation Evidence.

The MUMOSA dashboard's panels are intended to provide for user perception of essential elements of information (SA level 1) about the complex event they select in the form of multi-modal evidence. The workflow design enables users to explore and compare information across evidence panels, as well as edit and annotate the content of the complex schema graphs and scenario simulation. This aims to support them in interpreting and retaining the panel content with multiple elements of information, and in building their own narrative of the complex event (level 2).

Users engage in interactive multi-modal question-answering (Q/A) and exploration of events and simulated environments. The user initializes the dashboard for the complex event of interest and time frame. After inputting a question, they receive a text answer and access to supporting evidence from text documents and photographic visuals. They may simultaneously explore the event in its entirely through schema graph structures and 3D simulations. Each of these modalities of evidence pertaining to the incident appears in a separate interactive panel, as shown in Figure 1.

In this paper, we select one unexpected crisis to focus on—the Ohio 2023 train derailment—as we describe the design and capabilities of the dashboard for the following applications:

1. to assemble *crisis documentation* for those writing 'lessons learned' investigative reports

2. to create *training resources* for those responsible in the future for handling crises

For background, Section 2 describes existing resources we build on in constructing the dashboard, and basic facts about the Ohio derailment. Sections 3 and 4 cover the dashboard implementation and workflow (SA levels 1 and 2 respectively) for the crisis documentation and training resources. Section 5 envisions the dashboard of the future sup-

designated as progressive levels 1, 2, and 3 of SA.

porting real-time crisis response, akin to the needs of SA level 3. We briefly overview related research that differs from our approach in Section 6 and conclude in Section 7.[3]

2 Background

We briefly overview here existing resources that we build on in four panels of our dashboard.

Textual evidence. To show textual evidence, we leverage text-based Q/A and Frequently Asked Questions (FAQs), where a set of common user questions pertaining to a particular topic are compiled into an accessible list where the user may look up answers if their query is common (Tekumalla, 2020). Prior work has shown how to find these matches in a dialogue Q/A. By using statistical text classifiers, Leuski and Traum (2011) compared a user question in real-time against a distributions of common user questions paired with responses. After successfully matching the input question to the pre-processed question set, the paired answer was returned. The same statistical classifier was leveraged in human-robot dialogue extending beyond the constraint of a 'question,' allowing for different types of frequently issued robot-directed commands (Lukin et al., 2018; Gervits et al., 2021). The matching was re-implemented in Lukin et al. (2024) using sentence embeddings and cosine similarity to find close matches between vectorized input and pre-stored questions, and showed significant improvement in accuracy over the statistical approach in the same domain of human-robot dialogue. Section 3.1.1 covers our work incorporating a modified version of this approach with LLMs in responding to user input.

Visual evidence. Prior to VLMs, comprehensive text generation from images required several different tools: OCR for text recognition, object recognition and segmentation for object annotation, visual-question-answering models for short answers to specific questions about the image, and captioners to generate a one sentence description of the image. Now, VLMs are able to accomplish all of these tasks (with the present exception of producing segmentation and bounding boxes) in a unified, context-sensitive way. To show visual evidence in answering a text question, Section 3.1.2 describes our use of Idefics3 (Laurençon et al., 2024) to generate text descriptions of images that we can match on in a similar way as carried out for textual evidence. Idefics3 was developed by Huggingface and builds off of Google's SigLIP (Zhai et al., 2023) and Meta's Llama 3.1 (AI@Meta, 2024).

Schema evidence. Schemas provide structured representations of real-world occurrences. They are event-centric, and as such, serve as abstract templates for understanding and analyzing complex sets of events. Event schemas typically consist of:

- Events: High-level (e.g., "transport accident") and granular sub-events (e.g., "damage," "investigation.")
- Entities: Actors or objects involved in events (e.g., "train," "residents," "authorities.")
- Relations: Connections between entities or events, often temporal or causal in nature.

Schema visualizers allow for complex events to be viewed in an intuitive way via a graph-like structure of nodes with directed edges. Schemas may be compared against source documents to find when an event mentioned matches an event node. Section 3.2.1 describes the RESIN pipeline are used to extract and match events to the schema (Du et al., 2022; Wen et al., 2021) and the RESIN visualizer (Nguyen et al., 2023) to view and edit them within our dashboard.

Simulation evidence. Reconstructing scenes from a set of images is an emerging research area in 3D computer vision, enabling novel view synthesis and embodied scene understanding, both of which could be crucial for crisis response. Advancements in Neural Radiance Fields (NeRF) and 3D Gaussian Splatting (3DGS) have resulted in 3D models that achieve state-of-the-art in rendering appearance, rendering speed, and training efficiency. Section 3.2.2 covers the use of 3DGS (Kerbl et al., 2023). A 3DGS scene is represented as a set G of discrete Gaussian primitives each with parameters (μ, o, s, r, SH) where $\mu \in \mathbb{R}^3$ is for the spatial center, $o \in \mathbb{R}$ for opacity, $s \in \mathbb{R}^3$ for scale, $r \in \mathbb{R}^4$ for quaternion rotation, and SH for spherical harmonics coefficients which represent view-dependent colors. We extend this formulation with additional parameters to capture language features from 2D foundation models (Kirillov et al., 2023; Bowser and Lukin, 2024).

Scenario: Ohio Train Derailment. On February 3, 2023, in East Palestine, Ohio, USA, about 50 train cars derailed from a 150 Norfolk Southern

[3]We plan to release the dashboard as an artifact of our research towards enabling higher levels of SA following systematic evaluation in future work.

freight train.[4] Eleven of the derailed cars were carrying hazardous materials including vinyl chloride, ethylene glycol, ethylhexyl acrylate, butyl acrylate and isobutylene. Some cars caught fire, and others spilled hundred thousand gallons of hazardous materials into a stream that eventually empties into the Ohio River. A number of federal and state government agencies were immediately mobilized. Clean-up efforts included real-time testing of air, soil, and water. A controlled burn of remaining chemicals was ordered on February 6, 2023 to prevent further explosions. However, after extensive investigation of the incident, this course of action was assessed over a year later to have been unnecessary. We select this real-world incident since news articles, government reports, photos, and other data about it are openly available for populating our dashboard panels and assessing ways these varied information sources may help immediate responders more reliably gain SA in novel and unexpected events.

3 MUMOSA Dashboard Evidence Panels

The user starts their interactions with the MUMOSA dashboard by initializing it for a particular incident and date of interest. They can then proceed by posing questions about events in the incident and exploring the source data evidence provided with the system responses along with full incident visualizations in the dashboard panels. We focus here and in Section 4 on interactions specifically for *forensic* use cases of the dashboard with pre-processed data for *investigators* and *first responders.* We postpone till Section 5 discussion of future dashboard research for *real-time* conditions with dynamic changes to both data availability and user information needs.

The intent for the dashboard panels is to provide users with essential elements of information (SA level 1). User workflow across panels for building their understanding of the sequences of events within the incident (SA level 2) will be addressed in the section that follows.

3.1 Interactive Multi-Modal Q/A

During the multi-modal Q/A interaction, the user enters questions or makes directed requests using natural language, and the dashboard responds, as information is available, with both a text answer (Figure 1**A**) and panels populated with supportive evidence from source texts and visuals (Figure 1**B**). The system provides next-search alternatives to Q/A interactions for the users within the panels, enabling them to look for other evidence deeper within the reply stack or browse the source document collection.

3.1.1 Textual Evidence Panel

Textual evidence is shown in its own panel with the system answer (the text returned to the user in response to their question in the Q/A interaction) highlighted, and surrounding context and source information provided for further exploration. *In advance of the user's question*, the dashboard contains a collection of texts. For our case study scenario, we gathered news articles from different sources published on different days following the derailment. The text from these articles was scraped from the websites and segmented into sentences. Next, we created Q/A pairs, where the questions had answers contained in the sentences. We ran different large language models (ChatGPT and Llama 3.1) to generate numerous questions from the sentences, and then with manual review, as feasible for this forensic use case, we validated or adjusted each generated question as reasonable for inclusion in our stored Q/A pairs. For subsequent run-time comparison with user questions, all the stored questions were also vectorized through sentence embeddings using SBERT (Reimers, 2019).

After the input of the user's question, we run a semantic sentence matching, as described in Lukin et al. (2024). The user question is vectorized with SBERT and compared against every pre-stored vectorized question using cosine similarity. The stored questions are ranked in descending order, and the answer, found in the pair with the top question, is displayed to the user in the answer box immediately below the user question. The answer also appears contextualized within the Textual Evidence Panel containing: the source document passage with answer highlighted, the document title, link to the source document, and two buttons for further exploration. The "Show other evidence" button enables users to examine other lower-ranked answers retrieved in response to their request. The "Browse collection" button gives users access to the system's text document collection for more extensive investigation of source materials. Table 1 shows the user question *"What time did the derailment in East Palestine happen?"* as matched against the top-3 answers, corresponding to a request to show other evidence in Figure 1**B**.

[4]EPA website on derailment: https://www.epa.gov/east-palestine-oh-train-derailment/operational-updates

Table 1: Ranked answers to user question: *"What time did the derailment in East Palestine happen?"*

Score	Answer
0.82	About 50 cars derailed in East Palestine at about 9 p.m. EST Friday...
0.71	The 50-car Norfolk Southern train derailed around 9 p.m. Friday night.
0.53	East Palestine officials said 68 agencies from three states and a number of counties responded to the derailment...

3.1.2 Visual Evidence Panel

Visual evidence is shown in its own dashboard panel in response to the user's question. In *advance of the user's question*, the dashboard requires a collection of images paired with natural language text. This text may come from different sources, including:

- human-written captions or alt-texts associated with the image, if retrieved from a document;
- machine-generated captions or descriptions as generated by a VLM;
- annotated labels or bounding boxes associated with objects in an image as annotated by a computer vision object detection model;
- texts within an image generated by OCR.

For our forensic use case in the case study, we manually gathered photographs from different sources showing the derailment. We then extracted the relevant text sources (i.e., the caption, alt-text, OCR) and generated text descriptions using Idefics3-8B-Llama3.

After the input of the user's question, we follow a paired-vector comparison process, similar to the one described for textual evidence: the user's question is vectorized using SBERT and compared against pre-stored, vectorized image texts. The pair with the highest match is selected, the matched image text is returned to the user as the answer to their question, and the associated image is shown in the Visual Evidence Panel alongside the image texts. For example, a different user question inquiring into the aftermath of the derailment might be, *"How does the wastewater get cleaned?"* This question might have a high match to the human-authored text caption "This centrifuge separates solid waste from liquid wastewater in holding bins to determine whether the waste is hazardous and then disposed properly" that is associated with an image of a centrifuge. This caption is returned to the user as the answer, and the retrieved image will appear together with its text caption in the Visual Evidence Panel (Figure 2). The user may follow up with two button choices, asking the system to show other visual evidence found, or browsing the source collection of images to inspire new questions.

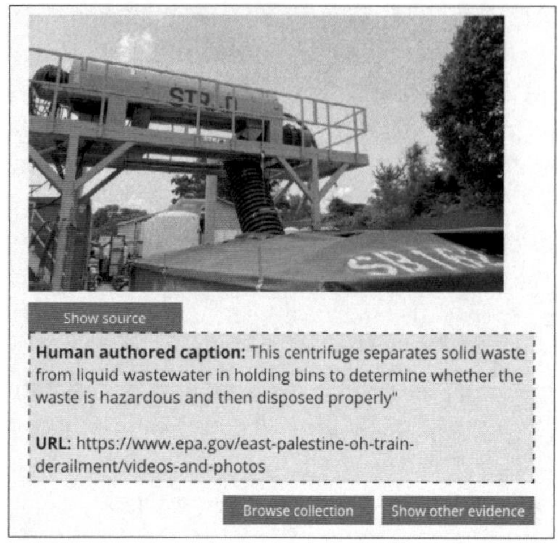

Figure 2: Visual Evidence Panel following the user question *"How does the wastewater get cleaned?"*

In cases where the user's question yields a high match from both the collection of documents and images, the dashboard will inform the user through the Q/A interface to inspect both Textual and Visual Evidence Panels.

3.2 Interactive Multi-Modal Event Exploration

In addition to asking questions or making directed requests, the user can explore the event as a whole using two representations of the incident: a schema panel view showing a graph of event nodes and either hierarchical or temporal event-event relations as edges, and a 3D simulated panel view showing a visualization of event itself. The Schema and Simulation Evidence Panels are not extrinsically tied to the user's question. At any point during the user's interaction with the dashboard, they may choose to explore these panels.

3.2.1 Schema Evidence Panel

The Schema Evidence Panel provides the user with an event-centric exploration of the incident. First, documents are preprocessed to identify events using the information extraction module of the RESIN pipeline (Du et al., 2022; Wen et al., 2021). The resulting extractions are then matched to events in incident schemas by executing the matching module in the RESIN pipeline. Finally, a separate program consumes the matching module's output for visualizing the schema graph in the evidence panel where the user can explore and edit it (Nguyen et al., 2023).

The schema the user sees is based on their selection of the incident and timeframe at the top of the dashboard. Figure 1**C** shows a screenshot of the *transport accident* schema[5], and so the visualized graph displays events within this type of incident. Blue diamonds represent complex events in the schema that typically happen or could happen within this incident. Clicking a blue diamond, e.g., *damage*, expands the graph with its subevents containing different color and shaped nodes. Circles are primitive events, as leaf nodes (no subevents). A red circle indicates actual evidence was extracted from the source material that matched the primitive event type, whereas events not included in the original schema appear as yellow (see Figure 4 in Appendix A).

Clicking a red circle, e.g., *damage*, expands the panel with further information about the event, including the matched phrase in the source material, and the participants and their roles in the event (i.e., A0 agent causer, A1 patient entity damaged, and location). The user has hands-on access to explore all events within the schema, opening nodes to see where matches occurred in event fields from document content reported during the selected timeframe.

3.2.2 Simulation Evidence Panel

The Simulation Evidence Panel provides the user with an interactive 3D model that has been reconstructed from photographs of the incident, resulting in a bird's-eye view of the scene. The user can navigate the scene through the first-person perspective using a mouse and keyboard.

The simulation is constructed using a 3D Gaussian Splatting point cloud structure (Kerbl et al., 2023). Figure 1**C** shows a snapshot from our simulation after scene reconstruction from the angle the user selected by moving their cursor. This simulation was created using only 24 references images that were captured by an aerial drone flying overhead of the derailment incident,[6] thus the reconstruction shows the user novel views unavailable from the original source. Figure 7 in Appendix B shows the full flattened view of the 3D simulation from which the view in Figure 1**C** was taken. The geometry and visual appearance of the simulation is improved as more images are added.

The simulation can be annotated using user-specified keypoints and image segmentation masks which are unprojected onto the underlying model for 3D segmentation. Sections of the 3D map can then be highlighted with unique colors and icons.

4 User Workflow

The MUMOSA dashboard represents a powerful tool for users to query events by enabling Q/A over multi-modal data sources where the modalities offer complementary supporting evidence. While the evidence in the individual panels provides users with essential elements of information (SA level 1), the MUMOSA dashboard itself provides for an easy-access workflow to detect and compare events across panels and modalities. By using all the panels together, the dashboard provides unique opportunities for users to iterate in their information foraging and annotate the underlying data to enhance their understanding of the sequence of events (SA level 2).

In our forensic use of this case study, a user may want to understand the initial response of the derailment by asking the question, *"What time did the derailment in East Palestine happen?"* to which the answer was *"about 9 p.m. EST Friday"* with the textual evidence showing an article published on February 4, 2023. This answer may prompt the user towards several lines of inquiry, one of which may be to ask *"Was it hard to see at night during the initial incident response?"* This might return a photograph of the nighttime scene in the Visual Evidence Panel, which may in turn inspire another question that could be answered by the Textual Evidence Panel, e.g., *"What challenges did the first responders face in the dark?"*

We also readily imagine that the open-ended workflow with schema and simulation panels will elicit follow-up questions. When exploring the schema view, users can navigate the hierarchical structure of events related to the train derailment. For example, they might explore sub-events under *investigation*, as seen Figure 6 in Appendix A. This exploration may prompt a user to follow-up with *"What criminal charges are being reported?"* The response in the schema evidence would highlight the node of interest within the schema, and search

[5]The *transport accident* schema was independently curated by RESIN team on DARPA KAIROS.

[6]Source video from Youtube: "National Transportation Safety Board B-Roll: Train Derailment in East Palestine, OH" https://www.youtube.com/watch?v=7AyXTVkVBT4

stored documents for supportive textual evidence.

Giving users access to the simulation affords them greater situational awareness to ask questions pertaining to accessibility and route planning, obstacle and target identification, and scene overview. Examination of the simulation might prompt not only new questions, but the ability to display answers within the simulation using annotations. The user may ask the question *"Where is the immediate danger?"* and the simulation would highlight the clusters of train cars in orange and red, as seen in Figure 3. This may be followed up by *"What buildings are in immediate danger?"* and would highlight the buildings in green (also Figure 3). In this way, the simulation view displays portions of visual evidence to the user without constraining their viewpoint to the original camera pose.

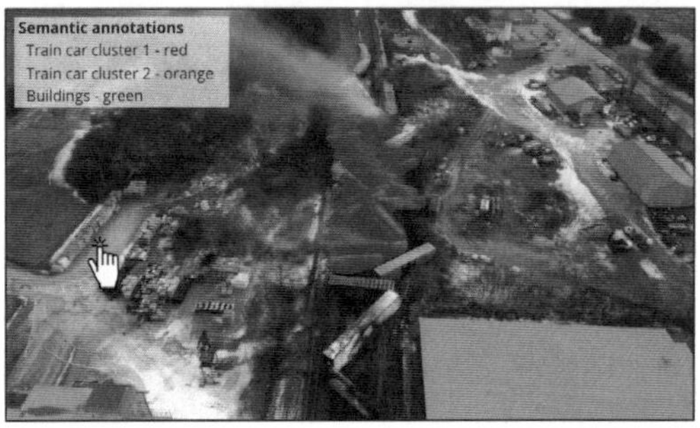

Figure 3: Simulation evidence augmented with semantic segmentation masks as a result of user questions

5 Discussion: Toward Real-Time Event Tracking

The MUMOSA dashboard currently aims to serve as an interactive *forensic resource,* providing support to post-crisis incident investigations and training exercises for first responders at SA levels 1 and 2. The questions we have included above showcase how users may search for information looking back at events within an incident across modalities. The evidence supplied in one modality may inspire new questions or may lead to further insights in conjunction with evidence from another modality. With this groundwork in place, we now shift our discussion to how we envision the dashboard will support *real-time* crisis responses.

5.1 Dynamic Timeframes

The MUMOSA dashboard is designed to show grounded evidence for the incident and timeframe the user selects at the start of a session to build their own understanding of time-stamped incident events. It remains an open design research question how we might modify the dashboard to *automatically visualize* incident changes for the user in real-time, without also cognitively overloading them by viewing too much information across the multiple modalities. One UI/UX design opportunity is augmenting the dashboard with a timeline and adjustable slider for the user to control the sequenced, connected display of photos, news report summaries, 3D reconstructions and schema graphs. Photographs from news reports of ongoing events could be presented along a timeline to show the progression of events together with generated text summaries based on and time-aligned to those reports for augmenting a Situation Report, such as SmartBook (Reddy et al., 2024). The 3DGS simulation within the Simulation Evidence panel, in conjunction with an adjustable slider on the timeline, could display changes to the simulation by adjusting the opacity of Gaussians belonging to dynamic objects (Shen et al., 2024; Wu et al., 2024). Similarly, the slider could be connected to the graph display in the Schema Evidence panel, enabling the user to move through the progression of photos on the timeline in conjunction with visible changes to the schema, displaying automated detection of events in red graph nodes (Appendix A shows different timescales of schema evidence).

Additional modalities may extend to time series data collected at the incident site from sensors deployed that are constantly recording and storing measurements. In particular, we are exploring how time series data from the air[7], water[8], and soil sample measurements[9] can be incorporated into the dashboard to allow a user to examine quantitative data changes over time and location and further query these new modalities through the Q/A interaction.

5.2 Scalability for Responding to Rapidly Evolving Incidents

In order for the dashboard to be responsive to real-time event tracking, the back-end storage and processing requirements must be scalable to support streaming data, as well as filter the incoming data for content, such as for misinformation. Though these issues fall beyond the scope of this paper, they

[7]https://www.epa.gov/east-palestine-oh-train-derailment/air-sampling-data

[8]https://www.orsanco.org/east-palestine-train-derailment-spill-response/

[9]https://www.epa.gov/east-palestine-oh-train-derailment/soil-and-sediment-sampling-data

help sharpen the criteria and distinctions to keep in mind as we are in the process of selecting metrics and designing an evaluation of the current MUMOSA dashboard with its strictly forensic goals. For example, the intended end-users of the forensic MUMOSA dashboard will not be subject to the time pressure, cognitive distractions, and levels of noise in an emergency operations center or an incident command post that end-users of a real-time dashboard would be. The speed of processing (velocity), the amount of data (volume), the range of data modalities (variety), the timeliness and accuracy of the data content (value and veracity)—all well-known "V"s of information overload—will differ along with stakeholder and user expectations and requirements of a dashboard, depending on whether it will serve forensic or real-time goals. These all need to be understood in advance of any dashboard evaluation.

5.3 Evaluating User Priorities

Ultimately, our goal is to support end-users of a real-time dashboard at SA levels 1, 2, and 3, that includes scenario planning and "what-if" analysis using all available modalities. In determining how effective the dashboard can be for investigators and responders at SA levels 1 and 2, we have begun to assess the accuracy of the technology in each evidence panel. Before we can measure how well the dashboard can support different user needs, as we are not subject matter experts for their tasks, we need to design and conduct interviews with individuals in the relevant communities.

Investigators, who examine past events with particular questions in mind, will benefit from training on the dashboard before any evaluation, with guided learning of panel workflows and in-depth searches that support chronological reconstruction (such as browsing the document collection and schema visualization over time). This already suggests additional value to prioritizing the development of the timeline mentioned above for a real-time dashboard. Furthermore, a future dashboard that provides automated detection and highlighting of discrepancies between conflicting event reports would also help expedite the investigator's work. For now, we plan to task participants involved in our *investigator evaluation* with manually constructing a timeline of events and their trusted sources, to assess the ease with which they can make use of the current dashboard.

Responders, who are in training to deal with crisis events, will benefit from learning to view the 3D simulations and annotations that document immediate dangers in physical environments, for discerning what constitutes sufficient information for rapid decision-making. Thus, a future dashboard that provides for automatic detection and highlighting of key crisis regions in the physical environment as the incident unfolds, would help expedite the responder processing of incoming information. For now, we are designing a pilot study for participants in the *responder evaluation* where their task will be to create a situation report with summaries of levels of danger at different locations, as more information becomes known over time.

5.4 Event Tracking with a Dialogue Agent

The dashboard as presented thus far relies on the user to "pull" information by typing and submitting their own questions as inspired by their viewing of the different evidence panels. We envision a future iteration where the dashboard becomes more like an *agent* that can also "push" information to the end-user, taking an active role in the interaction. The agent could engage in a dialogue with the user by supporting a fact-seeking conversation, requesting clarifications to the user's question, and making suggestions of follow-up questions. The agent may be designed to recognize changes to a situation as time progresses, and alert the user so they may further inquire.

Additionally, we expect to extend the dashboard beyond text input only to support various modality input, where the user could submit text questions about particular image(s) previously retrieved as visual evidence. We envision an additional interaction mode within the dashboard that can reference prior images and engage in a new dialogue session about them. This further would support new images to be uploaded as incidents unfold in real-time. In these cases of unlabeled data, human-authored captions may not be available, and instead, automatically generated descriptions can be used for Q/A matching. Table 2 shows both the human-authored descriptions about the image in Figure 2, as well as automatically generated ones, which provide extensive detail and attempted analysis.

6 Related Work

Text-based search methods, begun in the 1950's, have been central to modern information retrieval systems (Sanderson and Croft, 2012). Most recently, generative AI has been leading a new

Human-written caption	"This centrifuge separates solid waste from liquid wastewater in holding bins to determine whether the waste is hazardous and then disposed properly."
Alt-text	"Huge machine called a centrifuge separates the solid waste."
Text in image	"STRAD" and "SB162"
Generated description from Idefics3-8B-Llama3 (Prompt: "Describe this image")	"The object is most likely a type of pump station designed for heavy-duty use, probably utilized in industries like construction, mining, or wastewater management due to its robust build and extensive piping setup. Pumps labeled with identifiers like SB168 often denote standardized models within these sectors, known for their reliability and durability. Given the context clues provided by the surrounding environment (industrial equipment, trees), we infer that this equipment plays a critical role in managing fluid flow efficiently across different sites where liquid transfer is necessary." (See Appendix C for the full generated output)

Table 2: Texts associated with the photograph retrieved in Figure 2

wave of search-related technologies (Najork, 2023). Nonetheless, it is quite striking that reports suggest half of all web searches are not answered.[10] Thus, for complex tasks such as those build situational awareness, there remain significant opportunities to develop, deploy, and assess interactive systems for the impact of providing multiple modalities of information to dashboard users for their detection and understanding of events over time.

We know of no other research that combines information for user access across modalities as we have within an interactive dashboard. MUMOSA provides an interactive, multi-modal interface where users can iteratively forage for answers about complex events to meet their information requirements. Our approach, by retaining a dialogue history with text and visual evidence for documenting user searches, paves the way to building an AI agent-based system (White, 2024).

Event detection has recently been expanded by novel methods of embedding and extracting events across modalities from multimedia sources. For example, by constructing shared semantic vector spaces for texts and images (Radford et al., 2021; Jia et al., 2021), systems can generate text descriptions of events detected in images where only objects have been identified (Li et al., 2020a). Image retrieval has seen advances by using global features (Shao et al., 2023), augmenting query or image vectors (Zhu et al., 2023), and general purpose VLMs (Wang et al., 2022). Our FAQ approach on documents and images is intended to achieve high accuracy to support our investigator users looking forensically at data, and serve as a strong feasibility test in bringing together the evidence panels. We also give users access to the document and image collections using the semantic search ranking to enable users to forage in a less constrained way by exposing the evidence directly to the user.

The automated construction of regular patterns of events from news reports, where the task of event schema induction applies, continues to challenge researchers (Devare et al., 2023; Li et al., 2023). The innovation of building path language models by connecting shared arguments across events within instance graphs has provided for more complete schema induction (Li et al., 2020b).

Recent advances in 3DGS for 3D reconstruction have begun to support natural language querying of a scene (Shi et al., 2024), however these approaches presently only highlight segmentation masks based on keywords, e.g., 'train cars.' There is no framework in place to support interactive querying of the 3D reconstruction from natural language questions. In order to understand that the question we pose *"Where is the immediate danger?"* refers to the train cars requires greater understanding of 'danger' in the context of the simulation.

7 Conclusion

Our MUMOSA dashboard aims to provide a user with level 1 and 2 situational awareness for understanding essential elements of information and complex events by uniting complimentary modalities and interactions. We further envision how the dashboard will support real-time crisis response (SA level 3). By integrating document-based Q/A, visual evidence retrieval, event schema visualization, and 3D scene simulation, our dashboard offers a comprehensive solution for complex event understanding. This multifaceted approach not only supports various levels of situational awareness, from initial perception to comprehensive understanding, but also provides a flexible, future-ready framework that can evolve with advancements in AI and data processing technologies.

[10] https://blogs.microsoft.com/blog/2023/02/07/reinventing-search-with-a-new-ai-powered-microsoft-bing-and-edge-your-copilot-for-the-web

References

AI@Meta. 2024. Llama 3 model card.

Shawn Bowser and Stephanie M. Lukin. 2024. 3D Gaussian Splatting for Human-Robot Interaction. In *Interactive AI for Human-Centered Robotics Workshop*.

Sugam Devare, Mahnaz Koupaee, Gautham Gunapati, Sayontan Ghosh, Sai Vallurupalli, Yash Kumar Lal, Francis Ferraro, Nathanael Chambers, Greg Durrett, Raymond Mooney, et al. 2023. Sageviz: Schema generation and visualization. In *Proceedings of the 2023 Conference on Empirical Methods in Natural Language Processing: System Demonstrations*, pages 328–335.

Xinya Du, Zixuan Zhang, Sha Li, Pengfei Yu, Hongwei Wang, Tuan Lai, Xudong Lin, Ziqi Wang, Iris Liu, Ben Zhou, Haoyang Wen, Manling Li, Darryl Hannan, Jie Lei, Hyounghun Kim, Rotem Dror, Haoyu Wang, Michael Regan, Qi Zeng, Qing Lyu, Charles Yu, Carl Edwards, Xiaomeng Jin, Yizhu Jiao, Ghazaleh Kazeminejad, Zhenhailong Wang, Chris Callison-Burch, Mohit Bansal, Carl Vondrick, Jiawei Han, Dan Roth, Shih-Fu Chang, Martha Palmer, and Heng Ji. 2022. RESIN-11: Schema-guided event prediction for 11 newsworthy scenarios. In *Proceedings of the 2022 Conference of the North American Chapter of the Association for Computational Linguistics: Human Language Technologies: System Demonstrations*, pages 54–63, Hybrid: Seattle, Washington + Online. Association for Computational Linguistics.

Mica R. Endsley. 1995. Toward a theory of situation awareness in dynamic systems. *Journal of the Human Factors and Ergonomics Society*, 37(1):32–64.

Mica R. Endsley. 2015. Situation awareness misconceptions and misunderstandings. *Journal of Cognitive Engineering and Decision Making*, 9(1):4–32.

Felix Gervits, Anton Leuski, Claire Bonial, Carla Gordon, and David Traum. 2021. A classification-based approach to automating human-robot dialogue. Increasing Naturalness and Flexibility in Spoken Dialogue Interaction: 10th International Workshop on Spoken Dialogue Systems.

Ralph Grishman. 2019. Twenty-five years of information extraction. *Natural Language Engineering*, 25(6):677–692.

Chao Jia, Yinfei Yang, Ye Xia, Yi-Ting Chen, Zarana Parekh, Hieu Pham, Quoc V Le, Yunhsuan Sung, Zhen Li, and Tom Duerig. 2021. Scaling up visual and vision-language representa- tion learning with noisy text supervision. In *Proceedings of the 38 th International Conference on Machine Learning, PMLR 139*.

Bernhard Kerbl, Georgios Kopanas, Thomas Leimkuehler, and George Drettakis. 2023. 3D Gaussian Splatting for Real-Time Radiance Field Rendering. *ACM Transactions on Graphics (TOG)*, 42(4):1–14.

Alexander Kirillov, Eric Mintun, Nikhila Ravi, Hanzi Mao, Chloe Rolland, Laura Gustafson, Tete Xiao, Spencer Whitehead, Alexander C. Berg, Wan-Yen Lo, Piotr Dollár, and Ross Girshick. 2023. Segment anything. *Preprint*, arXiv:2304.02643.

Hugo Laurençon, Andrés Marafioti, Victor Sanh, and Léo Tronchon. 2024. Building and better understanding vision-language models: insights and future directions. *Preprint*, arXiv:2408.12637.

Anton Leuski and David Traum. 2011. Npceditor: Creating virtual human dialogue using information retrieval techniques. *Ai Magazine*, 32(2):42–56.

Manling Li, Alireza Zareian, Qi Zeng, Spencer Whitehead, Di Lu, Heng Ji, and Shih-Fu Chang. 2020a. Cross-media structured common space for multimedia event extraction. In *Proceedings of ACL*.

Manling Li, Qi Zeng, Ying Lin, Kyunghyun Cho, Heng Ji, Jonathan May, Nathanael Chambers, and Clare Voss. 2020b. Connecting the dots: Event graph schema induction with path language modeling. In *Proceedings of Conference on Empirical Methods in Natural Language Processing (EMNLP)*.

Sha Li, Ruining Zhao, Manling Li, Heng Ji, Chris Callison-Burch, and Jiawei Han. 2023. Open-domain hierarchical event schema induction by incremental prompting and verification. *Preprint*, arXiv:2307.01972.

Stephanie M Lukin, Felix Gervits, Cory J Hayes, Anton Leuski, Pooja Moolchandani, John G Rogers III, Carlos Sanchez Amaro, Matthew Marge, Clare R Voss, and David Traum. 2018. Scoutbot: a dialogue system for collaborative navigation.

Stephanie M. Lukin, Jaci South, and Shawn Bowser. 2024. CHRIS-Bot: A Robot for Dialogue and Scene Understanding of Anomalous Environments in Virtual Reality. Technical Report ARL-TR-9906, DEVCOM Army Research Laboratory.

N Najork. 2023. Generative information retrieval. In *Proceedings of the 46th Intern. ACM SIGIR Conf. on Research and Development in Information Retrieval*, volume 1.

Khanh Duy Nguyen, Zixuan Zhang, Reece Suchocki, Sha Li, Martha Palmer, Susan Brown, Jiawei Han, and Heng Ji. 2023. Resin-editor: A schema-guided hierarchical event graph visualizer and editor. *Preprint*, arXiv:2312.03093.

Alec Radford, Jong Wook Kim, Chris Hallacy, Aditya Ramesh, Gabriel Goh, Sandhini Agarwal, Girish Sastry, Amanda Askell, Pamela Mishkin, Jack Clark, Gretchen Krueger, and Ilya Sutskever. 2021. Learning transferable visual models from natural language supervision. In *Proceedings of the 38 th International Conference on Machine Learning, PMLR 139*.

Revanth Gangi Reddy, Daniel Lee, Yi R. Fung, Khanh Duy Nguyen, Qi Zeng, Manling Li, Ziqi Wang, Clare Voss, and Heng Ji. 2024. Smartbook: Ai-assisted situation report generation for intelligence analysts. *Preprint*, arXiv:2303.14337.

N Reimers. 2019. Sentence-bert: Sentence embeddings using siamese bert-networks. *arXiv preprint arXiv:1908.10084*.

Mark Sanderson and W. Bruce Croft. 2012. The history of information retrieval research. In *Proceedings of the IEEE, Issue: Special Centennial Issue*, volume 100, pages 1444–1451.

Shihao Shao, Kaifeng Chen, Arjun Karpur, Qinghua Cui, André Araujo, and Bingyi Cao. 2023. Global features are all you need for image retrieval and reranking. In *Proceedings of the IEEE/CVF International Conference on Computer Vision*, pages 11036–11046.

Licheng Shen, Ho Ngai Chow, Lingyun Wang, Tong Zhang, Mengqiu Wang, and Yuxing Han. 2024. Gaussian time machine: A real-time rendering methodology for time-variant appearances. *Preprint*, arXiv:2405.13694.

Jin-Chuan Shi, Miao Wang, Hao-Bin Duan, and Shao-Hua Guan. 2024. Language embedded 3d gaussians for open-vocabulary scene understanding. In *Proceedings of the IEEE/CVF Conference on Computer Vision and Pattern Recognition (CVPR)*, pages 5333–5343.

Lavanya Sita Tekumalla. 2020. NLP Tutorial : Automatic Question Answering from information in FAQ. https://github.com/lavanyats/QuestionAnswering_From_FAQ_Tutorial. Published: 2020. Accessed: 2024-10-01.

Wenhui Wang, Hangbo Bao, Li Dong, Johan Bjorck, Zhiliang Peng, Qiang Liu, Kriti Aggarwal, Owais Khan Mohammed, Saksham Singhal, Subhojit Som, et al. 2022. Image as a foreign language: Beit pretraining for all vision and vision-language tasks. *arXiv preprint arXiv:2208.10442*.

Haoyang Wen, Ying Lin, Tuan Lai, Xiaoman Pan, Sha Li, Xudong Lin, Ben Zhou, Manling Li, Haoyu Wang, Hongming Zhang, Xiaodong Yu, Alexander Dong, Zhenhailong Wang, Yi Fung, Piyush Mishra, Qing Lyu, Dídac Surís, Brian Chen, Susan Windisch Brown, Martha Palmer, Chris Callison-Burch, Carl Vondrick, Jiawei Han, Dan Roth, Shih-Fu Chang, and Heng Ji. 2021. RESIN: A dockerized schema-guided cross-document cross-lingual cross-media information extraction and event tracking system. In *Proceedings of the 2021 Conference of the North American Chapter of the Association for Computational Linguistics: Human Language Technologies: Demonstrations*, pages 133–143, Online. Association for Computational Linguistics.

Ryen W. White. 2024. Advancing the search frontier with ai agents. *Communications of the ACM*, 67(9):54–65.

Guanjun Wu, Taoran Yi, Jiemin Fang, Lingxi Xie, Xiaopeng Zhang, Wei Wei, Wenyu Liu, Qi Tian, and Xinggang Wang. 2024. 4d gaussian splatting for real-time dynamic scene rendering. *Preprint*, arXiv:2310.08528.

Xiaohua Zhai, Basil Mustafa, Alexander Kolesnikov, and Lucas Beyer. 2023. Sigmoid loss for language image pre-training. *Preprint*, arXiv:2303.15343.

Qiusi Zhan, Sha Li, Kathryn Conger, Martha Palmer, Heng Ji, and Jiawei Han. 2023. Glen: General-purpose event detection for thousands of types. *Preprint*, arXiv:2303.09093.

Yutao Zhu, Huaying Yuan, Shuting Wang, Jiongnan Liu, Wenhan Liu, Chenlong Deng, Zhicheng Dou, and Ji-Rong Wen. 2023. Large language models for information retrieval: A survey. *arXiv preprint arXiv:2308.07107*.

A Appendix: Schema Visualization and Sources

This section lists the four article sources used to create the different schema timeframes.

Article 1:

- Title: 50-car train derailment causes big fire, evacuations in Ohio
- Date Published: February 4, 2023
- Source: Associated Press (AP)
- https://apnews.com/article/pennsylvania-ohio-evacuations-fires-5d399dc745f51ef746e22828083d8591

Article 2:

- Title: East Palestine under mandatory evacuation, possible explosion warning after toxic train derailment
- Date Published: February 5, 2023
- Source: Ideastream Public Media
- https://www.ideastream.org/community/2023-02-05/east-palestine-under-mandatory-evacuation-possible-explosion-warning-after-toxic-train-derailment

Article 3:

- Title: Ohio crews conduct a 'controlled release' of toxic chemicals from derailed train cars
- Date Published: February 6, 2023
- Source: National Public Radio (NPR)
- https://www.npr.org/2023/02/06/1154760911/ohio-train-derailment

Article 4:

- Title: Is the Ohio River contaminated? East Palestine train derailment sparks concerns over water
- Date Published: February 14, 2023
- Source: The Columbus Dispatch
- https://www.dispatch.com/story/news/local/2023/02/14/is-the-ohio-river-contaminated-east-palestine-train-derailment-sparks-concerns-over-water/69900528007/

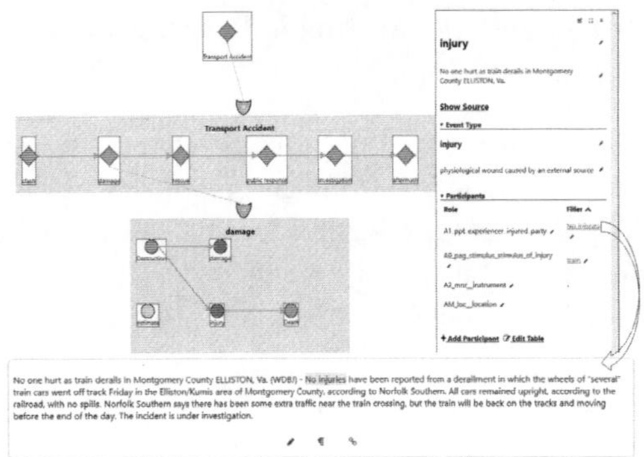

Figure 4: Schema Evidence Panel using the transport accident schema, matched on events in news reports over 10 days. Selecting 'injury' (red) node and matched text "No injuries" in role filler, opens panel below with that text highlighted in source context.

As more documents are analysed over time, additional extracted events are incorporated into MUMOSA. Some event nodes may be newly matched (previously blue, turn red), such as "injury", while newly extracted events not included in the original schema may appear (yellow), such as "estimate", as shown in Figure 4. Selecting the linked filler in the panel of a matched node opens another window containing the matched phrase in the context of the source material.

Figure 5 presents two schemas side by side, to make evident the contrast between earlier and later date information within same schema. Both schemas match and visualize on the "damage" event, first with extracted information from just the earliest document (Article 1), and then from all four articles over ten days. Figure 6 similarly presents two schemas corresponds to the schema matching and visualization on "investigation" events, first with extracted information from just the earliest document (Article 1), and then from all four articles over ten days.

B Appendix: Simulation Space

Figure 7 displays a flattened view of the 3D simulation modeled using 3D Gaussian Splatting from the source video: "National Transportation Safety Board B-Roll: Train Derailment in East Palestine, OH" [11]

[11]https://www.youtube.com/watch?v=7AyXTVkVBT4

C Appendix: Full Image Description Output

Table 2 abbreviated the generated output by defics3-8B-Llama3 with the input image in Figure 2 using the prompt "Describe this image". Below is the full output from the model, verbatim (** indicates bold formatting):

The image depicts a piece of industrial equipment situated outdoors, likely in an area designated for construction or maintenance work. This apparatus appears to be part of a larger system used for pumping liquids or slurries, given the presence of hoses and pipes connected to it

Description of Objects Present in the Image:

1. **Main Equipment**:
- A large machine with multiple components:
- It has a rectangular base that supports several vertical elements.
- There is a prominent horizontal pipe extending from one side of the main structure, which seems to have black corrugated tubing attached to its end. This suggests that the device might be involved in transferring fluids or materials through pipelines.

2. **Safety Features**:
- Yellow guardrails are installed around the top section of the machinery, indicating safety measures to prevent falls during operation.
- Additional yellow handrail sections can also be seen on other parts of the structure, ensuring operator protection while working at height.

3. **Identification Markings**:
- "STR" is prominently displayed on the front panel of the machine, possibly denoting the manufacturer's name or model identifier.
- Below "STR," there's another label reading "SB168," which could represent a specific product line or serial number associated with the equipment.

4. **Covered Section**:
- At the bottom right corner of the image, there is a covered portion of the equipment. The cover bears white text that reads "SB168." This indicates either a storage compartment or a protective casing over sensitive internal mechanisms.

5. **Surrounding Environment**:
- In the background, various pieces of industrial equipment and containers are visible, suggesting a typical setting such as a warehouse, factory yard, or construction site.
- Trees and greenery indicate that the location may not be entirely urban but rather semi-rural or suburban.

6. **Sky Conditions**:
- Above, the sky is mostly clear with scattered clouds, implying fair weather conditions suitable for outdoor operations.

Analysis:
The described object is most likely a type of pump station designed for heavy-duty use, probably utilized in industries like construction, mining, or wastewater management due to its robust build and extensive piping setup. Pumps labeled with identifiers like SB168 often denote standardized models within these sectors, known for their reliability and durability. Given the context clues provided by the surrounding environment (industrial equipment, trees), we infer that this equipment plays a critical role in managing fluid flow efficiently across different sites where liquid transfer is necessary.

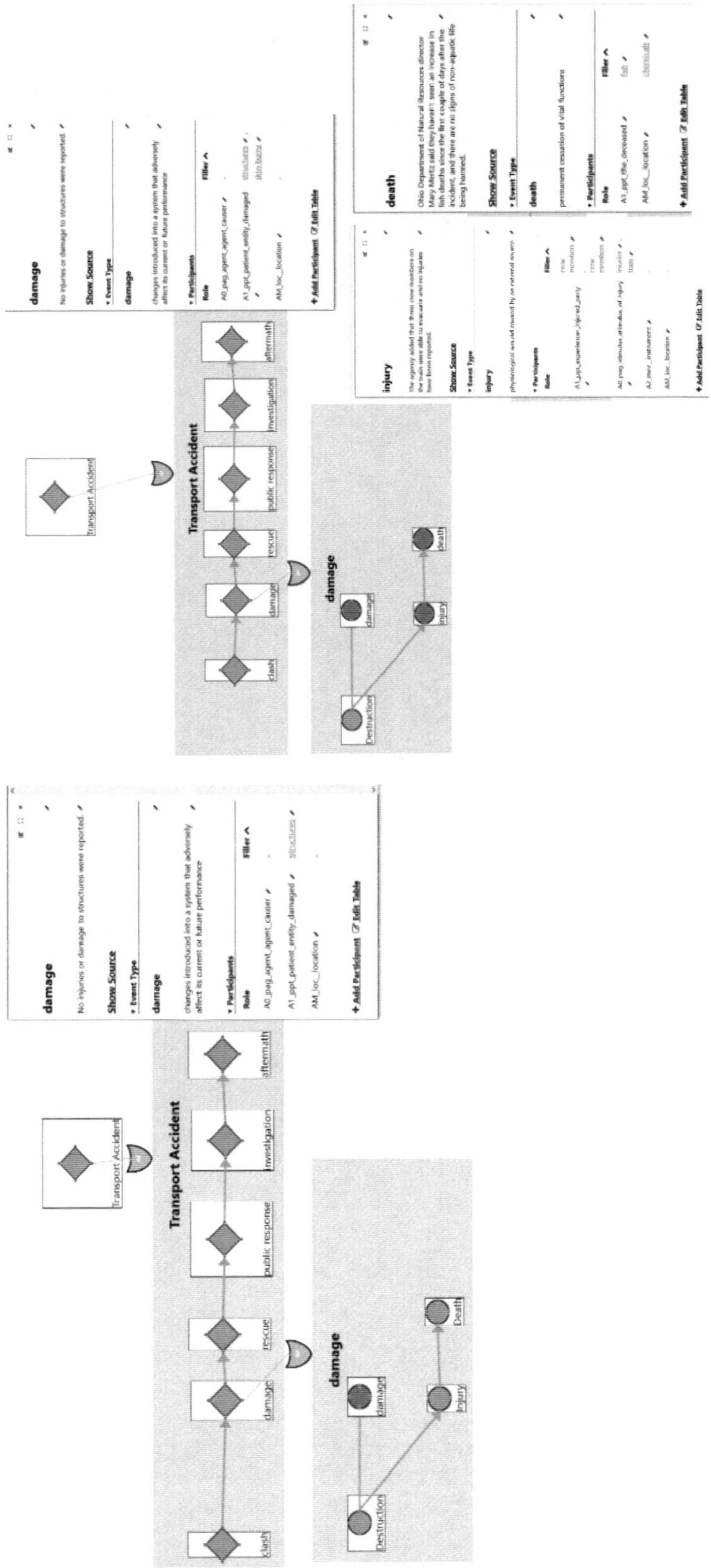

Figure 5: Same"transport accident" schema with "damage" events extracted from earliest date information and then with additional extracted information up to 10 days later

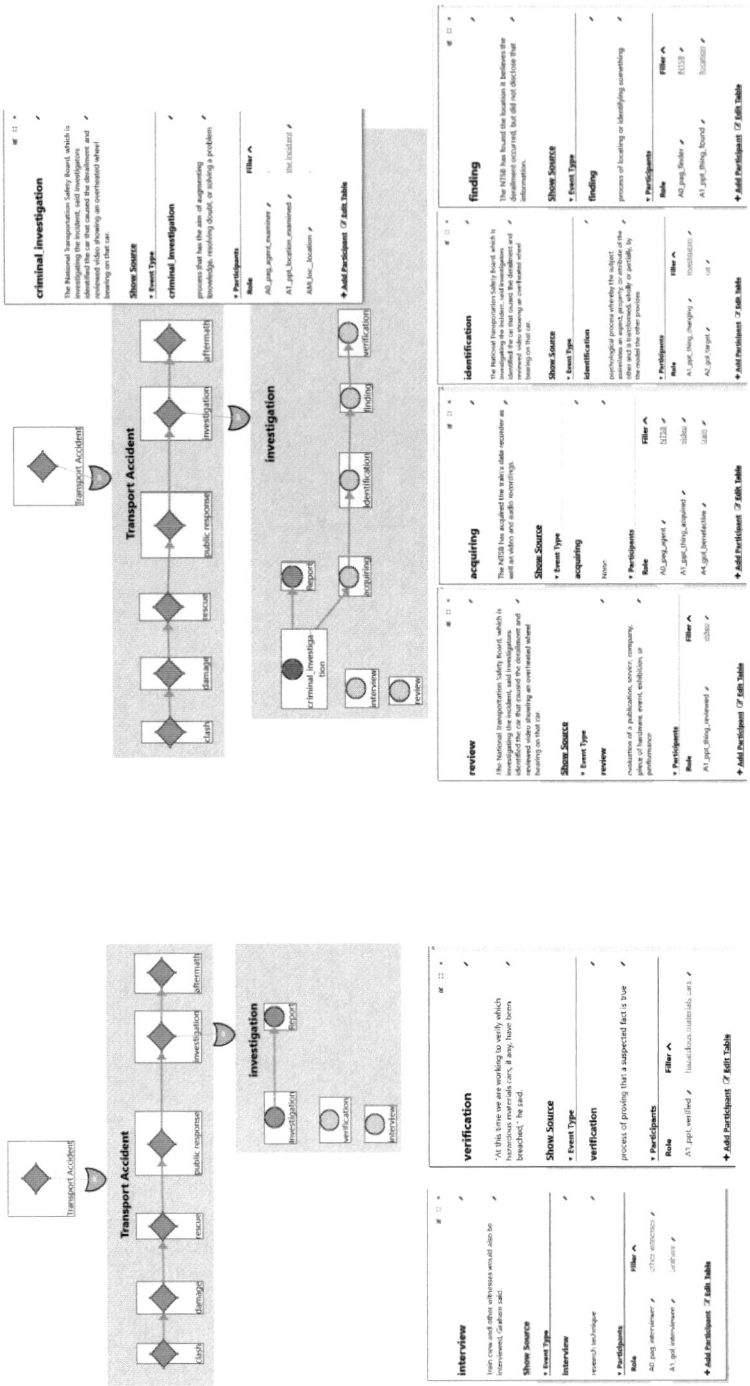

Figure 6: Same"transport accident" schema with "investigation" events extracted from earliest date information and then with additional extracted information up to 10 days later

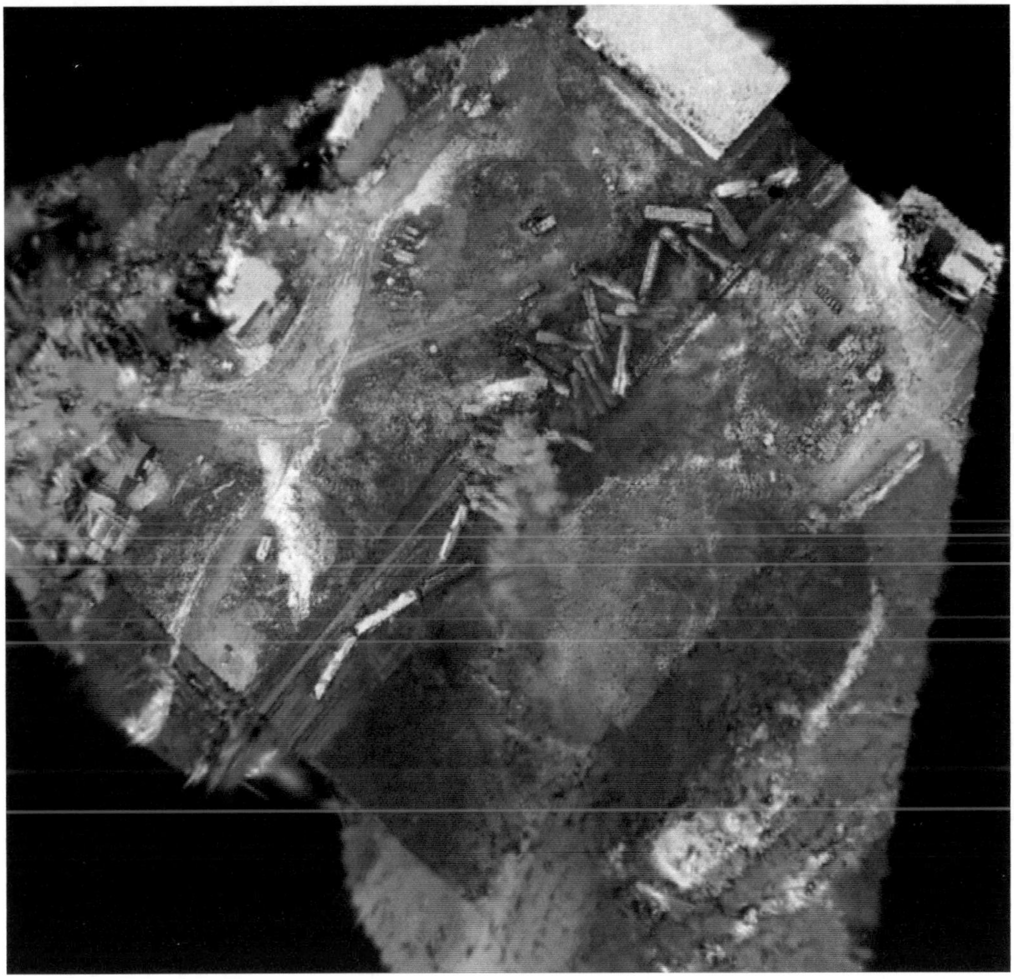

Figure 7: Flattened view of the 3D simulation

Reasoning and Tools for Human-Level Forecasting

Elvis Hsieh*, **Preston Fu***, **Jonathan Chen***

UC Berkeley
{htelvis92, prestonfu, jonchen25}@berkeley.edu

Abstract

Language models (LMs) trained on web-scale datasets are largely successful due to their ability to memorize large amounts of training data, even if only present in a few examples. These capabilities are often desirable in evaluation on tasks such as question answering but raise questions about whether these models can exhibit genuine reasoning or succeed only at mimicking patterns from the training data. This distinction is particularly salient in forecasting tasks, where the answer is not present in the training data, and the model must reason to make logical deductions. We present Reasoning and Tools for Forecasting (RTF), a framework of reasoning-and-acting (ReAct) agents that can dynamically retrieve updated information and run numerical simulation with equipped tools. We evaluate our model with questions from competitive forecasting platforms and demonstrate that our method is competitive with and can outperform human predictions. This suggests that LMs, with the right tools, can indeed think and adapt like humans, offering valuable insights for real-world decision-making.

1 Introduction

Forecasting is an essential tool today, playing a critical role in government, corporate, and personal decision-making. Weather forecasting provides essential information for agriculture, natural disaster preparedness for governments, and travel plans for individuals. During the COVID-19 pandemic, lockdown policies were largely determined by forecasts, which were required to be sufficiently accurate due to their global impact (Dubé et al., 2020).

Forecasting methodologies fall into two main categories (Webby and O'Connor, 1996): statistical and judgmental. Statistical forecasting leverages time-series modeling and excels with abundant data under stable conditions. Conversely, judgmental forecasting, which we refer to simply as "forecasting," typically relies on human expertise, integrating historical data, domain knowledge, and intuition to make predictions, and is particularly useful when data are sparse or conditions are volatile.

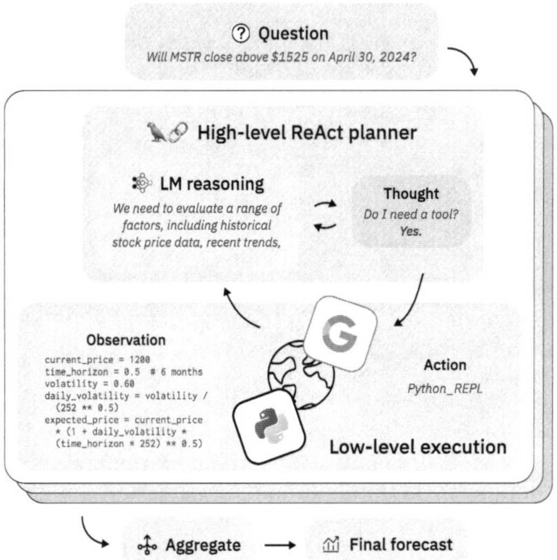

Figure 1: RTF: High-level ReAct agent oversees low-level agents, each equipped with distinct toolkits and data/document stores to accomplish various tasks, including Google API calling and Python simulation.

By nature, forecasting requires not only accuracy but also the ability to continuously adapt to dynamic data streams. This is where traditional LMs often struggle: timely data updates may cause predictions to change considerably and past data to be irrelevant.

2 Related Work

Information retrieval Reliable and accurate predictions are largely dependent on the information available to the predictor. This is especially the case of LMs, which are trained on data preceding a knowledge cutoff and have been shown to perform better with information retrieval (Shuster

*Authors contributed equally to this work.

Proceedings of the Workshop on the Future of Event Detection (FuturED), pages 48–57
November 15, 2024

et al., 2021).

Language models model the likelihood $p_\theta(y_i|x, y_{<i})$ for input sequences x and target sequences y. Retrieval-augmented generation (RAG) (Lewis et al., 2021) proposes augmenting this approach with non-parametric memory, i.e. retrieving the top-k text documents z via $p_\eta(z|x)$ and conditioning the generator on the retrieved passages, $p_\theta(y_i|x, z, y_{<i})$. In a forecasting context, RAG enables us to search for relevant documents z that may contain timely information about the forecasting task x not present in the training data.

Prior approaches to LLM forecasting (Zou et al., 2022a) propose using neural networks to automate prediction in prediction markets. While language models can be trained to improve their performance on forecasting tasks, their accuracy remains significantly below those of human experts.

Current methods aim to improve the accuracy of LLM forecasting by fine-tuning and scratchpad prompting (Nye et al., 2021; Halawi et al., 2024; Yan et al., 2024) or ensembling (Bassamboo et al., 2018; Schoenegger et al., 2024) to first approach human-level forecasting. Concurrent work (Pratt et al., 2024) benchmarks LLMs' forecasting capabilities using the GleanGen prediction market, an internal tool at Google. However, this approach did not accurately reflect real human crowd prediction distributions, and it relied on PaLM2 (Anil et al., 2023), which was suboptimal than GPT models.

We propose a zero-shot tool-usage LLM framework without costly fine-tuning and laborious tedious scratchpad format prompting.

Ensembles Leveraging multiple LLM agents has demonstrated strong performance on a variety of tasks, and improve performance beyond that of a single agent (Talebirad and Nadiri, 2023; Liu et al., 2023). Recent work in tool learning has implemented task planning and execution with separate agents (Song et al., 2023; Shi et al., 2024). LLM forecasting in particular has relied on the wisdom of crowds effect, and has shown that taking ensemble sizes up to 36 outperforms any individual forecasting agent (Bassamboo et al., 2018; Schoenegger et al., 2024).

We propose bridging this gap with a hierarchical structure to facilitate cooperation between high-level reasoning and low-level execution agents, and demonstrate that a small ensemble suffices for human-level performance.

3 Reasoning and Tools for Forecasting

Forecasting is a complex task solving environment, for which we would like to leverage a frozen LM p_θ as reasoning. Successful forecasting agents rely on the most up-to-date information, and accordingly operate as agents that collect observations $\mathbf{o}_t \in \mathcal{O}$ and take actions $\mathbf{a}_t \in \mathcal{A}$. The observation space $\mathcal{O}$ is natural language, as collected from the prompt itself or information on the internet. The agent's actions are distributed according to $\mathbf{a}_t \sim \pi(\mathbf{a}_t|\mathbf{c}_t)$, where $\mathbf{c}_t = (\mathbf{o}_1, \mathbf{a}_1, \ldots, \mathbf{o}_{t-1}, \mathbf{a}_{t-1})$ is the context to the agent.

Our proposed approach π satisfies the following criteria:

(i) It is **simple, scalable, and time-invariant**. As we consider different datasets of forecasting questions or language models at least as capable as the current state-of-the-art, we would like our approach to work at least as well.

(ii) It can produce comprehensive responses through zero-shot prompting from factual information, which can be used to **reliably support decision-making** in downstream scenarios.

(iii) These responses should be **consistent**, i.e. they should correctly synthesize the up-to-date information the model collects.

(Yao et al., 2023) shows that CoT prompting, even with in-context examples, can iteratively hallucinate to produce incorrect responses on complex tasks. CoT satisfies (i) but neither (ii) nor (iii). We find that CoT's lack of interaction with the environment (i.e. sole reliance on its training data) limits its reasoning abilities and over-emphasizes irrelevant information.

(Yao et al., 2023) proposes ReAct for this setting: $\mathcal{A} = \{\texttt{search}, \texttt{lookup}, \texttt{finish}\}$, and observations $\mathbf{o}_t$ from `search` and `lookup` are collected from $\mathcal{O} \subseteq$ Wikipedia web API. The context is then augmented a thought $\hat{\mathbf{a}}_t \sim p_\theta(\hat{\mathbf{a}}_t|\mathbf{c}_t)$ that composes information about the existing context. This method has shown to significantly enhance the model's ability to refine its responses continuously, reducing the likelihood of erroneous outputs due to lacking critical context information. Vanilla ReAct satisfies (i); as part of our framework, we show that it can additionally satisfy (ii) and (iii).

Hierarchical planning We define π by an aggregate of a collection of hierarchical ReAct agents with tools for real-time data retrieval and simulation, expanding π's observations $\mathbf{o}_t$ collected from $\mathcal{O} \subseteq$ Google Search API and Python interpreter.

We propose hierarchical ReAct planning, where a LM agent acts as a high-level planner for handling abstract logic and forecasting principles based on the outputs collected from the low-level agents (Figure 1). When LLMs handle API directly with individual agents, it can consume a large portion of the context window. We delegate the reasoning and API calling to specialized agents to enhances efficiency, conserves tokens, and allows for more complex operations. The high-level agent interacts with the low-level agent by invoking it as a tool. We wrap API tools with another ReAct agent to form the low-level agent, which significantly increases API call success rates due to its self-correction mechanism (Yao et al., 2023). Both classes of agents are implemented with GPT-4o backbones.

Ensemble Motivated by (Schoenegger et al., 2024), we use GPT-4o as the sole backbone for our method, and aggregate outputs from just 3 agents. Despite our small ensemble, our approach of ensembling highly calibrated agents shows robust performance (Section 4.2).

4 Experiments

4.1 Setup

Models and data (Jin et al., 2021; Zou et al., 2022b) have proposed forecasting benchmarks to assess models' forecasting abilities, simulating forecasting by leveraging that models are only trained up to a cutoff date. However, these benchmarks, consisting of questions that resolved in 2022, are now outdated for evaluating the performance of models such as GPT-4o due to answer leakage in training data (knowledge cutoff October 2023; see Appendix A.1).

We curated the dataset on April 15, 2024, when we scraped the platform for questions resolving within the next two weeks and corresponding human crowd predictions. We then filtered out vague questions through an LLM with an filtering system prompt, and ran every prediction method on these questions, enabling a fair comparison between each method and the human crowd. A example of a vague question filtered was "Is AP Chemistry harder than AP Physics 1?" since no objective answer could be given (see Appendix D.1). To prevent answer leakage from the Google API, we set the search range to prior to this date.

None of our baselines have direct access to prediction market data, and empirically we found that this information was never scraped via Google search. That is, the prediction given by the ensemble of agents relies on only the agents themselves, with no human crowd influence. (By contrast, if deployed in the real world, this approach could benefit from incorporating the current human crowd performance as an input to the prediction due to the wisdom-of-crowds effect. Indeed, we observe in our experiments that human crowds are fairly well-calibrated.) For the model details, we set the high-level agent using GPT-4-0 with a temperature of 0.1, and the low-level agent using GPT-4-0 with a temperature of 0.

Performance metrics Our n forecasting questions have true outcomes $o_i \in \{0,1\}$ and probabilistic forecasts $f_i \in [0,1]$. We evaluate our forecasts using Brier scores (Brier, 1950), i.e. $\frac{1}{n}\sum_{i=1}^{n}(f_i - o_i)^2$, and accuracy, i.e. $\frac{1}{n}\sum_{i=1}^{n}\mathbf{1}\{\mathbf{1}\{f_i > 0.5\} = o_i\}$.[1][2] In case LMs decline to give numerical answers, the question is dropped over all methods when evaluating scores.

Table 1: Performance of different models with the same prompt on forecasting questions. "Base LM" refers to {GPT-4o, 4, 3.5, Llama 3}. "Acc" is accuracy, and "Std" is ensemble standard deviation.

Method	Brier $\downarrow$	Acc % $\uparrow$	Std $\downarrow$
Crowd	0.172	73.8	
RTF Median of 3	**0.169**	72.4	0.092
RTF Mean of 3	0.170	**73.9**	0.092
RTF Sampled	0.180	71.6	
Halawi et al. (2024) GPT-4o	0.177	68.7	
GPT-4o	0.210	65.5	
Base LM Mean	0.218	62.9	0.150
Base LM Median	0.228	61.3	0.150
Llama 3	0.256	56.2	
GPT-3.5	0.261	53.5	
GPT-4	0.265	54.8	

Baselines In Table 1, we compare RTF ensemble to multiple baselines: (a) crowd scores given by the current traded values on Manifold Markets (see

[1] The optimal strategy to minimize Brier scores is to forecast $f_i = \mathbb{P}(o_i = 1)$, so this scoring metric is unbiased. It is typical to compare Brier scores to 0.25, which can be achieved by $f_i = 0.5$ for all i.

[2] Accuracy denotes whether f_i and o_i are on the same side of 0.5.

Appendix A.2), (b) scratchpad prompting, ensemble, and fine-tuning (Halawi et al., 2024), and (c) base models from different providers.

4.2 Results and Observations

Table 1 demonstrates that RTF significantly improves over CoT and scratchpad with fine-tuning. We also achieve comparable Brier score (0.169 vs. 0.172) and superior accuracy (73.9% vs. 73.8%) compared to human predictors using the median and mean of our ensemble, respectively.

We also demonstrate that ensembles for RTF yield better performance than individual agents (Brier 0.169 vs. 0.180). However, this is not the case for base LMs (Brier 0.218 vs. 0.210 for GPT-4o). Base LMs tend to produce higher-variance outputs (standard deviation in ensemble size 4 of 0.150) compared to our better-calibrated ReAct agents (standard deviation in ensemble size 3 of 0.092), which satisfied (iii) as defined in Section 3.

Ensembles only contribute to the final performance if each ensemble member is already sufficiently calibrated. Indeed, Brier scores given by randomly sampling our ReAct ensemble outputs, "React Sampled" in the table, achieved a score of 0.180, far better than was achieved by any of the base methods (which, aside from GPT-4o, perform worse than guessing 0.5 every time by Brier score).

Ablation study To demonstrate the effectiveness of our introduced components, we conduct the ablation study. We showed each component is necessary for the fully functioning RTF framework.

- **ReAct:** RTF itself without adequate guidance from ReAct struggles to properly use the tools provided by our low-level agents, which leads to misguided lines of reasoning that cascade downstream. This is consistent with the observation (B) in (Yao et al., 2023), where groundedness and trustworthiness come at the cost of higher reasoning error rates.

- **Hierarchical Planning:** Empirically, without the cooperation of high- and low-level agents, a single agent fails to call APIs and perform necessary reasoning, as it exhausted available tokens on API schemas. In our experiments, the single-agent approach frequently encountered time-out errors or exceeded rate limits when handling complex queries.

Qualitative analysis While the baselines systematically evaluate multiple considerations, they do not consider interactions between these considerations. Empirically, we find in our samples that the prompting style we present is useful in generating a wide variety of arguments and providing reasonable estimates for how to weight each of those arguments. On the other hand, we see that this same prompt GPT-4o directly does this calibration in a sequential manner to update its final estimate, which may result in over- or under-estimate based on the recency of its considerations. In general, we find that RTF yield human-like reasoning trajectories, showing the robustness of interactive decision making, supporting goal (ii) from Section 3 (see Appendix D).

Calibration index In Table 2, we evaluate our methods by calibration index, which compares binned forecast probabilities to observed outcomes. A well-calibrated model means that if a forecast predicts an event with a certain probability, the event should occur approximately that fraction of the time over many predictions.

We calculate the calibration index as

$$CI = \frac{1}{N}\sum_{k=1}^{K} N_k(f_k - o_k)^2,$$

where N is the total number of forecasts, N_k is the number of forecasts in bin k, f_k is the mean forecast probability in bin k, and o_k is the observed probability with which events occur in bin k. We select bins as the K-quantiles of the forecasts.

Comparing GPT-4o and React Mean, we see a significant decrease in calibration index (0.0194 vs. 0.0129), which shows that ensembling with ReAct not only increases forecasting accuracy, but also more accurately measures the specific magnitudes with which events occur.

Table 2: Calibration index with $K = 5$

Method	Calibration Index ↓
Crowd	0.0101
ReAct Mean	**0.0129**
ReAct Median	0.0137
ReAct	0.0164
GPT-4o	0.0194
GPT-4	0.0290
GPT-3.5	0.0298
Llama 3	0.0301

5 Conclusion

We present Reasoning and Tools for Forecasting, a framework to leverage LMs' reasoning capabilities by interacting with the latest information. It is competitive with the predictive capabilities of human forecasters on forecasting platforms. The RTF synthesizes information through a structured decision-making process, ensuring that the predictions are both current and relevant. Additionally, while previous work has shown that ensembling can improve prediction accuracy, a carefully calibrated smaller set of models is often more cost-effective than larger ensembles.

By advancing LMs' abilities to reason and dynamically interact with new data, RTF offers a robust tool for real-world decision-making for tasks like forecasting.

Limitations The evaluation dataset is based on prediction market data and popular questions rather than domain-specific questions. This facilitates a comparison with crowd prediction performance, but may not fully capture the nuances of more specialized domains. In addition, our work focused on predicting binary rather than numerical outcomes.

Acknowledgments We appreciate the inspiration from Prof. Jacob Steinhardt's amazing forecasting class at UC Berkeley. We thank OpenAI for granting API credits.

References

Rohan Anil, Andrew M. Dai, and Orhan Firat. 2023. Palm 2 technical report. *Preprint*, arXiv:2305.10403.

Achal Bassamboo, Ruomeng Cui, and Antonio Moreno. 2018. Wisdom of crowds: Forecasting using prediction markets. In *Technical Report*. Working paper, Kellogg School of Management, Northwestern University.

Glenn W Brier. 1950. Verification of forecasts expressed in terms of probability. *Monthly weather review*, 78(1):1–3.

Mirette Dubé, Alyshah Kaba, Theresa Cronin, Sue Barnes, Tara Fuselli, and Vincent Grant. 2020. COVID-19 pandemic preparation: using simulation for systems-based learning to prepare the largest healthcare workforce and system in Canada. *Advances in Simulation*, 5:22.

Danny Halawi, Fred Zhang, Chen Yueh-Han, and Jacob Steinhardt. 2024. Approaching human-level forecasting with language models. *Preprint*, arXiv:2402.18563.

Woojeong Jin, Rahul Khanna, Suji Kim, Dong-Ho Lee, Fred Morstatter, Aram Galstyan, and Xiang Ren. 2021. Forecastqa: A question answering challenge for event forecasting with temporal text data. *Preprint*, arXiv:2005.00792.

Patrick Lewis, Ethan Perez, Aleksandra Piktus, Fabio Petroni, Vladimir Karpukhin, Naman Goyal, Heinrich Küttler, Mike Lewis, Wen tau Yih, Tim Rocktäschel, Sebastian Riedel, and Douwe Kiela. 2021. Retrieval-augmented generation for knowledge-intensive nlp tasks. *Preprint*, arXiv:2005.11401.

Zijun Liu, Yanzhe Zhang, Peng Li, Yang Liu, and Diyi Yang. 2023. Dynamic llm-agent network: An llm-agent collaboration framework with agent team optimization. *Preprint*, arXiv:2310.02170.

Manifold Markets. 2022. Maniswap.

Metaculus. 2023. Wisdom of the Crowd vs. the Best of the Best of the Best.

Maxwell Nye, Anders Johan Andreassen, Guy Gur-Ari, Henryk Michalewski, Jacob Austin, David Bieber, David Dohan, Aitor Lewkowycz, Maarten Bosma, David Luan, et al. 2021. Show your work: Scratchpads for intermediate computation with language models. *arXiv preprint arXiv:2112.00114*.

Sarah Pratt, Seth Blumberg, Pietro Kreitlon Carolino, and Meredith Ringel Morris. 2024. Can language models use forecasting strategies? *Preprint*, arXiv:2406.04446.

Philipp Schoenegger, Indre Tuminauskaite, Peter S. Park, and Philip E. Tetlock. 2024. Wisdom of the silicon crowd: Llm ensemble prediction capabilities rival human crowd accuracy. *Preprint*, arXiv:2402.19379.

Zhengliang Shi, Shen Gao, Xiuyi Chen, Yue Feng, Lingyong Yan, Haibo Shi, Dawei Yin, Pengjie Ren, Suzan Verberne, and Zhaochun Ren. 2024. Learning to use tools via cooperative and interactive agents. *Preprint*, arXiv:2403.03031.

Kurt Shuster, Spencer Poff, Moya Chen, Douwe Kiela, and Jason Weston. 2021. Retrieval augmentation reduces hallucination in conversation. *Preprint*, arXiv:2104.07567.

Yifan Song, Weimin Xiong, Dawei Zhu, Wenhao Wu, Han Qian, Mingbo Song, Hailiang Huang, Cheng Li, Ke Wang, Rong Yao, et al. 2023. Restgpt: Connecting large language models with real-world restful apis. *arXiv preprint arXiv:2306.06624*.

Yashar Talebirad and Amirhossein Nadiri. 2023. Multi-agent collaboration: Harnessing the power of intelligent llm agents. *Preprint*, arXiv:2306.03314.

Richard Webby and Marcus O'Connor. 1996. Judgemental and statistical time series forecasting: a review of the literature. *International Journal of Forecasting*, 12(1):91–118. Probability Judgmental Forecasting.

Qi Yan, Raihan Seraj, Jiawei He, Lili Meng, and Tristan Sylvain. 2024. Autocast++: Enhancing world event prediction with zero-shot ranking-based context retrieval. *Preprint*, arXiv:2310.01880.

Shunyu Yao, Jeffrey Zhao, Dian Yu, Nan Du, Izhak Shafran, Karthik Narasimhan, and Yuan Cao. 2023. React: Synergizing reasoning and acting in language models. *Preprint*, arXiv:2210.03629.

Andy Zou, Tristan Xiao, Ryan Jia, Joe Kwon, Mantas Mazeika, Richard Li, Dawn Song, Jacob Steinhardt, Owain Evans, and Dan Hendrycks. 2022a. Forecasting future world events with neural networks. *Preprint*, arXiv:2206.15474.

Andy Zou, Tristan Xiao, Ryan Jia, Joe Kwon, Mantas Mazeika, Richard Li, Dawn Song, Jacob Steinhardt, Owain Evans, and Dan Hendrycks. 2022b. Forecasting future world events with neural networks. *Preprint*, arXiv:2206.15474.

A Models and Knowledge Accuracy

A.1 Models

Table 3: Models we evaluated

Model	Knowledge Cutoff	Evaluation Cost
GPT-4o	Oct 2023	$0.005/1K tokens
GPT-4-Turbo	Apr 2023	$0.01/1K tokens
GPT-3.5-Turbo	Sep 2021	$0.0005/1K tokens
Llama-3-7B	Mar 2023	One GPU

We list the details of models we evaluated in Table 3, where the cutoffs have been retrieved from the model cards. For GPT models, we run them via the OpenAI API. We host Llama-3-7B on a single NVIDIA TITAN RTX 24GB via Ollama for roughly 0.5 GPU-hours. All other approaches are run through the OpenAI API, for roughly 1 hour per naive baseline, 6 hours for our reproduction of (Halawi et al., 2024), and 2.5 hours for our proposed method. For GPT models, we use temperature 0.5 for all the experiments.

(Halawi et al., 2024) finds that GPT-3.5 and GPT-4 do not have leakage due to post-training. We find that the same is true of GPT-4o and Llama-3-7B: prompting with "Answer this question without searching the web: Who was appointed to the Governor-General of Australia in 2024?" yielded a statement about its cutoff date, whereas the correct answer was given when prompted for the answer in 2019.

A.2 Crowd Predictions

On Manifold Markets, players make bets on the outcome of various events where the prices of bets are determined by a current aggregate of crowd predictions, which are prices in $[0, 1]$. As bets are made, the prices are adjusted by their automated market-makers (Markets, 2022). As shown in (Metaculus, 2023), the crowd prediction is a strong baseline and consistently outperform top forecaster in the prediction market.

B Dataset

B.1 Questions

Our final dataset consisted of 201 questions from Manifold Markets. These question were all resolved after April 15, 2024, which was the knowledge cutoff date for our low-level agent supporting the Google Search API. We include a subset of the dataset for reference.

Table 4: 5 example questions from dataset

1. Will Congress pass bill banning Tiktok by April 30?
2. 2024-04-30: Will ETH close above $3700?
3. Will "Challengers" (2024) receive a CinemaScore of B+ or above?
4. Will >10 NYU student pro-Palestinian protesters be arrested by the end of April?
5. Will Adeel Mangi be confirmed by the U.S. Senate before May 1st?

From Manifold Markets, we initially filtered for questions that resolve between April 16, 2024 and May 15, 2024, inclusive. Then, to improve the quality of our questions, we filtered the question as described in Appendix D.1. Finally, after the markets have resolved, we re-collect data using the API to extract the answers and compute Brier scores and accuracies. In the future, researchers can use our questions data for forecasting using LMs and information retrieval tools with cutoff dates before April 15, 2024 (see Section 4.1).

B.2 Knowledge Evaluation by Category

Table 5: Category frequencies

Count	Category
Economics & Business	68
Politics & Governance	34
Science & Tech	29
Arts & Recreation	29
Sports	16
Security & Defense	13
Healthcare & Biology	5
Environment & Energy	4
Social Sciences	3
Total	201

We show the diversity of our dataset in Table 5, with categories determined by GPT-3.5. Due to the popularity of Economics & Business and Politics & Governance questions on the forecasting platform, we have higher proportions of data in those categories.

C Forecasting Principles Guidance

Our system prompt requested that the output satisfy elementary forecasting principles. Due to its length, the full prompt will be released along with the codebase and dataset. The forecasting principles are as follows:

```
- You may find relevant time series data online. If the
      data is recent, you can use zeroth-order or first-
      order approximations (but for longer time horizons,
      recall that these may break down due to saturation
      effects).
```

```
- Don't ignore base rates for low-probability events that
      haven't happened, but rather attempt to estimate
      those probabilities to inform your estimate.
- Attempt to approximate the same quantity in multiple
      different ways. You are welcome to split your
      reasoning into multiple sections, where in each
      section you describe how you reached an estimate
      independently. If your estimates in these sections
      are very far off, reason through why the estimates
      are so different, potentially update those estimates,
       and theorize how confident you are in each estimate.
       Then, combine those forecasts using a weighted or
      trimmed mean or median.

 - Some data can be modeled well using a common
      distribution, e.g., normal, log-normal, power law,
      or Poisson distribution (but this is by no means a
      guarantee). If there's a good reason to believe this
       is the case, you should use information about those
       distributions.
```

D Prompts and Workflows

Due to length, we have only included one full sample below. In general, we observe that RTF yields more robust CoT-style outputs, whereas base LMs use more linear reasoning that may result in outputs unnecessarily biased towards specific considerations.

D.1 Question Filtering

By inspection, we observed that many questions on forecasting markets like Manifold are overly specific or too vague. We filter these questions with the following data wrangling prompt, which contains a mix of flagged and unflagged examples. The prompt aims to restrict the data to reasonably forecastable questions, and empirically in Section B we see that the unflagged questions are suitably diverse. The prompt was run with a temperature of 0.1.

```
I'm trying to assess the quality of an old forecasting dataset.


Here is a forecasting question from the dataset: {question}.

Please flag questions that (i) don't sound like binary
      forecasting questions or (ii) involve people you couldn'
      t know about (e.g. any instance of "I" without further
      qualification) by outputting "flag".
If it sounds like a reasonable question, output "ok".

Examples of strings that should be flagged:
"Will I finish my homework tonight?"
"Metaculus party 2023"
"Will Hell freeze over?"
"Will this video reach 100k views by the EOD?"
"Will Michael Huang's first declared MIT major be Course 3 (
      Material Science)?"
"When I flip a coin in 10 minutes, will it land on heads?"
"Will my prediction streak end (or will I lose a streak freeze
      ) while I touch grass this weekend?"
"Am I tied for 7th place on TST?"

Examples of strings that should not be flagged:
"Will Megan Markle and Prince Harry have a baby by the end of
      the year?"
"Will the Brain Preservation Foundation's Large Mammal
      preservation prize be won by Feb 9th, 2017?"
"Will there be more novel new drugs approved by the FDA in
      2016 than in 2015?"

Your response should take the following structure:
Insert thinking:
{{ insert your concise thoughts here }}
Classification:
{{ insert "flag" or "ok"}}
```

D.2 Sample Question

```
Will ETH close above $3700?
Background: None
Resolution criteria: None
Closure time: April 30, 2024
```

For reference, this prompt resolved as NO (0).

D.3 RTF Output

```
[Entering new AgentExecutor chain...]
To forecast the probability that ETH (Ethereum) will close
      above $3700 on April 30, 2024, I'll follow a structured
      approach:

1. **Reference Classes and Base Rates**:
   - Historical price trends of Ethereum.
   - Historical performance of similar cryptocurrencies.
   - General market conditions and trends in the
        cryptocurrency market.

2. **Recent News and Distinctive Features**:
   - Recent developments in Ethereum technology.
   - Regulatory news affecting cryptocurrencies.
   - Broader economic conditions impacting the cryptocurrency
        market.

3. **Statistical Modeling**:
   - Use historical price data to model potential future price
         movements.
   - Consider volatility and distribution patterns typical for
         Ethereum.

### Step-by-Step Analysis

#### 1. Reference Classes and Base Rates
First, let's look at the historical price data of Ethereum. We
       want to understand how often Ethereum has closed above
      $3700 in the past and under what conditions it has done
      so.

Thought: Do I need to use a tool? Yes
Action: Google Search Snippets
Action Input: "historical price data of Ethereum"
To forecast the probability that ETH (Ethereum) will close
      above $3700 on April 30, 2024, I'll follow a structured
      approach:

1. **Reference Classes and Base Rates**:
   - Historical price trends of Ethereum.
   - Historical performance of similar cryptocurrencies.
   - General market conditions and trends in the
        cryptocurrency market.

2. **Recent News and Distinctive Features**:
   - Recent developments in Ethereum technology.
   - Regulatory news affecting cryptocurrencies.
   - Broader economic conditions impacting the cryptocurrency
        market.

3. **Statistical Modeling**:
   - Use historical price data to model potential future price
         movements.
   - Consider volatility and distribution patterns typical for
         Ethereum.

### Step-by-Step Analysis

#### 1. Reference Classes and Base Rates
First, let's look at the historical price data of Ethereum. We
       want to understand how often Ethereum has closed above
      $3700 in the past and under what conditions it has done
      so.

Thought: Do I need to use a tool? Yes
Action: Google Search Snippets
Action Input: "historical price data of Ethereum"
```

Ethereum Price History. Daily. Weekly. Monthly. 3/28 ... Historical Data. Frequently Asked Questions (FAQs) ... What Does Ethereum's Market Cap History Reveal About... Jan 8, 2023 ... Price history of ETH: On August 7, 2015, the first Ethereum transaction was carried out using the transaction hash of block 46147. Since its... Ethereum's (ETH) highest price in late 2021 was much higher than any other price seen in a chart that looks at the previous 5 years as well as 2023. Track the latest Ethereum price, market cap, trading volume, news and more with CoinGecko's live ETH price chart and popular... Features real-time (live) charts, ethereum blockchain, news and videos. Learn about ETH, the current hashrate, crypto trading and more. Dec 18, 2016 ... There is no canonical ETH or BTC price, each exchange has its own. Exchange may or may not collect historical data, and granularity of such data... Sep 1, 2017 ... Ethereum price history API? I am working on a personal project to develop graphs of the 7 day, 1 month, 3 month, etc. price history of ethereum. Jan 30, 2022 ... ... ethereum-get ... ETH price as an integer on an IoT device like the ESP8266 3 Read all historical price data of a Chainlink price feed in... Mar 21, 2023 ... Historical tick and granular OHLC price data for Ethereum tokens based on DEX swaps. Low resolution (can only get hourly or daily price data... Ethereum Price History. Crypto prices are volatile in the sense that they can explode to the upside or blow up your life savings. Since its launch, ETH has made...]The search results indicate that there are multiple sources for historical Ethereum price data. For a thorough analysis, we'll need to pull specific historical data points. Let's proceed by gathering detailed historical price data for Ethereum.

1. Reference Classes and Base Rates (Continued)
To get a sense of the base rate, we need to know how often Ethereum has closed above $3700 in the past and under what conditions.

Thought: Do I need to use a tool? Yes
Action: Google Search Snippets
Action Input: "Ethereum historical price data 2021 2022 2023"
The search results indicate that there are multiple sources for historical Ethereum price data. For a thorough analysis, we'll need to pull specific historical data points. Let's proceed by gathering detailed historical price data for Ethereum.

1. Reference Classes and Base Rates (Continued)
To get a sense of the base rate, we need to know how often Ethereum has closed above $3700 in the past and under what conditions.

Thought: Do I need to use a tool? Yes
Action: Google Search Snippets
Action Input: "Ethereum historical price data 2021 2022 2023"
Ethereum's (ETH) highest price in late 2021 was much higher than any other price seen in a chart that looks at the previous 5 years as well as 2023. Jan 8, 2023 ... Ethereum was first conceptualized in 2013. Ether (ETH) is the native cryptocurrency of Ethereum. On November 9, 2021, Ethereum briefly attained... Frequently Asked Questions (FAQs). How Has Ethereum's Price History Influenced the Cryptocurrency Market? Nov 18, 2022 ... As one of the more innovative crypto projects, Ethereum has seen a historic low of about 42 cents and a high of about $4800 in November 2021... Jan 9, 2022 ... A friend of mine recently asked me about finding historical open, high, low, and close (OHLC) data for cryptocurrency pairs. Jul 27, 2023 ... Source: https://coinmarketcap.com/currencies/ethereum/historical-data/ ... Over the past two years (July 9, 2021 to July 9, 2023) ... 2022, when ETH... ETH Historical Price ; $3,747.13 minus $3,875.64. $3,664.40 minus $3,959.28. $4,878.26 22.8%. Nov 10, 2021 (over 2 years). $0.433 869871.6%. Oct 20... Historical annualised electricity consumption ... 2021 2022 2023 2024 0 40 80 120 160 200 240 280 ... The electricity cost parameter plays a crucial role in... 2021 to 2023. Bitcoin took less than a month in 2021 to smash its 2020 price record, surpassing $40,000 by Jan. 7, 2021. By mid-April, Bitcoin prices reached... May 29, 2023, 20.80, 20.97, 20.30, 20.59, 20.59, 228,295,637. Related Tickers. BTC-USD Bitcoin USD. 68,466.40. -1.09%. ETH-USD Ethereum USD. 3,843.49. -0.85%.]The search results indicate that Ethereum reached its all-time high in November 2021, with prices briefly surpassing $4800. For a thorough analysis, we need to look at historical data points from 2021, 2022, and 2023 to understand the frequency and conditions under which Ethereum has closed above $3700.

Historical Price Data Analysis

1. Reference Classes and Base Rates (Continued)
Let's consider the following data points:
- **All-Time High (ATH)**: Ethereum reached an ATH of approximately $4800 in November 2021.
- **2021**: Ethereum frequently traded above $3700 during the latter part of the year, especially around its ATH.
- **2022**: The cryptocurrency market experienced significant volatility, and Ethereum's price dropped below $3700 for a considerable period.
- **2023**: The price of Ethereum has been fluctuating, with occasional spikes but generally trading below $3700.

Based on this historical data, we can establish a base rate for Ethereum closing above $3700. However, we need to adjust for recent trends and market conditions.

2. Recent News and Distinctive Features
- **Technological Developments**: Ethereum's transition to Ethereum 2.0 and the implementation of Proof of Stake (PoS) could influence its price positively.
- **Regulatory Environment**: Increased regulation of cryptocurrencies could introduce uncertainty and affect market sentiment.
- **Macroeconomic Conditions**: Broader economic factors, such as inflation and interest rates, can impact investment in cryptocurrencies.

3. Statistical Modeling
To model Ethereum's potential future price movements, we need to consider its historical volatility and distribution patterns. Cryptocurrencies often exhibit high volatility, and their price movements can be modeled using distributions like log-normal or power law.

Combining Estimates
Let's combine our estimates from different approaches:

1. **Base Rate Estimate**:
   - During the peak of the 2021 bull market, Ethereum frequently traded above $3700. Assuming a 30% chance based on historical data.

2. **Recent Trends and News**:
   - Positive technological developments and potential regulatory impacts. Adjusting the base rate slightly upwards to 35%.

3. **Statistical Modeling**:
   - Considering the high volatility and potential for significant price movements, we can use a log-normal distribution to model future prices. However, without precise modeling tools, we estimate a 40% chance based on volatility patterns.

Final Probability Estimate
Let's combine these estimates using a weighted average approach:
- Base Rate: 30%
- Recent Trends and News: 35%
- Statistical Modeling: 40%

Weighted Average Calculation:
\[
\text{Final Probability} = \frac{30\% + 35\% + 40\%}{3} = 35\%
\]

Thought: Do I need to use a tool? No
Final Answer: 0.35The search results indicate that Ethereum reached its all-time high in November 2021, with prices briefly surpassing $4800. For a thorough analysis, we need to look at historical data points from 2021, 2022, and 2023 to understand the frequency and conditions under which Ethereum has closed above $3700.

Historical Price Data Analysis

1. Reference Classes and Base Rates (Continued)
Let's consider the following data points:
- **All-Time High (ATH)**: Ethereum reached an ATH of approximately $4800 in November 2021.

- **2021**: Ethereum frequently traded above $3700 during the latter part of the year, especially around its ATH.
- **2022**: The cryptocurrency market experienced significant volatility, and Ethereum's price dropped below $3700 for a considerable period.
- **2023**: The price of Ethereum has been fluctuating, with occasional spikes but generally trading below $3700.

Based on this historical data, we can establish a base rate for Ethereum closing above $3700. However, we need to adjust for recent trends and market conditions.

2. Recent News and Distinctive Features
- **Technological Developments**: Ethereum's transition to Ethereum 2.0 and the implementation of Proof of Stake (PoS) could influence its price positively.
- **Regulatory Environment**: Increased regulation of cryptocurrencies could introduce uncertainty and affect market sentiment.
- **Macroeconomic Conditions**: Broader economic factors, such as inflation and interest rates, can impact investment in cryptocurrencies.

3. Statistical Modeling
To model Ethereum's potential future price movements, we need to consider its historical volatility and distribution patterns. Cryptocurrencies often exhibit high volatility, and their price movements can be modeled using distributions like log-normal or power law.

Combining Estimates
Let's combine our estimates from different approaches:

1. **Base Rate Estimate**:
   - During the peak of the 2021 bull market, Ethereum frequently traded above $3700. Assuming a 30% chance based on historical data.

2. **Recent Trends and News**:
   - Positive technological developments and potential regulatory impacts. Adjusting the base rate slightly upwards to 35%.

3. **Statistical Modeling**:
   - Considering the high volatility and potential for significant price movements, we can use a log-normal distribution to model future prices. However, without precise modeling tools, we estimate a 40% chance based on volatility patterns.

Final Probability Estimate
Let's combine these estimates using a weighted average approach:
- Base Rate: 30%
- Recent Trends and News: 35%
- Statistical Modeling: 40%

Weighted Average Calculation:
\[
\text{Final Probability} = \frac{30\% + 35\% + 40\%}{3} = 35\%
\]

Thought: Do I need to use a tool? No
Final Answer: 0.35]

[Finished chain.]
prompt: 2024-04-30: Will ETH close above $3700?
response: 0.35, index: 6

D.4 GPT-4o Output

To forecast whether ETH (Ethereum) will close above $3700 by April 30, 2024, we need to consider several factors, including historical price data, market trends, and current events that could influence the price. Let's break down the analysis step-by-step.

Step 1: Historical Data and Base Rates

First, we need to look at the historical price data for ETH to understand its past performance and volatility. We can use this data to establish a base rate for how often ETH has closed above $3700 in the past.

Historical Price Data

- ETH has been highly volatile, with significant price swings over the past few years.
- ETH reached an all-time high of around $4800 in November 2021.
- Since then, the price has fluctuated, with periods of both significant gains and losses. Let's assume we have the following historical data for ETH closing prices over the past few years: - 2021: ETH closed above $3700 on 50 days.
- 2022: ETH closed above $3700 on 20 days.
- 2023 (up to October): ETH closed above $3700 on 10 days. Given this data, we can calculate the base rate for ETH closing above $3700.

Base Rate Calculation Total number of days in the dataset: 365 (2021) + 365 (2022) + 273 (2023 up to October) = 1003 days Total number of days ETH closed above $3700: 50 (2021) + 20 (2022) + 10 (2023) = 80 days Base rate = 80 / 1003 approximate to 0.08 (8%)

Step 2: Current Market Trends and News

Next, we need to consider the current market trends and any recent news that could impact the price of ETH.

Market Trends

- The cryptocurrency market has been experiencing increased institutional interest and adoption.
- Regulatory developments could either positively or negatively impact the market.
- Macroeconomic factors, such as inflation and interest rates, could influence investor sentiment. #### Recent News - Ethereum's transition to a proof-of-stake (PoS) consensus mechanism (Ethereum 2.0) could have a significant impact on its price.
- Any major security breaches or technological advancements could also affect the price. ### Step 3: Adjusting the Base Rate Based on the current market trends and recent news, we need to adjust our base rate. #### Positive Factors
- Increased institutional interest and adoption could drive the price higher.
- The successful implementation of Ethereum 2.0 could boost investor confidence.

Negative Factors
- Regulatory crackdowns could negatively impact the price.
- Macroeconomic factors such as rising interest rates could lead to reduced investment in riskier assets like cryptocurrencies.

Step 4: Combining Estimates

We can combine our base rate with adjustments for current trends and news to arrive at a final probability estimate.

Adjusted Probability

- Base rate: 8%
- Positive adjustment: +5% (for increased adoption and Ethereum 2.0)
- Negative adjustment: -3% (for potential regulatory and macroeconomic risks)

Final adjusted probability = 8% + 5% - 3% = 10%

Step 5: Final Probability Estimate

After considering all factors, my best prediction for the probability of ETH closing above $3700 by April 30, 2024, is: **0.10 (10%)**
This estimate balances the historical base rate with current market trends and potential risks, aiming to minimize the Brier score by being well-calibrated and resolved.

A Comprehensive Survey on Document-Level Information Extraction

Hanwen Zheng[1], **Sijia Wang**[1], **Lifu Huang**[1,2]
[1]Virginia Tech, [2]University of California, Davis
{zoez,sijiawang,lifuh}@vt.edu

Abstract

Document-level information extraction (doc-IE) plays a pivotal role in the realm of natural language processing (NLP). This paper embarks on a comprehensive review and discussion of contemporary literature related to doc-IE. In addition, we conduct a thorough error analysis using state-of-the-art algorithms, shedding light on their limitations and remaining challenges for tackling the task of doc-IE. Our findings demonstrate that issues like entity coreference resolution and the lack of robust reasoning significantly hinder the effectiveness of document-level information extraction (doc-IE). Additionally, we uncover new challenges, including labeling noise and relation transitivity. The overarching objective of this survey paper is to provide valuable insights that can empower NLP researchers to further advance the performance of doc-IE.

1 Introduction

Natural language processing (NLP) triggers the present wave of artificial intelligence (Dosovitskiy et al., 2021; Liu et al., 2021; Zhang et al., 2021a; Zhang and Eskandarian, 2022). Information Extraction (IE) plays a vital role in all aspects of NLP by extracting structured information from unstructured texts (Lin et al., 2020; Wang et al., 2022). Document-level information extraction (**doc-IE**) has achieved significant progress, benefiting from the enormous data resources created by NLP researchers and the rapidly growing computational power resources (Yao et al., 2019; Xu et al., 2021b). However, several challenges persist within the realm of doc-IE research, such as entity coreference resolution, reasoning across long-span contexts, and lack of commonsense reasoning as shown in Figure 1. Furthermore, current doc-IE research predominantly focuses on restricted domains and languages (Zheng et al., 2019a; Yang et al., 2018; Tong et al., 2022; Li et al., 2021), which poses difficulties in fairly conducting model comparisons and hampers the generalizability of findings.

To gain a profound understanding of the current literature on doc-IE, we conduct a comprehensive survey of recent models and datasets for document-level relation extraction **(doc-RE)** and document-level event extraction **(doc-EE)**, focusing on those published in top NLP conferences such as ACL, EMNLP, and so on. These works span various languages and domains, providing a broad overview of advancements in the field. We also thoroughly analyze the errors of several state-of-the-art approaches and summarize several key remaining challenges and future research directions of doc-IE. The contributions of this survey paper include:

- To the best of our knowledge, we are the first to systematically review the literature on doc-IE, including both doc-EE and doc-RE.
- We conduct a thorough error analysis with the current state-of-the-art (SOTA) algorithms for doc-EE and doc-RE, and summarize several key remaining challenges that serve as a foundation for future advancements in doc-IE research and encourage researchers to further innovate and improve upon the various existing methodologies.

2 Task Definition

Event Extraction Event extraction (Grishman, 1997; Chinchor and Marsh, 1998; Ahn, 2006) is a task to identify and classify event triggers and relevant participants from natural language text. Formally, given a document consisting of a set of sentences where each sentence consists of a sequence of words, the objective of this task is to identify and extract the following components from a given document: **Event Mention**, which refers to the phrases or sentences denoting an event; **Event Trigger**, typically in the form of a verb that signals the occurrence of an event; **Event Type**, indicating the predefined type of event specified by the dataset, such as Conflict-Attack; **Argument Mention**, comprising entity mentions that provide additional details on the event, such as who, what, when, where, and how the event occurred; and finally, **Argument Role**, representing the role or type of argument associated with the entity.

Proceedings of the Workshop on the Future of Event Detection (FuturED), pages 58–72
November 15, 2024 ©2024 Association for Computational Linguistics

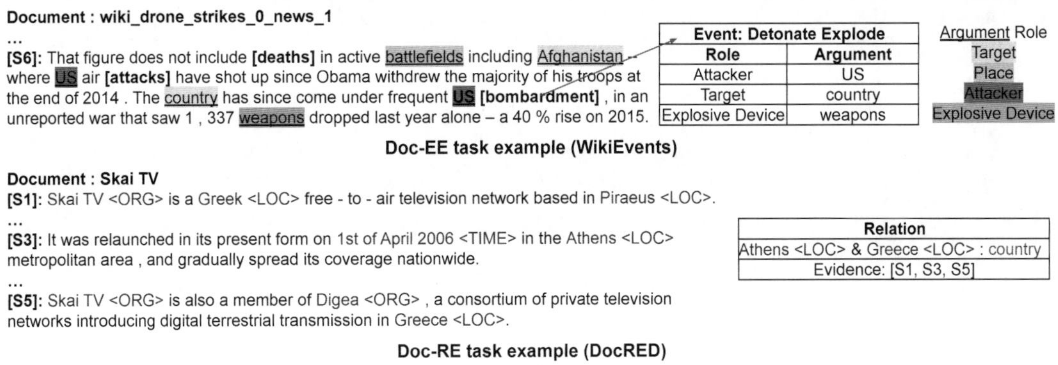

Figure 1: Examples of Document-Level Event Extraction (doc-EE) and Relation Extraction (doc-RE).

Relation Extraction Given a document D with a set of sentences, we assume that D also contains a set of entities $V = \{e_i\}_{i=1}^{N}$, which refer to units such as *People*, *Geographic Entity*, *Location*, *Organization*, *Date*, and *Number*. For each entity e_i, it might contain multiple entity mentions $e_i = \{m_j\}_{j=1}^{M}$, while each **Entity Mention** refers to a phrase within a text that identifies a specific entity. For instance, "NYC" and "the big apple" are both entity mentions for "New York City". The doc-RE task is to predict the relation types between an entity pair $(e_i, e_j)_{i,j \in \{1,\cdots,N\}, i \neq j}$, where e_i stands for the subject and e_j denotes the object. It is possible for an entity pair to have multiple relations, thereby rendering the task a multi-label classification problem. **Intra-sentence Relation** describes the relationship between entities within a single sentence, and the features within are often referred to as local features. **Inter-sentence Relation** refers to the relationship between entities across multiple sentences, and the features within are often referred to as global features.

3 Datasets

Doc-EE Datasets Existing doc-EE datasets are mainly collected from the news and financial domain. News is a large-scale accessible source of events like social emergencies and human life incidents, thus many datasets are created focusing on news events. Meanwhile, exploding volumes of digital financial documents, as a byproduct of continuous economic growth, have been created. Many datasets are created to help extract valuable structured information to detect financial risks or profitable opportunities. Statistics of the datasets for doc-EE are summarized in Table 1.

For news domain, **ACE-2005**[1] is a sentence-level event extraction (SEE) (Wang et al., 2022, 2023d) dataset but has been frequently used for evaluation in doc-EE. Unlike ACE-2005 which contains 5 groups of events covering *justice*, *life*, *business events*, etc, **MUC-4** (muc, 1992) focuses on one specific event type, *attack* events, containing 1,700 human-annotated news reports of terrorist attacks in Latin America collected by Federal Broadcast Information Services. MUC-4 includes six fine-grained incident types: *attack*, *kidnapping*, *bombing*, *arson*, *robbery*, and *forced work stoppage*, and four argument roles, including *individual perpetrator*, *organization perpetrator*, *physical target*, and *human target*. **Roles Across Multiple Sentences (RAMS)** (Ebner et al., 2020) is a crowd-sourced dataset with 9,124 event annotations on news articles from Reddit following the AIDA ontology[2]. **WikiEvents** (Li et al., 2021) follows the RAMS ontology containing 67 event types in a three-level hierarchy. Researchers used the BRAT interface for online annotation of event mentions (triggers and arguments) and event coreference separately. **CMNEE** (Zhu et al., 2024a) is a large-scale, open-source Chinese Military News Event Extraction dataset derived from the sentence-level military event detection dataset MNEE(Huang et al., 2022) and is manually annotated by human experts. **DocEE** (Tong et al., 2022) is the largest Doc-EE dataset to date. DocEE uses historical events and timeline events from Wikipedia as the candidate source to define 59 event types and 356 event argument roles. This dataset includes 27,485 document-level events and 180,528 event arguments that are manually labeled by humans.

For the financial domain, **ChFinAnn** (Zheng et al., 2019b) contains official disclosures such as

[1]https://catalog.ldc.upenn.edu/LDC2006T06

[2]https://aida.kmi.open.ac.uk/

Dataset	# Docs	# Events	# Event types	# Roles	# Arguments	Ratio
ACE-2005[1]	599	4,202	33	35	9,590	-
MUC-4 (muc, 1992)	1,700	1,514	4	5	2,641	13:2:2
RAMS (Ebner et al., 2020)	9,124	8,823	139	65	21,237	8:1:1
WikiEvents (Li et al., 2021)	246	3,951	67	59	5,536	10:1:1
DocEE (Tong et al., 2022)	27,485	27,485	59	356	180,520	-
CMNEE (Zhu et al., 2024a)	17,000	29,223	8	11	93,708	12:2:3
ChFinAnn (Zheng et al., 2019b)	32,040	47,824	5	35	289,871	8:1:1
DCFEE (Yang et al., 2018)	2,976	3,044	4	35	-	8:1:1
DuEE-Fin (Zheng et al., 2019b)	11,699	15,850	13	92	81,632	6:1:3

Table 1: Statistics of Doc-EE datasets. Ratio denotes training split ratio.

annual reports and earnings estimates, obtained from the Chinese Financial Announcement (CFA). The dataset has five event types: *Equity Freeze*, *Equity Repurchase*, *Equity Underweight*, *Equity Overweight* and *Equity Pledge*, with 35 different argument roles in total. In contrast to Doc-EE with one event in each document, 29.0% of the documents in ChFinAnn contain multiple events. **DCFEE** (Yang et al., 2018) comes from companies' official finance announcements and focuses on four event types: *Equity Freeze*, *Equity Pledge*, *Equity Repurchase*, and *Equity Overweight*. Data labeling was done through distant supervision. **DuEE-Fin** (Zheng et al., 2019b) is the largest human-labeled Chinese financial dataset. It is collected from real-world Chinese financial news and annotated with 13 event types. 29.2% of the documents contain multiple events and 16.8% of events consist of multiple arguments.

Several doc-RE datasets are from the biomedical domain. **Drug-gene-mutation (DGM)** (Jia et al., 2019) contains 4,606 PubMed articles, which are automatically labeled via distant supervision. DGM annotations include three entity types: *drugs*, *genes*, and *mutations*, and three relation types, including *drug-gene-mutation*, *drug-mutation*, and *gene-mutation relations*. **GDA** (Wu et al., 2019) gene-disease association corpus contains 30,192 titles and abstracts from PubMed articles that have been automatically labeled for *genes*, *diseases*, and *gene-disease associations* via distant supervision. **CDR** (Luan et al., 2018) is manually annotated for *chemicals*, *diseases*, and *chemical-induced disease (CID)* relations by domain experts. It contains the titles and abstracts of 1,500 PubMed articles and is split into training, validation, and test sets equally. **BioRED** (Luo et al., 2022) builds on previous biomedical datasets by including entity types such as gene/protein, disease, and chemical, along with gene-disease and chemical–chemical relations.

Additionally, doc-RE has been explored in other domains or languages. **DocRED** (Yao et al., 2019) is a human-annotated Doc-RE dataset, that includes 132,375 entities and 56,354 relational facts annotated on 5,053 Wikipedia documents. Doc-RED is generated by mapping Wikidata triples, originating from a comprehensive knowledge base closely intertwined with Wikipedia, onto complete English Wikipedia documents to get entity annotations. **RE-DocRED** (Tan et al., 2022b) refines 4,053 documents in the DocRED dataset targeting on resolving the problem of false negative samples. RE-DocRED increased the relation triples from 50,503 to 120,664 and decreased the *no_relation* samples by 3.1% by adding the missing relation triples back to the original DocRED. Moreover, **DocRED-FE** (Wang et al., 2023b) focus on fine-grained entity types; **DocRED-IE** (Bouziani et al., 2024) expands with five additional subtasks: *Mention Detection*, *Entity Typing*, *Entity Disambiguation*, *Coreference Resolution*, and their combinations, *Named Entity Recognition (NER) and Entity Linking* as in **DWIE** (Zaporojets et al., 2021). **KnowledgeNet** (Mesquita et al., 2019) offers links to a reference knowledge base (KB) for entity and relation annotations. **SciREX** (Jain et al., 2020) is a document-level relation extraction dataset that contains multiple IE tasks, such as Binary and N-ary relation classification. It consists of both automatic and human-annotated articles in the field of computer science. **HacRED** (Cheng et al., 2021) is a Chinese Doc-RE dataset collected from CN-DBpedia (Xu et al., 2017) that focuses on hard cases, such as long text and long distance between argument pairs, containing distractors or multiple homogeneous entity mentions. Statistics of the datasets for doc-RE are summarized in Table 2.

4 Methods

The fundamental challenge in doc-EE and doc-RE is to express document content in a concise and

Dataset	Annotation	# Types	# Facts	% Inter-rel	# Train	# Dev	#Test
DGM (Jia et al., 2019)	Distant Supervision	3	-	64.5%	32,040	-	-
CDR (Luan et al., 2018)	Human-annotated	1	-	29.8%	1,500	500	500
GDA (Wu et al., 2019)	Distant Supervision	1	-	15.6%	30,192	5,839	1,000
BioRED (Luo et al., 2022)	Combined	2	-	-	4,178	1,162	1,163
KnowledgeNet (Mesquita et al., 2019)	Human-annotated	15	13,000	-	-	-	-
DocRED (Yao et al., 2019)	Distant Supervision	96	50,345	12.5%	3,053	1,000	1,000
Re-DocRED (Tan et al., 2022b)	Combined	96	120,664	12.5%	3,053	500	500
DocRED-FE (Wang et al., 2023b)	Combined	96	32,366	-	2,596	1,000	-
DocRED-IE (Bouziani et al., 2024)	Automated	96	37,486	-	3,008	300	700
SciREX (Jain et al., 2020)	Human-annotated	2	-	99.0%	438	131	131
HacRED (Cheng et al., 2021)	Combined	26	65,225	25.4%	9,231	1,500	1,500
DWIE (Zaporojets et al., 2021)	Distant Supervision	65	21,749	-	700	-	100

Table 2: Statistics of Doc-RE datasets.

Task	Main Category	Sub Category	Approaches
Doc-EE	Multi-granularity-based	Sentence→ Paragraph→ Document	Yang et al. (2018), Huang and Jia (2021), Wang et al. (2023a)
	Graph-based	Heterogeneous graph	Zheng et al. (2019b), Xu et al. (2021d), Zhu et al. (2022), Xu et al. (2022), Zhang et al. (2024)
	Task-specific	Attention\Transformer	Yang et al. (2021), Liang et al. (2022), Liu et al. (2024)
		Other Networks	Huang and Peng (2021)
	Generation-based	-	Li et al. (2021), Zeng et al. (2022), Huang et al. (2023)
	Memory-based	-	Du et al. (2022), Cui et al. (2022)
	LLM-based	-	Gatto et al. (2024), Zhou et al. (2024), Uddin et al. (2024)
Doc-RE	Multi-granularity-based	Sentence→ Paragraph→ Document	Tang et al. (2020)
		Mention→ Entity	Jia et al. (2019)
	Graph-based	Heterogeneous graph	Quirk and Poon (2017), Peng et al. (2017), Song et al. (2018), Guo et al. (2019), Sahu et al. (2019), Christopoulou et al. (2019), Wang et al. (2020), Xu et al. (2021d), Zeng et al. (2020), Li et al. (2020), Zhang et al. (2020), Xu et al. (2023), Xu et al. (2021c), Zhu et al. (2024b), Mao et al. (2024)
		Homogeneous graph	Nan et al. (2020)
	Task-specific	Attention\Transformer	Zhou et al. (2021), Tan et al. (2022a)
		Other Networks	Xu et al. (2021a), Zhang et al. (2021b), Bouziani et al. (2024), Wang et al. (2023c), Ma et al. (2023)
	Evidence-based	Path reasoning	Huang et al. (2021)
		Evidence retrieval	Xie et al. (2022), Xiao et al. (2022)

Table 3: Typology of Doc-IE methods.

effective way such that key information is maintained. A typology of existing doc-EE and doc-RE approaches categorized by model design is shown in Table 3.

4.1 Doc-EE Approaches

Multi-granularity-based Models Multi-granularity-based designs employ two strategies: either addressing intermediate tasks using various models or utilizing the same model in a hierarchically ordered manner to independently tackle each subtask of information extraction, such as from sentence level to document level. The standard procedure involves concatenating features from each level to complete the IE tasks. **DCFEE** (Yang et al., 2018) first uses a sequence tagging model to automatically extract sentence-level events, and then proposes a key-event detection model based on a convolutional neural network (CNN) to predict document-level key event. **SCDEE** (Huang and Jia, 2021) uses graph attention network (GAT) to transform document-level features to event communities in order to detect event types at the sentence level. Wang et al. (2023a) collect sentence-level and document-level embeddings by various probing techniques to help probe event mentions in documents. Multi-granularity-based approaches improve the utilization of information across different granularities and the aggregation of global context, but they lose precision in co-reference resolution and capturing long-span dependencies.

Graph-based Models Graph-based models generally construct a graph with words, mentions, entities, arguments, or sentences as nodes and define different types of edges across the entire document, further predicting the relations by reasoning on the graph. **Doc2EDAG** (Zheng et al., 2019b) treats the doc-EE task as an event table-filling task by generating an entity-based directed acyclic graph. It decides which entity node to expand until the graph is fully recovered. **GIT** (Xu et al., 2021d) propose a heterogeneous graph to extract corresponding arguments by expanding a constrained event type tree while tracking and storing records in global memory. **PTPCG** (Zhu et al., 2022) prune the complete graph by deciding whether entity pairs retain an edge based on semantic similarity between entities. **TSAR** (Xu et al., 2022) prune the Abstract Meaning Representation (AMR) graph with span information and surrounding events, and treat event argument extraction (EAE) as a link prediction task. However, while dependency graphs contain rich structural information, the pruning strategy may not always preserve relevant details. **GAM** (Zhang et al., 2024) builds a semantic mention graph capturing co-existence, co-reference, and co-type relations. Graph-based models enhance document representation by allowing the model to learn in an aggregated format, but they may struggle to identify the same event across multiple events and establish their relationships.

Generation-based Models **Bart-Gen** (Li et al., 2021) ask a PLM to fill in the blank in the Doc-EE templates. **EA2E** (Zeng et al., 2022) focuses on event-aware argument extraction by labeling arguments from nearby events in the document to enhance context and extracting event iteratively during generation. **S2C** (Huang et al., 2023) generates all possible arguments and predict the corresponding event arguments in a simple to complex order. A typical challenge that generation-based approaches face is in identifying precise spans.

Memory-based Models Du et al. (2022) stores gold-standard and previously generated events in memory, allowing the decoder to dynamically retrieve event knowledge and decode arguments based on event dependencies. **HRE** (Cui et al., 2022) mimics human reading with a two-stage process: rough reading detects event types, and elaborate reading extracts complete event records with arguments, updating memory with event type and argument information. Memory-based models require additional storage capacity, which can be challenging for large datasets, but they enable the model to retain event and argument dependencies effectively.

LLM-based Models LLM-based models leverage the extensive prior knowledge of large language models like LLAMA2 (Touvron et al., 2023) and GPT-4(OpenAI, 2024) for in-context learning. Gatto et al. (2024) investigates two data augmentation strategies for synthesizing document-level EAE samples and utilizes LLMs for slot-filling to address EAE tasks. Zhou et al. (2024) introduces the Link-of-Analogy Prompting technique, which guides LLMs in generating analogies to facilitate retrieval, mapping, and evaluation processes in a cross-event context. Uddin et al. (2024) provides several question-generation strategies such as prompting using GPT-4 to ask questions about the arguments of an event and inputs those questions to BART-based models for EAE. LLM-based models don't require additional training or fine-tuning, but their limitations lie in their computational demands and difficulty in tuning and optimizing prompts.

Models with task-specific designs Models with task-specific designs mostly rely on attention-based architectures or other NN-based (neural networks), which replicate complex interactions among arguments by implicitly capturing long-distance dependencies. **DE-PPN** (Yang et al., 2021) uses an encoder-decoder structure where the document encoder captures document-aware sentence and argument embeddings, while the decoder simultaneously decodes events, arguments, and roles. **ReDEE** (Liang et al., 2022) is the first to use entity relation information for doc-EE tasks, which utilizes SSAN (Xu et al., 2021a) to extract relation triples as input and calculates the attention between entities and candidate arguments to gain dependency. **DEED** (Huang and Peng, 2021) is an end-to-end model that utilizes Deep Value Networks (DVN), a structured prediction algorithm that effectively bridges the disparity between ground truth and prediction. This model directly incorporates event trigger prediction into DVN, thereby efficiently capturing cross-event dependencies for document-level event extraction. **DEEIA** (Liu et al., 2024) proposes a multi-event argument extraction method using a dependency-guided encoding module to enhance the correlation between prompts and contexts, and an event-specific information aggregation module to provide event-specific information for better contextual understanding. These task-oriented approaches effectively capture long-span dependencies but may overlook sentence-level information and often require long input lengths.

4.2 Doc-RE Approaches

Multi-granularity-based Models The first work on doc-RE using a multi-granularity method is by Jia et al. (2019), employing multiscale representation learning to aggregate mention representations and ensemble sub-relations. The **HIN** (Hierarchical Inference Network) (Tang et al., 2020) uses Bi-LSTMs at the token, sentence, and document levels to extract features as sequences and weighs the overall features with the attention mechanism to obtain both local and global information.

Graph-based Models **DISCREX** (Quirk and Poon, 2017) constructs a document graph with word-based nodes and edges representing intra- and inter-sentence level relations including dependency, adjacency, and discourse relations. Peng et al. (2017) contributes a Graph-LSTM model with a Bi-LSTM to encode the document graph to two directed acyclic graphs (DAG). Song et al. (2018) compares bidirectional graph LSTM with bidirectional DAG LSTM and concludes that the former, which retains the original graph structure, performs better. **AGGCNs** (Guo et al., 2019) proposes an end-to-end graph convolutional network (GCN) that encodes the entire graph using multi-head self-attention to learn edge weights and uses densely connected layers to extract global information. Sahu et al. (2019) designates words as individual nodes and establishes five types of edges to represent inter- and intra-sentence dependency. The model then uses an edge-oriented GCN to retain aggregated node representations.

EoG (Christopoulou et al., 2019) is a pioneering graph-based model. It uses entities as nodes and forms unique edge representations through the paths between nodes to better capture the paired relations. To predict relations between entity pairs, EoG makes iterative inferences on the path between the entities and aggregates every edge to a direct entity-entity edge. Many papers adapted from EoG can be divided into two main categories: homogeneous and heterogeneous graphs. **LSR** (Nan et al., 2020) uses graph structure as a latent variable to form a homogeneous graph. Unlike EoG which uses a human-constructed graph, LSR learns structured attention to refine the graph dynamically and constructs latent structures based on the previous refinement. For heterogeneous graphs, different types of edges are defined, representing unique features, functions, and even dual graphs. **GLRE** (Wang et al., 2020) utilizes a multi-layer relational GCN to learn global entity representations as queries in self-attention, while using sentence-level information as keys to learn local entity representations. **HeterGSAN** (Xu et al., 2021d) constructs a heterogeneous graph based on EoG and encodes it using a GAT. HeterGSAN improves the performance of relation classification by reconstructing a dependency-based path between each pair of entities. **POR** (Xu et al., 2023) builds upon HeterGSAN using a path-retrieving method on paired entities to extract path features through an LSTM.

Dual graphs are normally used to capture hierarchical information. **GAIN** (Zeng et al., 2020) utilizes a heterogeneous mention-level graph to model interactions between the document and all mentions. **GEDA** (Li et al., 2020) optimizes entity representations with two attention layers and a heterogeneous GCN layer. **DHG** (Zhang et al., 2020) propose a framework with two heterogeneous graphs: a structure modeling graph using words and sentences as nodes to better capture document structure information and a relation reasoning graph using mentions and entities as nodes to perform multi-hop relation reasoning. **DRN** (Xu et al., 2021c) passes encoded sentences and entities as a heterogeneous graph to a multi-layer GCN and meanwhile uses a self-attention mechanism to learn better contextual document-level representations.

Models with task-specific designs Models with task-specific designs focus on capturing contexts and entity information through tailored designs for document-level tasks, utilizing either adequate neural network structures or novel loss functions. **SSAN** (Xu et al., 2021a) integrates structural dependencies within and throughout the encoding stage of the network, not only enabling simultaneous context reasoning and structure reasoning but also efficiently modeling these dependencies in all network layers. **ATLOP** (Zhou et al., 2021) leverages pre-trained attention weights for localized context pooling and adopts an adaptive thresholding loss (ATL) to ensure that each entity maintains the same representation and balances the logits of positive and negative labels. **DocuNet** (Zhang et al., 2021b) divides model construction into three parts leveraging a u-shaped semantic segmentation network to refine entity feature extraction. **KD** (Tan et al., 2022a) calculates self-attention in the vertical and horizontal directions of a paired entity table as the axial attention to enhance entity pair representations. The authors propose an adaptive focal loss (AFL) where the logits of entity relations are balanced with thresholds to address long-tailed classes.

Path (Evidence)-based Models Path-based models construct evidence paths and make relational decisions by reasoning on crucial information between entity pairs or sentences, instead of extracting features from the complete document. **THREE** (Huang et al., 2021) presents three kinds of paths to find the supporting sentences: consecutive paths, multi-hop paths, and default paths for entity pairs. **EIDER** (Xie et al., 2022) defines "evidence sentences", as a minimal number of sentences needed to predict the relations between certain pairs of entities in a document. **SAIS** (Xiao et al., 2022) utilizes two intermediary phases to obtain evidence information: pooled evidence retrieval, which distinguishes entity pairs with and without supporting sentences, and fine-grained evidence retrieval, which produces more interpretable evidence specific to each relation of an entity pair. Those approaches typically utilize supporting sentences to serve as evidence from existing datasets such as DocRED. The path-based approaches exhibit extraordinary performance because they align human perception and intuition in the doc-RE task, where we read through the whole document and evaluate sentences that are important for the task.

5 Discussion

To understand the limitations and remaining challenges of the current document-level IE approaches, we evaluate three state-of-the-art Doc-RE methods, **KD** (Tan et al., 2022a), **DRN** (Xu et al., 2021c), and **SAIS** (Xiao et al., 2022), on the DocRED and Re-DocRED datasets.Similarly, we also evaluate two state-of-the-art Doc-EE methods, graph-based model **TSAR** (Xu et al., 2022) and generative model **EA2E** (Zeng et al., 2022), on the WikiEvents dataset, and another two Doc-EE methods, graph-based model **PTPCG** (Zhu et al., 2022) and task-specific model **ReDEE** (Liang et al., 2022), on ChFinAnn dataset. For each work, we randomly select 50 errors and examine the cause of them. We finally conclude seven major types of errors for document-level information extraction. Figure 2, 3, 4 show the distribution of the seven types of errors on each dataset and Table 4 show several error examples.

Entity coreference resolution Document-level texts contain a large number of recognized entities

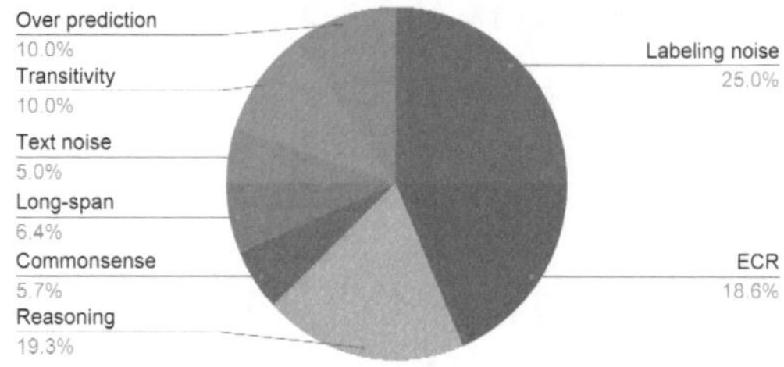

Figure 2: Doc-RE error distribution in DocRED and Re-DocRED

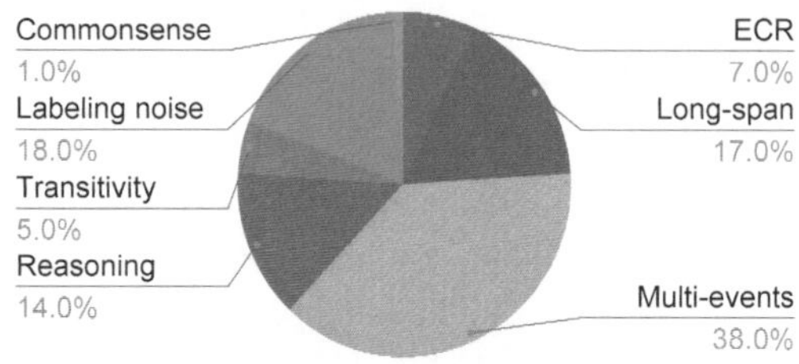

Figure 3: Doc-EE error distribution in ChFinAnn

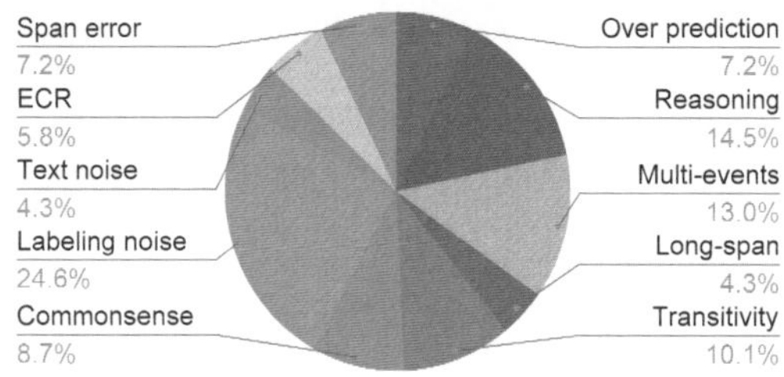

Figure 4: Doc-EE error distribution in WikiEvents

along with coreferential words such as them, he, which, etc. Entity coreference resolution errors happen when the model fails to resolve all mentions in a document that refer to the same entity.

Reasoning error This type of error mainly relates to multi-hop logical reasoning. Document-level texts contain considerable amounts of information, so models may fail to give correct logical inferences based on the given information. Inferring from multi-hop information requires a model to have a high level of natural language understanding ability.

Long-span Document contains multiple sentences in a long span. This error happens when the model fails to capture the full context of a document or uses global information for inference.

Commonsense knowledge The error occurs when models fail to correctly extract relations or events or assume the wrong semantics due to a lack of commonsense and background knowledge, which humans are able to learn or understand instinctively. Many datasets are specific to some domains, and in the absence of relevant background and domain-specific knowledge, models may inac-

Error Type	Text	GT	Pred
ECR	The game retains some common elements from previous **Zelda**<MISC> installments, such as the presence of **Gorons**<PER>, while introducing **Kinstones** <PER> and other new gameplay features.	The Legend of Zelda <MISC>, Gorons <PER> : characters	N/A
Multi-hop reasoning	**Parvathy**<PER> married film actor **Jayaram** <PER> who was her co-star in many films on... She has **two** <NUM> children, **Kalidas Jayaram**<PER> and **Malavika Jayaram**<PER>.	Jayaram<PER>, Kalidas Jayaram <PER>: child	N/A
Commonsense	**Olympic Gold** <MISC> is the official video game of the **XXV Olympic Summer Games** <MISC>, hosted by **Barcelona** <LOC>, **Spain** <LOC> in **1992** <TIME>.	XXV Olympic Summer Games <MISC> , Spain <LOC> : country	N/A
Over prediction	**The Link River** <LOC> is a short river connecting **Upper Klamath Lake** <LOC> to **Lake Ewauna** <LOC> in the city of **Klamath Falls** <LOC> in the **U.S.**<LOC> state of **Oregon** <LOC>.	N/A	Lake Ewauna <LOC>, Oregon <LOC> : located in the administrative territorial entity
Learned prior	**Ngoako Ramatlhodi** <PER>, a senior member of the **African National Congress** <ORG> , was **South Africa** <LOC> 's Minister	N/A	African National Congress <ORG>, South Africa <LOC> : country
Relation transitivity	At the **2007** <TIME> **European Indoor Athletics Championships** <MISC> he won a silver medal in the **4 x 400 metres** <NUM> relay , with teammates Ivan **Buzolin** <PER> , **Maksim Dyldin** <PER> and **Artem Sergeyenkov** <PER>	Artem Sergeyenkov <PER>, European Indoor Athletics Championships <MISC> : participant of	N/A

Table 4: Examples of Doc-RE errors: the column of GT shows the ground truth event annotations while the column of Pred shows the predicted event mentions.

curately reason or misinterpret information.

Relation transitivity error Documents tend to have many entities appearing in the same sentence or across sentences. Relation transitivity errors occur when a model fails to correctly infer a relation between two entities based on their individual relations with a third entity. Additionally, not all relations are transitive, thus the model should correctly recognize when transitivity applies.

Over prediction error This error type refers to the spurious error (as we presented in Table 4) where there is no ground truth relation between two entities but the model predicts a relation, and can be caused by a number of reasons. For instance, when using large pre-trained language models to encode the documents, learned prior can cause models to make overconfident predictions.

In addition to shared error types with Doc-RE, we observe two more types of errors based on the WikiEvents and ChFinAnn datasets.

Multi-events error In Doc-EE tasks, documents contain multiple events that overlap or occur simultaneously, which requires the model to have sufficient training or advanced techniques to learn the inherent complexity of multi-event documents. In an event-trigger-annotated dataset such as WikiEvents, the model can fail at assigning arguments to the correct events or matching roles to arguments. In a trigger-not-annotated dataset like ChFinAnn, event detection errors may occur when models try to identify and differentiate distinct events within the document due to the complex contextual structure of each event, as shown in the example of Figure 5.

Span errors Models face span error types mainly associated with previous tasks like entity recognition or caused by the different linguistic features and complexities of datasets. For example, nominal mention recognition and argument span mismatch errors are common in many works, particularly in generative methods.

Noisy data This issue comprises natural language noises and labeling noises. Real-world documents contain noisy, unstructured, or poorly formatted content, causing difficulties in identifying entities and extracting relations. See further discussion in Section C of the Appendix.

6 Remaining Challenges

Current difficulties can be broadly categorized into three areas: information spread out, multiple mentions and multiple entity pairs throughout the entire document, some information must be deduced from several sentences or transferred by other relations in order to be discovered. The first two issues have been addressed by existing approaches using attention mechanisms and graph networks, though multiple-step reasoning is less widely focused. Existing methods rely on LLMs to learn syntactic features while neglecting the relation transitivity between entity pairs and the evidence trace of reasoning. Progressively, more methods try to use evidence sentences or evidence paths to infer complicated relations. Models continue to struggle with capturing commonsense and knowledge-based information as it is difficult to from the training data. Previous works have tried adaptive losses for balancing the positive and negative examples to allevi-

成都三泰控股集团股份有限公司（以下简称“公司”）于2018年12月28日接到贺晓静女士、宋华梅女士、朱光辉先生通知，其均已完成股份增持计划。... 基于对公司持续稳健发展的信心及公司股票价值的认可，朱江先生、贺晓静女士、宋华梅女士、朱光辉先生（以下简称“增持主体”）计划自2018年7月5日起6个月内通过深圳证券交易所证券交易系统增持公司股份，其中朱江先生拟增持公司股份700000股至1000000股，贺晓静女士、宋华梅女士、朱光辉先生拟分别增持公司股份200000股至300000股。

Event: EquityOverweight		
Role	Evt1-pred	Evt2-pred
EquityHolder	朱江	朱江
TradedShares	Missing	Missing
EndDate	2018年12月28日	Missing

(English translation): Chengdu Santai Holding Group Co., Ltd. (Company) received a notification on December 28, 2018, from Ms. He Xiaojing, Ms. Song Huamei, and Mr. Zhu Guanghui, stating that they have all completed their share increase plans. Based on their confidence in the company's continuous and steady development, and acknowledgment of the value of the company's stock, Mr. Zhu Jiang, Ms. He Xiaojing, Ms. Song Huamei, and Mr. Zhu Guanghui (Increase Holders) plan to increase their holdings of the company's shares through the Shenzhen Stock Exchange trading system within 6 months from July 5, 2018. Specifically, Mr. Zhu Jiang intends to increase his holdings by 700,000 to 1,000,000 shares, while Ms. He Xiaojing, Ms. Song Huamei, and Mr. Zhu Guanghui each plan to increase their holdings by 200,000 to 300,000 shares.

Figure 5: Multi-event error example in ChFinAnn: The colors in the sentence highlight the gold standard event annotations (Event_0 , Event_1 , Event_2). The predicted event mentions and arguments are shown in the table. When predicting the arguments, e.g., *EquityHolder* role of Event_1 and Event_2, the model gets distracted by Event_0 and predicts *Zhu Jiang*. *December 28, 2018* and *200,000* are shared arguments of Event_1 and Event_2.

ate class imbalance problems. Existing works still struggle with long-tailed, ambiguous, and complicated classes, and have a hard time differentiating similar classes. Dataset-wise, creating annotated datasets for this task is time-consuming and expensive, which limits the amount of data available for training and evaluation. Domain-specific datasets differ from general datasets but are necessary for identifying relations that are specific to certain domains, understanding domain-specific terminology, and handling the high variability of language used in different domains.

There are several promising future directions. First, it is beneficial to incorporate entity coreference systems into doc-IE models, which we believe will play an important role in resolving ECR and multi-hop reasoning errors. Second, more investigations are needed to design a model with multi-hop reasoning capability. Finally, doc-EE and doc-RE can be supplementary tasks to each other. The information produced by these two tasks can provide a more complete picture of the information given in the document.

7 Conclusion

We conducted a thorough error analysis of current state-of-the-art algorithms, highlighting the limitations of existing approaches and identifying key challenges in document-level IE. Our analysis revealed that issues such as entity coreference resolution, insufficient reasoning capabilities, labeling noise, and relation transitivity significantly impact the performance of current models, providing insights for future research. Despite notable progress in the field, we conclude that persistent challenges within both datasets and models hinder the development of robust and generalizable solutions. Overcoming these obstacles will be essential for advancing document-level IE models in the future.

Limitations

Due to the constraint that some state-of-the-art models had not released their code at the time we conducted the error analysis, we carefully selected iconic models featuring key designs and unique characteristics for evaluation. The current datasets include only Chinese and English data in the news, finance, biomedical, and Wikipedia domains; therefore, our analysis primarily focuses on studies using English and Chinese datasets within these domains. Nevertheless, we believe that our conclusions will generalize to other domains, languages, and future datasets. The limitations identified in this survey are expected to provide valuable insights and may reflect similar challenges in unexplored areas.

This survey focuses exclusively on text-only document-level information extraction (IE) due to the lack of research and datasets available for multimodal document-level IE. However, the challenges identified in this survey are expected to be critical and may serve as motivation for future research efforts in this area.

Acknowledgements

This research is supported by the award No. 2238940 from the Faculty Early Career Development Program (CAREER) of the National Science Foundation (NSF). The views and conclusions contained herein are those of the authors and should not be interpreted as necessarily representing the official policies, either expressed or implied, of the U.S. Government. The U.S. Government is authorized to reproduce and distribute reprints for governmental purposes notwithstanding any copyright annotation therein.

References

1992. *Fourth Message Uunderstanding Conference (MUC-4): Proceedings of a Conference Held in McLean, Virginia, June 16-18, 1992.*

David Ahn. 2006. The stages of event extraction. In *Proceedings of the Workshop on Annotating and Reasoning about Time and Events*, pages 1–8.

Nacime Bouziani, Shubhi Tyagi, Joseph Fisher, Jens Lehmann, and Andrea Pierleoni. 2024. Rexel: An end-to-end model for document-level relation extraction and entity linking. *Preprint*, arXiv:2404.12788.

Qiao Cheng, Juntao Liu, Xiaoye Qu, Jin Zhao, Jiaqing Liang, Zhefeng Wang, Baoxing Huai, Nicholas Jing Yuan, and Yanghua Xiao. 2021. Hacred: A large-scale relation extraction dataset toward hard cases in practical applications. In *FINDINGS*.

Nancy Chinchor and Elaine Marsh. 1998. Muc-7 information extraction task definition. In *Proceeding of the seventh message understanding conference (MUC-7), Appendices*, pages 359–367.

Fenia Christopoulou, Makoto Miwa, and Sophia Ananiadou. 2019. Connecting the Dots: Document-level Neural Relation Extraction with Edge-oriented Graphs. *arXiv preprint*. ArXiv:1909.00228 [cs].

Shiyao Cui, Xin Cong, Bowen Yu, Tingwen Liu, Yucheng Wang, and Jinqiao Shi. 2022. Document-Level Event Extraction via Human-Like Reading Process. *arXiv preprint*. ArXiv:2202.03092 [cs].

Alexey Dosovitskiy, Lucas Beyer, Alexander Kolesnikov, Dirk Weissenborn, Xiaohua Zhai, Thomas Unterthiner, Mostafa Dehghani, Matthias Minderer, Georg Heigold, Sylvain Gelly, Jakob Uszkoreit, and Neil Houlsby. 2021. An image is worth 16x16 words: Transformers for image recognition at scale. In *International Conference on Learning Representations*.

Xinya Du and Claire Cardie. 2020. Event Extraction by Answering (Almost) Natural Questions. In *Proceedings of the 2020 Conference on Empirical Methods in Natural Language Processing (EMNLP)*, pages 671–683, Online. Association for Computational Linguistics.

Xinya Du, Sha Li, and Heng Ji. 2022. Dynamic Global Memory for Document-level Argument Extraction. *arXiv preprint*. ArXiv:2209.08679 [cs].

Seth Ebner, Patrick Xia, Ryan Culkin, Kyle Rawlins, and Benjamin Van Durme. 2020. Multi-sentence argument linking. In *Proceedings of the 58th Annual Meeting of the Association for Computational Linguistics*.

Joseph Gatto, Parker Seegmiller, Omar Sharif, and Sarah M. Preum. 2024. Large language models for document-level event-argument data augmentation for challenging role types. *Preprint*, arXiv:2403.03304.

Ralph Grishman. 1997. Information extraction: Techniques and challenges. In *International summer school on information extraction*, pages 10–27. Springer.

Zhijiang Guo, Yan Zhang, and Wei Lu. 2019. Attention Guided Graph Convolutional Networks for Relation Extraction. In *Proceedings of the 57th Annual Meeting of the Association for Computational Linguistics*, pages 241–251, Florence, Italy. Association for Computational Linguistics.

Hongbin Huang, Jiao Sun, Hui Wei, Kaiming Xiao, Mao Wang, and Xuan Li. 2022. A dataset of domain events based on open-source military news.

Kung-Hsiang Huang and Nanyun Peng. 2021. Document-level Event Extraction with Efficient End-to-end Learning of Cross-event Dependencies. In *Proceedings of the Third Workshop on Narrative Understanding*, pages 36–47, Virtual. Association for Computational Linguistics.

Quzhe Huang, Yanxi Zhang, and Dongyan Zhao. 2023. From simple to complex: A progressive framework for document-level informative argument extraction. In *Findings of the Association for Computational Linguistics: EMNLP 2023*, pages 6129–6140, Singapore. Association for Computational Linguistics.

Quzhe Huang, Shengqi Zhu, Yansong Feng, Yuan Ye, Yuxuan Lai, and Dongyan Zhao. 2021. Three Sentences Are All You Need: Local Path Enhanced Document Relation Extraction. In *Proceedings of the 59th Annual Meeting of the Association for Computational Linguistics and the 11th International Joint Conference on Natural Language Processing (Volume 2: Short Papers)*, pages 998–1004, Online. Association for Computational Linguistics.

Yusheng Huang and Weijia Jia. 2021. Exploring Sentence Community for Document-Level Event Extraction. In *Findings of the Association for Computational Linguistics: EMNLP 2021*, pages 340–351, Punta Cana, Dominican Republic. Association for Computational Linguistics.

Sarthak Jain, Madeleine van Zuylen, Hannaneh Hajishirzi, and Iz Beltagy. 2020. SciREX: A challenge dataset for document-level information extraction. In *Proceedings of the 58th Annual Meeting of the Association for Computational Linguistics*, pages 7506–7516, Online. Association for Computational Linguistics.

Robin Jia, Cliff Wong, and Hoifung Poon. 2019. Document-Level N-ary Relation Extraction with Multiscale Representation Learning. In *Proceedings of the 2019 Conference of the North American Chapter of the Association for Computational Linguistics: Human Language Technologies, Volume 1 (Long and Short Papers)*, pages 3693–3704, Minneapolis, Minnesota. Association for Computational Linguistics.

Kamran Kowsari, Kiana Jafari Meimandi, Mojtaba Heidarysafa, Sanjana Mendu, Laura Barnes, and Donald

Brown. 2019. Text classification algorithms: A survey. *Information*, 10(4):150.

Bo Li, Wei Ye, Zhonghao Sheng, Rui Xie, Xiangyu Xi, and Shikun Zhang. 2020. Graph Enhanced Dual Attention Network for Document-Level Relation Extraction. In *Proceedings of the 28th International Conference on Computational Linguistics*, pages 1551–1560, Barcelona, Spain (Online). International Committee on Computational Linguistics.

Sha Li, Heng Ji, and Jiawei Han. 2021. Document-Level Event Argument Extraction by Conditional Generation. *arXiv preprint*. ArXiv:2104.05919 [cs].

Yuan Liang, Zhuoxuan Jiang, Di Yin, and Bo Ren. 2022. RAAT: Relation-Augmented Attention Transformer for Relation Modeling in Document-Level Event Extraction. In *Proceedings of the 2022 Conference of the North American Chapter of the Association for Computational Linguistics: Human Language Technologies*, pages 4985–4997, Seattle, United States. Association for Computational Linguistics.

Ying Lin, Heng Ji, Fei Huang, and Lingfei Wu. 2020. A joint neural model for information extraction with global features. In *Proceedings of the 58th Annual Meeting of the Association for Computational Linguistics*, pages 7999–8009, Online. Association for Computational Linguistics.

Wanlong Liu, Li Zhou, Dingyi Zeng, Yichen Xiao, Shaohuan Cheng, Chen Zhang, Grandee Lee, Malu Zhang, and Wenyu Chen. 2024. Beyond single-event extraction: Towards efficient document-level multi-event argument extraction. *Preprint*, arXiv:2405.01884.

Z. Liu, Y. Lin, Y. Cao, H. Hu, Y. Wei, Z. Zhang, S. Lin, and B. Guo. 2021. Swin transformer: Hierarchical vision transformer using shifted windows. In *2021 IEEE/CVF International Conference on Computer Vision (ICCV)*, pages 9992–10002, Los Alamitos, CA, USA. IEEE Computer Society.

Yi Luan, Luheng He, Mari Ostendorf, and Hannaneh Hajishirzi. 2018. Multi-task identification of entities, relations, and coreference for scientific knowledge graph construction. In *Proceedings of the 2018 Conference on Empirical Methods in Natural Language Processing*, pages 3219–3232, Brussels, Belgium. Association for Computational Linguistics.

Ling Luo, Po-Ting Lai, Chih-Hsuan Wei, Cecilia N Arighi, and Zhiyong Lu. 2022. Biored: a rich biomedical relation extraction dataset. *Briefings in Bioinformatics*, 23(5):bbac282.

Youmi Ma, An Wang, and Naoaki Okazaki. 2023. DREEAM: Guiding Attention with Evidence for Improving Document-Level Relation Extraction. *arXiv preprint*. ArXiv:2302.08675 [cs] version: 1.

Yanxu Mao, Peipei Liu, and Tiehan Cui. 2024. Gega: Graph convolutional networks and evidence retrieval guided attention for enhanced document-level relation extraction. *Preprint*, arXiv:2407.21384.

Filipe Mesquita, Matteo Cannaviccio, Jordan Schmidek, Paramita Mirza, and Denilson Barbosa. 2019. KnowledgeNet: A benchmark dataset for knowledge base population. In *Proceedings of the 2019 Conference on Empirical Methods in Natural Language Processing and the 9th International Joint Conference on Natural Language Processing (EMNLP-IJCNLP)*, pages 749–758, Hong Kong, China. Association for Computational Linguistics.

Guoshun Nan, Zhijiang Guo, Ivan Sekulić, and Wei Lu. 2020. Reasoning with Latent Structure Refinement for Document-Level Relation Extraction. *arXiv preprint*. ArXiv:2005.06312 [cs].

OpenAI. 2024. Chatgpt (gpt-4). `https://chat.openai.com`. Accessed: 2024-08-19.

Nanyun Peng, Hoifung Poon, Chris Quirk, Kristina Toutanova, and Wen-tau Yih. 2017. Cross-Sentence N-ary Relation Extraction with Graph LSTMs. *Transactions of the Association for Computational Linguistics*, 5:101–115. Place: Cambridge, MA Publisher: MIT Press.

Chris Quirk and Hoifung Poon. 2017. Distant Supervision for Relation Extraction beyond the Sentence Boundary. *arXiv preprint*. ArXiv:1609.04873 [cs].

Sunil Kumar Sahu, Fenia Christopoulou, Makoto Miwa, and Sophia Ananiadou. 2019. Inter-sentence Relation Extraction with Document-level Graph Convolutional Neural Network. *arXiv preprint*. ArXiv:1906.04684 [cs].

Linfeng Song, Yue Zhang, Zhiguo Wang, and Daniel Gildea. 2018. N-ary Relation Extraction using Graph-State LSTM. In *Proceedings of the 2018 Conference on Empirical Methods in Natural Language Processing*, pages 2226–2235, Brussels, Belgium. Association for Computational Linguistics.

Qingyu Tan, Ruidan He, Lidong Bing, and Hwee Tou Ng. 2022a. Document-Level Relation Extraction with Adaptive Focal Loss and Knowledge Distillation. *arXiv preprint*. ArXiv:2203.10900 [cs].

Qingyu Tan, Lu Xu, Lidong Bing, Hwee Tou Ng, and Sharifah Mahani Aljunied. 2022b. Revisiting DocRED – Addressing the False Negative Problem in Relation Extraction. *arXiv preprint*. ArXiv:2205.12696 [cs].

Hengzhu Tang, Yanan Cao, Zhenyu Zhang, Jiangxia Cao, Fang Fang, Shi Wang, and Pengfei Yin. 2020. HIN: Hierarchical Inference Network for Document-Level Relation Extraction. In *Advances in Knowledge Discovery and Data Mining*, Lecture Notes in Computer Science, pages 197–209, Cham. Springer International Publishing.

MeiHan Tong, Bin Xu, Shuai Wang, Meihuan Han, Yixin Cao, Jiangqi Zhu, Siyu Chen, Lei Hou, and Juanzi Li. 2022. DocEE: A Large-Scale and Fine-grained Benchmark for Document-level Event Extraction. In *Proceedings of the 2022 Conference of the North American Chapter of the Association for Computational Linguistics: Human Language Technologies*, pages 3970–3982, Seattle, United States. Association for Computational Linguistics.

Hugo Touvron, Louis Martin, Kevin Stone, Peter Albert, Amjad Almahairi, Yasmine Babaei, Nikolay Bashlykov, Soumya Batra, Prajjwal Bhargava, Shruti Bhosale, Dan Bikel, Lukas Blecher, Cristian Canton Ferrer, Moya Chen, Guillem Cucurull, David Esiobu, Jude Fernandes, Jeremy Fu, Wenyin Fu, Brian Fuller, Cynthia Gao, Vedanuj Goswami, Naman Goyal, Anthony Hartshorn, Saghar Hosseini, Rui Hou, Hakan Inan, Marcin Kardas, Viktor Kerkez, Madian Khabsa, Isabel Kloumann, Artem Korenev, Punit Singh Koura, Marie-Anne Lachaux, Thibaut Lavril, Jenya Lee, Diana Liskovich, Yinghai Lu, Yuning Mao, Xavier Martinet, Todor Mihaylov, Pushkar Mishra, Igor Molybog, Yixin Nie, Andrew Poulton, Jeremy Reizenstein, Rashi Rungta, Kalyan Saladi, Alan Schelten, Ruan Silva, Eric Michael Smith, Ranjan Subramanian, Xiaoqing Ellen Tan, Binh Tang, Ross Taylor, Adina Williams, Jian Xiang Kuan, Puxin Xu, Zheng Yan, Iliyan Zarov, Yuchen Zhang, Angela Fan, Melanie Kambadur, Sharan Narang, Aurelien Rodriguez, Robert Stojnic, Sergey Edunov, and Thomas Scialom. 2023. Llama 2: Open foundation and fine-tuned chat models. *Preprint*, arXiv:2307.09288.

Md Nayem Uddin, Enfa George, Eduardo Blanco, and Steven Corman. 2024. Generating uncontextualized and contextualized questions for document-level event argument extraction. In *Proceedings of the 2024 Conference of the North American Chapter of the Association for Computational Linguistics: Human Language Technologies (Volume 1: Long Papers)*, pages 5612–5627, Mexico City, Mexico. Association for Computational Linguistics.

Barry Wang, Xinya Du, and Claire Cardie. 2023a. Probing representations for document-level event extraction. In *Findings of the Association for Computational Linguistics: EMNLP 2023*, pages 12675–12683, Singapore. Association for Computational Linguistics.

Difeng Wang, Wei Hu, Ermei Cao, and Weijian Sun. 2020. Global-to-Local Neural Networks for Document-Level Relation Extraction. In *Proceedings of the 2020 Conference on Empirical Methods in Natural Language Processing (EMNLP)*, pages 3711–3721, Online. Association for Computational Linguistics.

Hongbo Wang, Weimin Xiong, Yifan Song, Dawei Zhu, Yu Xia, and Sujian Li. 2023b. Docred-fe: A document-level fine-grained entity and relation extraction dataset. In *ICASSP 2023-2023 IEEE International Conference on Acoustics, Speech and Signal Processing (ICASSP)*, pages 1–5. IEEE.

Jize Wang, Xinyi Le, Xiaodi Peng, and Cailian Chen. 2023c. Adaptive hinge balance loss for document-level relation extraction. In *Findings of the Association for Computational Linguistics: EMNLP 2023*, pages 3872–3878, Singapore. Association for Computational Linguistics.

Sijia Wang, Mo Yu, Shiyu Chang, Lichao Sun, and Lifu Huang. 2022. Query and extract: Refining event extraction as type-oriented binary decoding. In *Findings of the Association for Computational Linguistics: ACL 2022*, pages 169–182, Dublin, Ireland. Association for Computational Linguistics.

Sijia Wang, Mo Yu, and Lifu Huang. 2023d. The art of prompting: Event detection based on type specific prompts. In *ACL 2023*. Association for Computational Linguistics.

Ye Wu, Ruibang Luo, Henry C. M. Leung, Hing-Fung Ting, and Tak Wah Lam. 2019. Renet: A deep learning approach for extracting gene-disease associations from literature. In *RECOMB*.

Yuxin Xiao, Zecheng Zhang, Yuning Mao, Carl Yang, and Jiawei Han. 2022. SAIS: Supervising and Augmenting Intermediate Steps for Document-Level Relation Extraction. In *Proceedings of the 2022 Conference of the North American Chapter of the Association for Computational Linguistics: Human Language Technologies*, pages 2395–2409, Seattle, United States. Association for Computational Linguistics.

Yiqing Xie, Jiaming Shen, Sha Li, Yuning Mao, and Jiawei Han. 2022. Eider: Empowering Document-level Relation Extraction with Efficient Evidence Extraction and Inference-stage Fusion. In *Findings of the Association for Computational Linguistics: ACL 2022*, pages 257–268, Dublin, Ireland. Association for Computational Linguistics.

Benfeng Xu, Quan Wang, Yajuan Lyu, Yong Zhu, and Zhendong Mao. 2021a. Entity Structure Within and Throughout: Modeling Mention Dependencies for Document-Level Relation Extraction. *Proceedings of the AAAI Conference on Artificial Intelligence*, 35(16):14149–14157. Number: 16.

Bo Xu, Yong Xu, Jiaqing Liang, Chenhao Xie, Bin Liang, Wanyun Cui, and Yanghua Xiao. 2017. Cn-dbpedia: A never-ending chinese knowledge extraction system. In *International Conference on Industrial, Engineering and Other Applications of Applied Intelligent Systems*.

Runxin Xu, Tianyu Liu, Lei Li, and Baobao Chang. 2021b. Document-level event extraction via heterogeneous graph-based interaction model with a tracker. *Preprint*, arXiv:2105.14924.

Runxin Xu, Peiyi Wang, Tianyu Liu, Shuang Zeng, Baobao Chang, and Zhifang Sui. 2022. A Two-Stream AMR-enhanced Model for Document-level Event Argument Extraction. *arXiv preprint*. ArXiv:2205.00241 [cs].

Wang Xu, Kehai Chen, and Tiejun Zhao. 2021c. Discriminative Reasoning for Document-level Relation Extraction. *arXiv preprint*. ArXiv:2106.01562 [cs].

Wang Xu, Kehai Chen, and Tiejun Zhao. 2021d. Document-Level Relation Extraction with Reconstruction. *Proceedings of the AAAI Conference on Artificial Intelligence*, 35(16):14167–14175. Number: 16.

Wang Xu, Kehai Chen, and Tiejun Zhao. 2023. Document-Level Relation Extraction with Path Reasoning. *ACM Transactions on Asian and Low-Resource Language Information Processing*, 22(4):1–14.

Hang Yang, Yubo Chen, Kang Liu, Yang Xiao, and Jun Zhao. 2018. DCFEE: A Document-level Chinese Financial Event Extraction System based on Automatically Labeled Training Data. In *Proceedings of ACL 2018, System Demonstrations*, pages 50–55, Melbourne, Australia. Association for Computational Linguistics.

Hang Yang, Dianbo Sui, Yubo Chen, Kang Liu, Jun Zhao, and Taifeng Wang. 2021. Document-level Event Extraction via Parallel Prediction Networks. In *Proceedings of the 59th Annual Meeting of the Association for Computational Linguistics and the 11th International Joint Conference on Natural Language Processing (Volume 1: Long Papers)*, pages 6298–6308, Online. Association for Computational Linguistics.

Yuan Yao, Deming Ye, Peng Li, Xu Han, Yankai Lin, Zhenghao Liu, Zhiyuan Liu, Lixin Huang, Jie Zhou, and Maosong Sun. 2019. DocRED: A Large-Scale Document-Level Relation Extraction Dataset. In *Proceedings of the 57th Annual Meeting of the Association for Computational Linguistics*, pages 764–777, Florence, Italy. Association for Computational Linguistics.

Klim Zaporojets, Johannes Deleu, Chris Develder, and Thomas Demeester. 2021. Dwie: An entity-centric dataset for multi-task document-level information extraction. *Information Processing & Management*, 58(4):102563.

Qi Zeng, Qiusi Zhan, and Heng Ji. 2022. EA2E: Improving Consistency with Event Awareness for Document-Level Argument Extraction. In *Findings of the Association for Computational Linguistics: NAACL 2022*, pages 2649–2655, Seattle, United States. Association for Computational Linguistics.

Shuang Zeng, Runxin Xu, Baobao Chang, and Lei Li. 2020. Double Graph Based Reasoning for Document-level Relation Extraction. *arXiv preprint*. ArXiv:2009.13752 [cs].

Ce Zhang and Azim Eskandarian. 2022. A quality index metric and method for online self-assessment of autonomous vehicles sensory perception. *ArXiv*, abs/2203.02588.

Ce Zhang, Azim Eskandarian, and Xuelai Du. 2021a. Attention-based neural network for driving environment complexity perception. *2021 IEEE International Intelligent Transportation Systems Conference (ITSC)*, pages 2781–2787.

Jian Zhang, Changlin Yang, Haiping Zhu, Qika Lin, Fangzhi Xu, and Jun Liu. 2024. A semantic mention graph augmented model for document-level event argument extraction. In *Proceedings of the 2024 Joint International Conference on Computational Linguistics, Language Resources and Evaluation (LREC-COLING 2024)*, pages 1577–1587, Torino, Italia. ELRA and ICCL.

Ningyu Zhang, Xiang Chen, Xin Xie, Shumin Deng, Chuanqi Tan, Mosha Chen, Fei Huang, Luo Si, and Huajun Chen. 2021b. Document-level Relation Extraction as Semantic Segmentation. *arXiv preprint*. ArXiv:2106.03618 [cs] version: 2.

Zhenyu Zhang, Bowen Yu, Xiaobo Shu, Tingwen Liu, Hengzhu Tang, Wang Yubin, and Li Guo. 2020. Document-level Relation Extraction with Dual-tier Heterogeneous Graph. In *Proceedings of the 28th International Conference on Computational Linguistics*, pages 1630–1641, Barcelona, Spain (Online). International Committee on Computational Linguistics.

Shun Zheng, Wei Cao, Wei Xu, and Jiang Bian. 2019a. Doc2EDAG: An End-to-End Document-level Framework for Chinese Financial Event Extraction. In *Proceedings of the 2019 Conference on Empirical Methods in Natural Language Processing and the 9th International Joint Conference on Natural Language Processing (EMNLP-IJCNLP)*, pages 337–346, Hong Kong, China. Association for Computational Linguistics.

Shun Zheng, Wei Cao, Wei Xu, and Jiang Bian. 2019b. Doc2EDAG: An end-to-end document-level framework for chinese financial event extraction. In *EMNLP*.

Hanzhang Zhou, Junlang Qian, Zijian Feng, Hui Lu, Zixiao Zhu, and Kezhi Mao. 2024. Llms learn task heuristics from demonstrations: A heuristic-driven prompting strategy for document-level event argument extraction. *Preprint*, arXiv:2311.06555.

Wenxuan Zhou, Kevin Huang, Tengyu Ma, and Jing Huang. 2021. Document-Level Relation Extraction with Adaptive Thresholding and Localized Context Pooling. *Proceedings of the AAAI Conference on Artificial Intelligence*, 35(16):14612–14620. Number: 16.

Mengna Zhu, Zijie Xu, Kaisheng Zeng, Kaiming Xiao, Mao Wang, Wenjun Ke, and Hongbin Huang. 2024a. CMNEE:a large-scale document-level event extraction dataset based on open-source Chinese military news. In *Proceedings of the 2024 Joint International Conference on Computational Linguistics, Language Resources and Evaluation (LREC-COLING 2024)*, pages 3367–3379, Torino, Italia. ELRA and ICCL.

Tong Zhu, Xiaoye Qu, Wenliang Chen, Zhefeng Wang, Baoxing Huai, Nicholas Jing Yuan, and Min Zhang. 2022. Efficient Document-level Event Extraction via Pseudo-Trigger-aware Pruned Complete Graph. *arXiv preprint*. ArXiv:2112.06013 [cs].

Xudong Zhu, Zhao Kang, and Bei Hui. 2024b. FCDS: Fusing constituency and dependency syntax into document-level relation extraction. In *Proceedings of the 2024 Joint International Conference on Computational Linguistics, Language Resources and Evaluation (LREC-COLING 2024)*, pages 7141–7152, Torino, Italia. ELRA and ICCL.

A Evaluation Metrics

In document-level information extraction (IE), the primary evaluation metrics are Precision (P), Recall (R), and Macro-F1 score (Kowsari et al., 2019). Additionally, for doc-RE, Ign F1 is also used as an evaluation metric (Yao et al., 2019) which refers to the F1 score that excludes relational facts shared by the training and dev/test sets. This metric is important for evaluating the generalizability of the model, as it disregards triples that have already been included in the annotated training dataset.

B Performance of Existing Methods

Performance of Doc-RE Existing Methods are shown in Table 8, Table 5, and Table 6. Performance of Doc-EE Existing Methods are shown in Table 9 and Table 7.

Model	**F1**
SAIS$^{O}_{RE+CR+ET}$-SciBERT (Xiao et al., 2022)	87.10
DocuNet-SciBERT-base (Zhang et al., 2021b)	85.30
Eider(Rule)-SciBERT-base (Xie et al., 2022)	84.54
ATLOP-SciBERT-base (Zhou et al., 2021)	83.90
SSAN-SciBERT (Xu et al., 2021a)	83.70

Table 5: Doc-RE GDA rank

Model	**F1**
SAIS$^{O}_{RE+CR+ET}$-SciBERT (Xiao et al., 2022)	79.00
DocuNet-SciBERT-base (Zhang et al., 2021b)	76.30
Eider(Rule)-SciBERT-base (Xie et al., 2022)	70.63
ATLOP-SciBERT-base (Zhou et al., 2021)	69.40
SSAN-SciBERT (Xu et al., 2021a)	68.70

Table 6: Doc-RE CDR rank

Model	**F1**
ReDEE (Liang et al., 2022)	81.90
Git (Xu et al., 2021d)	80.30
PTPCG (Zhu et al., 2022)	79.40
SCDEE (Huang and Jia, 2021)	78.90
DE-PPN (Yang et al., 2021)	77.90
HRE (Cui et al., 2022)	76.80
Doc2EDAG (Zheng et al., 2019b)	76.30

Table 7: Doc-EE ChFinAnn rank

C Additional error analysis

Noisy data Natural language can be ambiguous or vague, leading to uncertainty in model inference. To overcome the limitations of the cost of creating annotated datasets, researchers commonly apply

Model	F1	Ign-F1
KD-Rb-l (Tan et al., 2022a)	67.28	65.24
SSAN-RoBERTa-large+Adaptation (Xu et al., 2021a)	65.92	63.78
SAIS-RoBERTa-large (Xiao et al., 2022)	65.11	63.44
Eider-RoBERTa-large (Xie et al., 2022)	64.79	62.85
DocuNet-RoBERTa-large (Zhang et al., 2021b)	64.55	62.40
ATLOP-RoBERTa-large (Zhou et al., 2021)	63.40	61.39

Table 8: Doc-RE DocRED rank

Model	Arg Identification		Arg Classification	
	Head F1	Coref F1	Head F1	Coref F1
TSAR$_{large}$ (Xu et al., 2022)	76.62	75.52	69.70	68.79
EA^{2}E (Zeng et al., 2022)	74.62	75.77	68.61	69.70
BART-Gen(Li et al., 2021)	71.75	72.29	64.57	65.11
OneIE(Li et al., 2021)	61.88	63.63	57.61	59.17
BERT-QA(Du and Cardie, 2020)	61.05	64.59	56.16	59.36

Table 9: Doc-EE WikiEvent rank

automatic labeling strategies like distant supervision to generate large-scale training data. However, this leads to several minor problems due to noise and bias: nested entities (i.e., some entities can be embedded within other entities), false negative labels (i.e., entity pairs not known to be related but getting labeled as such in the dataset), and missing ground truth labels.

Note that Doc-EE errors vary between ChFinAnn and WikiEvents. There could be a number of factors behind the different Doc-EE error distribution between ChFinAnn and WikiEvents. One crucial factor is the diversity in underlying statistics between datasets due to their distinct domains and languages. Compared to the news dataset WikiEvents, the Chinese financial dataset ChFinAnn requires less commonsense comprehension. Each dataset contains unique linguistic features and complexities. WikiEvents has annotated trigger words, and arguments tend to be near the trigger words, whereas ChFinAnn can have events spread across the entire document and is more likely to interfere with other events. Therefore, long-span and multi-events are major error types in ChFinAnn. Moreover, various model designs and approaches usually aim to address specific challenges and optimize performance on the respective dataset.

Generative Approaches to Event Extraction: Survey and Outlook

Étienne Simon[*1] Helene Bøsei Olsen[*1] Huiling You[1]
Samia Touileb[2] Lilja Øvrelid[1] Erik Velldal[1]
[1] University of Oslo, [2] University of Bergen

Abstract

This paper aims to map out the current landscape of generative approaches to the task of event extraction. In surveying the emerging literature on the topic, we identify the distinctive properties of existing studies and catalogue them to build a comprehensive view of the various techniques employed. Finally, looking ahead, we argue for a new generative formulation of event extraction, allowing for a better fit between methodology and task – a proposal that could also pertain to many other traditional NLP tasks currently based on annotations of text-spans.

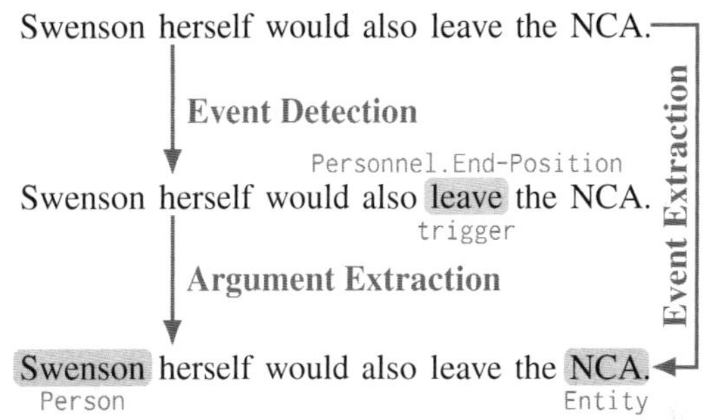

Figure 1: The two subtasks of event extraction on a sample from ACE. The event type is shown in blue over the trigger highlighted in orange. The event arguments are highlighted in green with their role specified under each argument.

1 Introduction

Event extraction is one of the core applications in Natural Language Processing (NLP), aiming to create structured representations of events described in unstructured text. The task revolves around the identification and categorisation of predefined types of events within texts. This is typically broken down into identifying and categorising so-called event triggers and their respective arguments, along with their relevant properties and relationships, such as time, location, and participants.

Recently, generative language models have seen widespread uptake across many subfields of NLP, and event extraction is no exception. Generative approaches to event extraction sometimes deviate from the traditional way of identifying and categorising events and their arguments, introducing new opportunities and challenges with respect to both training and evaluation.

This paper provides an overview of the current landscape of generative approaches to event extraction by focusing on a representative set of techniques across different dimensions. We survey how the task of event extraction is approached across the range of decoder-only and encoder–decoder models with regards to generating the extracted event fields as natural language – as opposed to the traditional sequence labelling or boundary identification approaches. For readers seeking a broader overview of event extraction approaches, the surveys by Xiang and Wang (2019), Liu et al. (2021) and Li et al. (2022) can be explored.

Event extraction (EE) is traditionally approached as a sequence labelling problem. The annotations identify specific text spans that highlight event triggers with their associated arguments. This leads to the task being broken up into two parts as shown in Figure 1: (1) *event detection* (ED) where event triggers are identified and the event is categorised into a type. An event trigger typically corresponds to the word(s) in the text that most clearly describes an event. In the example of Figure 1, "leave" evokes an "`End-Position`"-type event. (2) *event argument extraction* (EAE) where event arguments are identified along with their role. The role is the semantic relationship of the argument to the event. In the example of Figure 1, "Swenson" is identified as relevant to the `End-Position` event as the `Person` leaving. When two distinct models are used to tackle each subtask, the approach is referred to as a

[*]Equal contribution.

Proceedings of the Workshop on the Future of Event Detection (FuturED), pages 73–86
November 15, 2024 ©2024 Association for Computational Linguistics

pipeline, while approaching both subtasks together is denoted a *joint* approach. Only a third of the models we survey perform ED. The two subtasks are also evaluated separately. However, the argument extraction scores are not always comparable as some models use a pipeline setup where the gold trigger is used in the evaluation of argument extraction, while other models only work in a joint setup where the arguments can only be extracted together with the trigger (Peng et al., 2023). We therefore elect to not include reported results as comparison can be misleading. Before we dive into the description of the different modelling approaches, we start by discussing some of the most prominent event extraction datasets.

2 Datasets

In this section, we discuss the event datasets most commonly used across the different generative approaches we assess in Section 3. While some of the datasets cover multiple languages, most primarily focus on English language sources.

The highly influential Automatic Content Extraction (ACE) program released manual event annotations for text spans at the sentence-level, also including rich information about entities, temporal expressions, and relations between entities. The event annotation in the ACE tradition has become a *de facto* standard for the evaluation of event extraction systems in the field of NLP. The 5th iteration of the dataset, ACE 2005 (Doddington et al., 2004), consists of broadcast transcripts in addition to newswire and newspaper texts. It provides manual annotation for entities, relations, and events for joint evaluation of multiple information extraction tasks in multiple languages (Arabic, Chinese, and English) at the sentence level. The ACE dataset is annotated for 8 general event types (e.g. `Life`, `Conflict`, `Transaction`), along with 33 subtypes (e.g. `Conflict.Attack`), and 22 argument roles (e.g. `Attacker`, `Agent`, and `Recipient`). The English version of the dataset comprises 599 documents. Depending on the pre-processing approach, ACE features two main variants, where ACE covers only events with single-token triggers, and ACE+ keeps all events with either single- or multi-token triggers. Four F1 scores are usually reported on ACE: the trigger identification, the trigger classification into an event type, the argument identification, and the argument classification into a role.

The evaluation of ACE and similar datasets is structured primarily for sequence labelling models. It typically involves comparing the predicted position offsets (specific locations of event mentions in the text) with the corresponding correct offsets. Consequently, if a name appears multiple times within a sentence, only one of those occurrences is considered correct.[1] Since generative models only extract and generate out-of-context surface forms without incorporating position offsets, evaluating them on datasets like ACE may give these approaches an unfair advantage. The current best practice for generative approaches is to search for the text generated by the model in the input text, transform the output to offsets to simulate a sequence labelling model, and subsequently evaluate it as such.

More recently, the ERE annotation effort (Entities, Relations, and Events, Song et al., 2015) has contributed both data and annotation guidelines for event extraction purposes. The ERE effort has evolved from the Light ERE to Rich ERE datasets, advancing from simple ACE-based annotations to more complex handling of entities and events, ultimately enabling document-level event co-reference. The ERE effort covers English, Spanish and Chinese documents from discussion forums, newswire, and proxy sources. The Rich ERE extends the annotation scheme of ACE, covering 9 main event types and 38 event subtypes. In Light ERE, only asserted events are annotated (events that have occurred), with each event trigger linked to a single event. In contrast, Rich ERE allows for event triggers to be annotated for multiple events and includes annotations for event modality, capturing events that did not actually occur.

Another sentence-level event dataset is MAVEN (MAssive eVENt detection dataset, Wang et al., 2020). It aims to alleviate problems of data scarcity and low coverage and contains 111 611 distinct events across 4480 human-annotated documents in total, corresponding to event-related articles from English Wikipedia. It comprises 168 hierarchically organised event types derived from FrameNet (Baker et al., 1998), intended to cover general-domain events.

Li et al. (2021) introduce a document-level annotated dataset based on English Wikipedia articles and their referenced news articles called WIKIEVENTS. While only containing 246 documents

[1]The ACE corpora include coreference information. However, it is not an established part of the standard formulation when evaluating the event extraction task.

with 8544 sentences, the dataset serves as an essential benchmark for event extraction systems beyond the sentence-level. Each document is annotated with event types, event mentions (triggers and arguments), and co-references across sentences, even in sentences lacking an explicit event trigger. Annotating co-references enables a fairer evaluation of generative models, as an extracted argument is considered correct if the model generates any coreference of the gold argument. In WIKIEVENTS parlance, these are referred to as coref scores. The annotators also aimed to annotate the most informative event mention, giving precedence to name mentions over nominal mentions rather than focusing solely on the mention closest to the trigger word. This allows for another evaluation mode for WIKIEVENTS termed informative argument extraction, where models are evaluated on their ability to extract the most informative argument mention. The annotations of the dataset resemble ACE, but expand the number of sub-events from 33 to 67 following the KAIROS ontology.[2] Additionally, WIKIEVENTS has a more fine-grained event-type hierarchy. For instance, whereas ACE identifies the event type and subtype such as `Conflict.Attack`, WIKIEVENTS introduces event types at three levels, such as `Conflict.Attack.DetonateExplode`.

In recent years, the fourth Message Understanding Conference (MUC-4, Sundheim, 1992) dataset has resurfaced in research on document-level event extraction. The dataset is based on English newswire provided by the Federal Broadcast Information Services. It is annotated with the event types `Arson`, `Attack`, `Bombing`, `Kidnapping`, `Robbery`, `Forced work stoppage`, covering political conflicts in Latin America. MUC-4 contains 1700 documents, which may be associated with zero or more events of each type. Moreover, the event type is associated with a template, each with the same set of 24 argument roles to be filled with either a numeric value, a categorical value, a text string, or a canonical form extracted or derived from the text. However, beyond event type classification, most recent works on the dataset are based on a simplified set of template slots restricted to five argument roles, where all have text string values that can be directly extracted from the source document (Du et al., 2021a,b; Gantt et al., 2024). Given that a large proportion of the documents are linked to empty templates, indicating the absence of relevant events, the ED task is important for MUC-4.

Some of the models discussed in this survey employ additional datasets alongside those outlined above. RAMS (Ebner et al., 2020) covers 9124 events from news articles and is annotated in a 5-sentence window around each event trigger. PHEE (Sun et al., 2022) is a biomedical domain-specific dataset focused on drug safety, consisting of nearly 5000 sentences extracted from public medical case reports. Finally, CASIE (Satyapanich et al., 2020), consisting of 5000 news articles, with 1000 of these annotated on the sentence-level for cyber-attack events.

3 Models

The majority of the models we survey follow a similar pattern as shown in Figure 2: the input text is fed to an encoder–decoder transformer that is fine-tuned to generate a representation of the events conveyed in said text. Most of them can be divided into one of two groups according to how the events are represented in the generated text. To structure this survey, we first consider the representation of events in the output of the model; two main approaches exist: i) either an event is represented using a formal structure template in line with Text2Event (Lu et al., 2021), or (ii) the event is represented using a natural language template in line with BART-Gen (Li et al., 2021). We present these two distinct approaches in two separate sections. A classification of all models is also given in Figure 3. Note that the organisation of this survey results from the fact that most of the models within the scope of this work build upon Text2Event and BART-Gen. However, this structure does not necessarily reflect a deep fundamental difference between the two sections.

The first model using a generative transformer to address EE falls partly outside this dichotomy. **TANL** (Paolini et al., 2021) introduces an ED model and an EAE model using T5 (Raffel et al., 2020). However, TANL does not focus solely on event extraction and can be trained on multiple information extraction (IE) tasks (named entity recognition, coreference resolution, etc). This is a recurring pattern in the papers we survey; different IE tasks are often similar enough that a single architecture can be reused. TANL goes one step further by simultaneously training on multiple tasks before

[2] https://www.darpa.mil/program/knowledge-directed-artificial-intelligence-reasoning-over-schemas

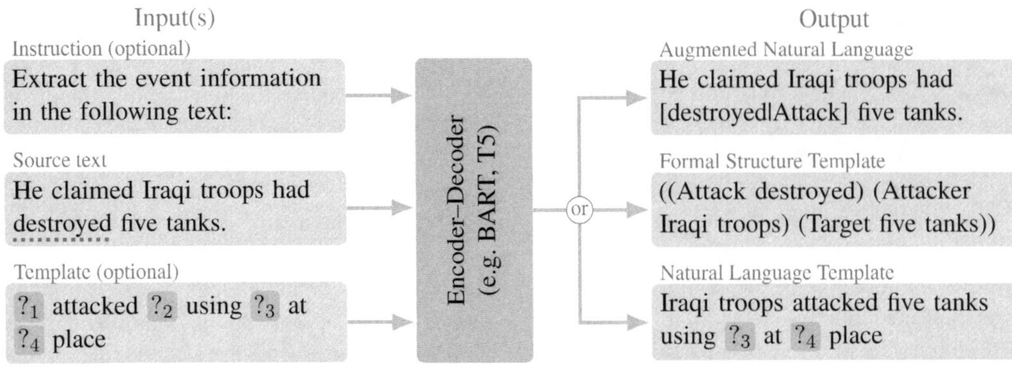

Figure 2: Schema of a standard generative event extraction model. On the left-hand side are common features given to the model as input. Some models rely only on the source text being present. A trigger word can be marked in the source text if the task being worked on is argument extraction. The inputs are generally given to an encoder–decoder model, which then generates a representation of the event. Three examples of possible outputs are shown on the right-hand side. TANL uses augmented natural language, while models based on generating a formal structure or natural language templates are described respectively in Sections 3.1 and 3.2 respectively. Note that some models do not follow this general pattern (see for example, QGA-EE).

evaluating event extraction. However, this setup is not common and makes direct comparisons of results difficult. TANL is also unique among generative models in that it is the only one that relies on offset-based annotation for training. This is because it uses an augmented text representation where the input text is generated in the model's output together with the extracted information. This can be seen in Figure 2, where the first box on the right showcases an example of TANL's output for event detection. Subsequent models only generate the structured information without generating the whole sentence. In this regard, TANL is more directly comparable to a sequence tagging scheme. For example, if the word "destroyed" appeared twice in the given example, the model would be able to distinguish between the two and tag only the relevant one.

3.1 Formal Structure Template

The first popular approach to represent events following TANL is to discard the source text from the output and keep only what is evaluated: the event structure. The exact structure used differs across models and needs only to be able to encode an associative dictionary between role and arguments (e.g. S-expression, JSON).

This approach was pioneered by **Text2Event** (Lu et al., 2021), which jointly models the ED and EAE subtasks. They use a T5 encoder–decoder model, where the encoder is given the source sentence alone and the decoder is supervised by an S-expression, as illustrated by Figure 2. The output of the model is therefore a mix of labels (event type, argument roles), structure tokens (separating the events and arguments), and input tokens (the extracted trigger and arguments) following a strict ordering. To enforce this ordering (e.g. an argument role must be followed by input tokens, then by a structure token), Text2Event introduces constrained decoding: the output vocabulary is restricted to valid tokens at each step (e.g. the softmax is only applied over tokens appearing in the input if an argument role was just generated). They show that this is particularly helpful with small training sets. Their ablation study also includes curriculum learning and shows that using natural language tokens for argument roles is preferable to arbitrary tokens. While TANL is often used as a baseline, it was not used as a basis for future work. Conversely Text2Event prompted a series of follow-up models bringing incremental improvements. For example, **Set Learning** (Li et al., 2023) improves Text2Event by attempting to enforce permutation-invariance of its output. In Text2Event a sample is supervised with a sequence of event arguments in an arbitrary order, whereas Li et al. (2023) supervises every sample with multiple orderings of the arguments and events.

The **KC-GEE** model (Wu et al., 2023) also follows most of the Text2Event architecture but uses prefix-tuning to enhance the performance on the task. Specifically, schema information – what are the possible event types and roles – is used to condi-

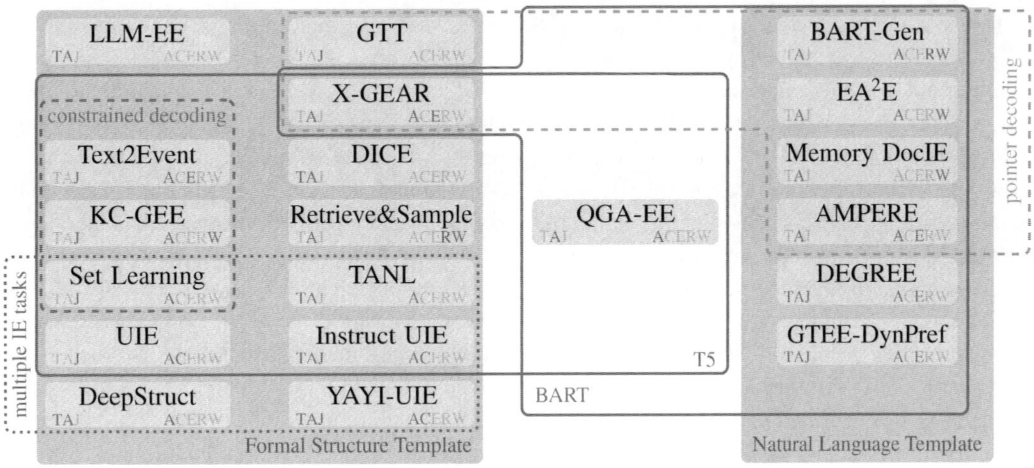

Figure 3: Overview of the models covered by the survey. The two shaded blocks correspond to the type of event representation generated by the models. The T5 and BART boxes indicate the backbone LLM of the different models. The constrained and pointer decoding boxes envelop models that do not freely generate from their entire vocabulary. Instead, their output is restricted either through a masking mechanism (constrained decoding) or by similarity with the input (pointer decoding). The multiple IE tasks box groups together models that are also used for other information extraction tasks such as named entity recognition and relation extraction. For each model, the lower left letters indicate which subtasks are tackled, while the lower right letters indicate the datasets they are evaluated on. The subtasks are: Trigger extraction & classification (ED), Argument extraction, and Joint trigger and argument extraction. A model can be used in a pipeline setup if it is marked for both trigger and argument extraction subtasks. The listed datasets are: ACE, CASIE, ERE, RAMS, and WIKIEVENTS. A slightly expanded version of this figure is presented in the appendix as Table 1.

tion both the encoder and the decoder through vector prefixes. This enables the model to generalise to unseen event types in a zero-shot setting. Additionally, KC-GEE targets document-level event extraction and incorporates a cross-attention mechanism to effectively process entire documents. KC-GEE achieves notable performance gains compared to Text2Event on WIKIEVENTS, and in the zero-shot setting.

Retrieve&Sample (Ren et al., 2023) focuses solely on document-level event argument extraction with retrieval-augmented generation (RAG). Specifically, they first retrieve top-k potentially helpful documents from the training corpus. The helpfulness of a document is computed using a T5-encoder-based siamese network from the input text and event schema. The retrieved documents are fed as an additional input to the model (Figure 2) together with the input document and schema information. They also explore two other retrieval strategies: context-consistent retrieval and schema-consistency retrieval. As it is designed for document-level extraction, the model is evaluated on RAMS and WIKIEVENTS.

Lu et al. (2022) introduce **UIE** as a unified information extraction framework via text-to-structure generation. Like TANL, the authors aim to tackle multiple IE tasks, however this is done with a formal structure similar to Text2Event. UIE formalise a unified structure for encoding different information elements (i.e. entities, relations, events), dubbed structural extraction language. The authors argue that any information extraction task can be decomposed into two atomic operations: *spotting* and *associating*; where the former operation locates relevant text spans and the latter connects the spans with a task-specific schema. The task to perform is indicated with a prefix referred to as *structural schema instructor*. For event extraction, this prefix contains the full dictionary of possible event types or roles, depending on the subtask. UIE is developed by the same team as Text2Event, and can be considered as its TANL-inspired generalisation. In particular they use an IE-specific pre-training that removes the need for constrained decoding. ACE, CASIE and PHEE are used to evaluate the models performance on the EE task. The UIE experimental setup composed of multiple IE tasks is subsequently re-used by other works we present in the next paragraphs. In parallel, Wang et al. (2022) introduce **DeepStruct**, a similar text-to-structure model which also addresses multiple IE tasks. However, they use GLM (Du et al., 2022b), a decoder-only transformer as a backbone, and only use ACE for evaluation.

Inspired by instruction tuning, Wang et al. (2023a) propose **InstructUIE** as a unified information extraction framework for multiple IE tasks in line with UIE. More specifically, all IE tasks are reformulated into the task of natural language generation with expert-designed instructions, which include a description of the output format (e.g. Output format is "type: trigger"). InstructUIE features joint training of multiple IE tasks on a collection of 32 datasets by creating a unified and consistent label set based on semantics, thus benefiting from cross-task knowledge sharing and more training data. Although InstructUIE is trained to extract the trigger and arguments jointly, it is only evaluated in a pipeline fashion on the same datasets as UIE.

Further extending instruction tuning, Xiao et al. (2024) propose **YAYI-UIE** as an end-to-end universal information extraction framework. Xiao et al. (2024) employ a two-step instruction tuning procedure: first, real-life dialogue data are used to enhance the model's capacity to understand human language instructions; second, the model is instruction fine-tuned for IE tasks on the InstructUIE datasets extended with Chinese-language datasets – in particular DuEE (Li et al., 2020b; Han et al., 2022) for event extraction. The instruction and output setup is somewhat similar to InstructUIE, except that a JSON-based format is used for the event structure. Similarly to DeepStruct, YAYI-UIE is based on a decoder-only model. They use Baichuan2 (Yang et al., 2023) as a backbone model, which is pre-trained using RLHF (Christiano et al., 2017) on English and Chinese data. YAYI-UIE achieves competitive results on the EAE subtask on the UIE experimental setup; the authors showcase in their ablation study the effectiveness of using real-life dialogue data to aid the model in understanding human instructions.

A few works evaluate decoder-only large language models (LLMs) for EE in a zero or few-shot fashion (Wang et al., 2024, 2022; Xiao et al., 2024; Wei et al., 2024), however outside of DeepStruct and YAYI-UIE, these efforts tend not to involve any fine-tuning. Worth noting is the work of Chen et al. (2024) that we refer to as **LLM-EE**. It sets out to assess the value of using pre-trained LLMs for EE, experimenting with a wide variety of different strategies. In a first suite of experiments, they prompt pre-trained LLMs to extract event information directly. Using ACE and MAVEN for evaluation, the LLMs tested include PaLM (Chowdhery et al., 2022), GPT-3.5-Turbo, and GPT-4 (OpenAI, 2024). Chen et al. (2024) report experiments for several different configurations; zero-shot and one-shot approaches, including both joint and pipeline strategies for the subtasks of ED and EAE, in addition to extraction of multiple events, for all event types simultaneously and individually. However, the results show that LLMs fall short of fine-tuned supervised approaches as was already shown by Gao et al. (2023). In a second suite of experiments, Chen et al. (2024) prompt the LLMs to generate annotated examples, aiming to improve the performance of fine-tuned models by augmenting the training data. This is motivated by the problems of data scarcity and class imbalance seen in many common datasets where certain low-frequent event types have very few annotated examples. The selection of models used for fine-tuning to evaluate the data augmentation comprises generative approaches like Text2Event discussed above. The results show that training on the augmented data yields a modest but consistent improvement in F-score (due to an increase in precision at the slight recall cost). An obvious avenue for future work left unexplored by Chen et al. (2024), is to further instruction fine-tune the LLM itself on EE specifically. Moreover, the context size of current LLMs would likely make them better positioned for document-level EE, rather than the sentence-level analysis required by datasets like ACE and MAVEN. Some works explore some specific characteristics of LLMs for EE, for example Code4Struct (Wang et al., 2023b) look at the possibility of transfer learning between python code and event structure using code-imitation prompts for few-shot event extraction. TISE (Fu et al., 2024) extends this by designing a method to select appropriate samples for the in-context learning prompts.

As described in Section 2, the template-filling dataset MUC-4 has reemerged in recent EE research. The **GTT** framework introduced by Du et al. (2021b) is one of the pioneering efforts in building an end-to-end generative model for the task of template filling, transforming it into a sequence generation problem. Although it is an encoder-only model, we include it in our survey for its seminal role. Extending the role filler entity extraction system GRIT (Du et al., 2021a), the framework relies on BERT with a partially-causal attention mask. Word prediction is done with a dot-product pointer selection mechanism to restrict output word predictions to the input vocabulary. The input includes a list of possible event types and structure tokens so that they can be generated, while the output is based on a formal structure template with a fixed set of (unlabelled) roles. In summary, GTT shows strong similarities with Text2Event, yet with some differences due to the use of BERT with a partial causal attention mask instead of an encoder–decoder. Compared to similar non-generative models, Du et al. (2021b) find that GTT performs better on MUC-4 documents with multiple events.

Some generative EE models focus on more specific problems. For example, **DICE** (Ma et al., 2023) is a T5-based model focused on the clinical domain, introducing a dataset alongside a Text2Event-like EAE model and a DEGREE-like ED model (described in the next section). Similarly, while most efforts focus on monolingual event extraction, Huang et al. (2022) explore zero-shot cross-lingual argument extraction on ACE and ERE using language-agnostic templates. They propose **X-GEAR** (Cross-lingual Generative Event Argument extractoR), which, given an input sentence, the trigger, and a type-dependent template, replaces the placeholder in the template either by generating a token or directly copying a token from the source text. The copy mechanism, adapted from See et al. (2017), conditions the generation of a token on a weighted sum of two distributions: the vocabulary distribution from the pre-trained mT5 model, serving as the backbone, and the copy probability derived from the cross-attention weights, which allows for directly copying tokens from the input sequence. Although X-GEAR is primarily developed for cross-lingual applications, it demonstrates strong performance in argument classification when both the source and target languages are English. While multiple studies (Paolini et al., 2021; Lu et al., 2021; Ren et al., 2023) highlight the benefit of using natural language for role labels in the generated template, X-GEAR conducts an ablation study showing that this approach does not generalise to cross-lingual settings.

3.2 Natural Language Template

Using natural language labels for event types and roles is expected to improve performance in the standard setup, as it allows models to leverage the LM pretraining of the backbone transformer (commonly BART). However, these architectures still use a non-natural formal structure to delimit different arguments. An alternative to this approach is to use a natural language template to structure the event as is shown on the right of Figure 2. We describe these approaches in what follows.

The first model of this type is **BART-Gen** (Li et al., 2021), a document-level EAE model. Argument extraction is framed as a conditional generation task, using a BART encoder–decoder model (Lewis et al., 2020). The output generated follows a predetermined natural language template given by the event ontology. The templates are specific to each event type and are also given in the input with special tokens in lieu of arguments. This allows BART-Gen to use a pointer-like mechanism for generation: the vectors at the output of BART-Gen are compared with the input embeddings, and the model then generates the token with the highest similarity, ensuring that all generated tokens appear in the input. Additionally, clarification statements in the form of type statements (e.g. `<arg>` is a Person), are included to avoid mismatches in entity types for arguments, and are used to re-rank the output sequences. A distinct trigger identification and classification model is introduced, as BART-Gen serves solely as an argument identification and classification system. However, this event detection model is not generative.

Zeng et al. (2022) introduce **EA^{2}E** (Event-Aware Argument Extraction) to solve document-level argument extraction by incorporating explicit event–event relations into an iterative inference process. Building upon BART-Gen (Li et al., 2021), the task is formulated as conditional generation, filling the argument placeholders of a pre-defined template. Moreover, event–event relations are also exploited by labelling the arguments of previously extracted events in the input. This allows the model to learn regularities, such as an entity previously extracted as a `Defendant` being more likely to be the `Perpetrator` in attack events. EA^{2}E performs this in an iterative fashion: first, the model generates the result for each target trigger, and then the predicted results will be used to augment the context for a second extraction. Evaluated on ACE and WikiEvents, EA^{2}E achieves advantageous results compared to previous works, such as BART-Gen. Du et al. (2022a) present a similar model evaluated on WikiEvents alone. Dubbed **Memory DocIE**, their approach takes as input a natural language template and a document, augmented with the most similar event already extracted from the document, where the latter is intended to act as a "document memory store". Event similarity is computed as the cosine between S-BERT embeddings of the filled event templates. Furthermore, all possible pairs of event roles are checked to mark incompatibilities, e.g. the `jailer` slot of an `arrest` event, is unlikely to be filled by the `attacker` of an `attack-detonate` event. The resulting constraints are enforced by masking incompatible tokens when generating arguments.

Hsu et al. (2022) propose the **DEGREE** model, targeting low-resource event extraction. While DEGREE still follows BART-Gen in that it uses BART to fill in a natural language template, it differs in how the event extraction task is approached. BART-Gen requires the event type to be known in order to select the appropriate template to be filled since the event type is traditionally extracted together with the trigger. In contrast, DEGREE still uses event-type-specific templates, but initiates them with "Event trigger is `<trigger>`" thus, it is able to perform trigger identification together with argument extraction given the event type. However, DEGREE is also trained to classify the event type. This is done by supervising the models with every possible template such that negative templates leave the `<trigger>` placeholder as-is in the output, while the correct templates would replace it with the trigger word. This means that all samples must be run through BART with all possible event templates during inference. This allows DEGREE to be used both in joint and pipeline settings. Furthermore, compared to BART-Gen, the input is extended with event type descriptions, such as "The event is related to conflict and some violent physical act.", and event keywords that are semantically similar to the event type. Compared to other generation-based models such as BART-Gen (Li et al., 2021), Text2Event (Lu et al., 2021), and TANL (Paolini et al., 2021), DEGREE shows comparable or inferior performance on sentence-level datasets. However, DEGREE's strength lies in low-resource settings, where it achieves significantly better performance even when trained on just 1% of the data.

Following DEGREE, Liu et al. (2022) introduce **GTEE-DynPref**, an approach using BART for conditional generation while attempting to ease event typing in the model's input. Usually, DEGREE's input is event-typed in two ways: through a type instruction "Event type `Meet`" and the natural language template. GTEE-DynPref replaces the type instruction with a vector representation similar to that of KC-GEE. Compared to DEGREE, an additional embedding matrix is used to associate type instruction prefix vectors to each event type. Each sample is associated with a distribution over event types using BERT. This distribution defines a convex combination of prefix vectors that are used in substitution to static type instruction. Since the type information is still enforced through the template, the model relies on training with negative event types. A 3-step curriculum learning approach used to bootstrap the type instruction embeddings further increases the complexity of the training procedure. Still, Liu et al. (2022) report competitive results on their evaluation datasets, ACE and ERE.

Hsu et al. (2023) introduce **AMPERE**, which also extends DEGREE by adding a dynamically generated prefix. This prefix incorporates structured information from abstract meaning representation (AMR) of the input passage. The AMR graph is encoded into prefix vectors using a BART-based AMR parser called SPRING (Bevilacqua et al., 2021). They show that explicit semantic structure from AMR aids event argument extraction. Compared to DEGREE, AMPERE injects AMR prefixes both into the encoder's self-attention blocks and into the decoder's cross-attention blocks. Additionally, they re-introduce a copy mechanism previously discarded by DEGREE but condition it with regularisation to encourage more frequent copying.

3.3 Iterative Question-Answering Approaches

In recent years, several efforts have approached EE as a Question-Answering (QA) task (Du and Cardie, 2020; Li et al., 2020a; Lyu et al., 2021). As a recent and generation-oriented study within this framework, Lu et al. (2023) propose the **QGA-EE** model for argument extraction, consisting of a question generation model (QG), and a question answering model (QA). Unlike models such as BART-Gen, which uses fixed templates for each event type, the sequence-to-sequence QG model generates context-aware questions tailored to the input sentence and the argument roles. A series of questions is generated for each sample, one for each role, each depending on the already extracted arguments. In order to generate the questions, the model is trained on manually created templates for each role in the ACE ontology, such as "Who was the attacking agent?" and "Who attacked `<target>`?". The QA model is trained with all possible questions as inputs and generates the answer strings corresponding to the role questions. The extracted arguments are then cross-checked with the input sentence, retaining only those that match perfectly. The authors explore the use of both BART and T5 architectures as the backbone for the QA model, finding that T5 yields better performance.

4 Summary and Outlook

This paper has surveyed the uptake of generative approaches to event extraction in NLP, presenting a range of different methods from encoder–decoders to decoder-only models. While some approaches take entire documents into account and others focus on the sentence-level, all evaluate performance based on matching predicted strings towards the strings found in the original input text.

We argue that the field has yet to embrace generative approaches to EE fully. Sticking to the traditional formulation of an "extraction" task makes it difficult to take full advantage of the capabilities of generative models like LLMs. The wide context windows of current LLMs also make them more suited for capturing more general or "complex events" – to use the words of Qi et al. (2022) – rather than the more granular and predicate-centered events typically targeted in the field so far. Going forward, we hope to see new formulations of the task itself, focusing on more high-level event analysis or understanding. By moving away from span-based and sentence-level annotations to more abstract and document-level annotations, with an evaluation methodology that correspondingly focuses on semantics rather than string matching towards a source text, we believe that the field can have a version of event analysis that will be more useful for many downstream applications (Olsen et al., 2024) and more attuned to the strengths and possibilities of generative approaches and LLMs. In fact, the arguments for such a shift from an "extractive" to an "abstractive" view could also be made for many other IE tasks in NLP where both modelling and evaluation are traditionally tied to span-based text annotations.

5 Limitations

In this survey, we adopt a narrow definition of generative methods – encoder–decoder and decoder-only transformers generating some natural language – to provide a detailed description of the systems rather than offering a broad overview. This focus allows for a more in-depth analysis but may limit the breadth of the discussion. Consequently, we are not discussing closely related work within information extraction, such as Named Entity Recognition and Relation Extraction. For readers seeking a broader perspective, we recommend the work of Huang et al. (2023) and Xu et al. (2023).

While this survey paper strives to cover all generative approaches to the task of event extraction within our scope, it is still possible that some relevant work has been unintentionally excluded, not due to a deliberate omission, but rather because it was not identified during our search. Our search was conducted across main NLP and AI venues such as ACL, EMNLP, and AAAI.

Some generative models were excluded as they did not generate natural language in their output, such as PAIE (Ma et al., 2022) and EEQA (Du and Cardie, 2020). We also excluded models such as RAP (Yao et al., 2023) as it is a generic method that could be plugged into any IE model generative or not. Some data-augmentation articles blur the line between dataset and model papers, most notably Gao et al. (2022) and are not included in our survey.

The page limit imposed on some articles made it hard to assess their characteristics, for example UIE (Lu et al., 2022) does not mention using constrained decoding in their article even though it is present in the code they provide. However, it is unclear whether this code path was actively used.

It is also worth noting that this survey does not extensively cover all datasets relevant to event extraction. The selection of datasets is guided by those used in evaluating the models the paper covers, which has led to a focus on English-language sources. Consequently, most datasets discussed in this survey are based on English, further reinforcing the overrepresentation of the English language.

Finally, while we address evaluation and performance in our discussions, we do not present evaluation scores for any of the models. Peng et al. (2023) describe several challenges in evaluating event extraction systems, highlighting issues such as discrepancies in output space and data processing, as well as the absence of pipeline evaluation, which impact the fair comparison of model performance. During the course of this research, we observed the same discrepancies in system evaluations.

6 Ethics

This work is intended to encourage further research within the framework of generative methods for event extraction. However, we acknowledge that several ethical concerns are inherent in this approach and may even be enhanced within this framework, warranting careful consideration.

Reliance on mainly English datasets for event extraction, coupled with the issue of hallucinations from large language models, might pose risks of harm and generate non-factual events, especially if not properly addressed. These risks should be given particular attention when moving towards more "abstractive" generative approaches.

Acknowledgements

This work was supported by the Research Council of Norway with funding to the *Peace Science Infrastructure* (project number 322425) and *MediaFutures: Research Centre for Responsible Media Technology and Innovation* (through the centers for Research-based Innovation scheme, project number 309339).

References

Collin F. Baker, Charles J. Fillmore, and John B. Lowe. 1998. The Berkeley FrameNet project. In *36th Annual Meeting of the Association for Computational Linguistics and 17th International Conference on Computational Linguistics, Volume 1*, pages 86–90, Montreal, Quebec, Canada. Association for Computational Linguistics.

Michele Bevilacqua, Rexhina Blloshmi, and Roberto Navigli. 2021. One spring to rule them both: Symmetric amr semantic parsing and generation without a complex pipeline. *Proceedings of the AAAI Conference on Artificial Intelligence*, 35(14):12564–12573.

Ruirui Chen, Chengwei Qin, Weifeng Jiang, and Dongkyu Choi. 2024. Is a large language model a good annotator for event extraction? *Proceedings of the AAAI Conference on Artificial Intelligence*, 38(16):17772–17780.

Aakanksha Chowdhery, Sharan Narang, Jacob Devlin, Maarten Bosma, Gaurav Mishra, Adam Roberts, Paul Barham, Hyung Won Chung, Charles Sutton, Sebastian Gehrmann, Parker Schuh, Kensen Shi, Sasha Tsvyashchenko, Joshua Maynez, Abhishek Rao, Parker Barnes, Yi Tay, Noam Shazeer, Vinodkumar Prabhakaran, Emily Reif, Nan Du, Ben Hutchinson, Reiner Pope, James Bradbury, Jacob Austin, Michael Isard, Guy Gur-Ari, Pengcheng Yin, Toju Duke, Anselm Levskaya, Sanjay Ghemawat, Sunipa Dev, Henryk Michalewski, Xavier Garcia, Vedant Misra, Kevin Robinson, Liam Fedus, Denny Zhou, Daphne Ippolito, David Luan, Hyeontaek Lim, Barret Zoph, Alexander Spiridonov, Ryan Sepassi, David Dohan, Shivani Agrawal, Mark Omernick, Andrew M. Dai, Thanumalayan Sankaranarayana Pillai, Marie Pellat, Aitor Lewkowycz, Erica Moreira, Rewon Child, Oleksandr Polozov, Katherine Lee, Zongwei Zhou, Xuezhi Wang, Brennan Saeta, Mark Diaz, Orhan Firat, Michele Catasta, Jason Wei, Kathy Meier-Hellstern, Douglas Eck, Jeff Dean, Slav Petrov, and Noah Fiedel. 2022. Palm: Scaling language modeling with pathways. *Preprint*, arXiv:2204.02311.

Paul F Christiano, Jan Leike, Tom Brown, Miljan Martic, Shane Legg, and Dario Amodei. 2017. Deep reinforcement learning from human preferences. In *Advances in Neural Information Processing Systems*, volume 30. Curran Associates, Inc.

George R Doddington, Alexis Mitchell, Mark A Przybocki, Lance A Ramshaw, Stephanie M Strassel, and Ralph M Weischedel. 2004. The automatic content extraction (ACE) program-tasks, data, and evaluation. In *International Conference on Language Resources and Evaluation*, volume 2, pages 837–840. Lisbon.

Xinya Du and Claire Cardie. 2020. Event extraction by answering (almost) natural questions. In *Proceedings of the 2020 Conference on Empirical Methods in Natural Language Processing (EMNLP)*, pages 671–683, Online. Association for Computational Linguistics.

Xinya Du, Sha Li, and Heng Ji. 2022a. Dynamic global memory for document-level argument extraction. In *Proceedings of the 60th Annual Meeting of the Association for Computational Linguistics (Volume 1: Long Papers)*, pages 5264–5275, Dublin, Ireland. Association for Computational Linguistics.

Xinya Du, Alexander Rush, and Claire Cardie. 2021a. GRIT: Generative role-filler transformers for document-level event entity extraction. In *Proceedings of the 16th Conference of the European Chapter of the Association for Computational Linguistics: Main Volume*, pages 634–644, Online. Association for Computational Linguistics.

Xinya Du, Alexander Rush, and Claire Cardie. 2021b. Template filling with generative transformers. In *Proceedings of the 2021 Conference of the North American Chapter of the Association for Computational Linguistics: Human Language Technologies*, pages 909–914, Online. Association for Computational Linguistics.

Zhengxiao Du, Yujie Qian, Xiao Liu, Ming Ding, Jiezhong Qiu, Zhilin Yang, and Jie Tang. 2022b. GLM: General language model pretraining with autoregressive blank infilling. In *Proceedings of the 60th Annual Meeting of the Association for Computational Linguistics (Volume 1: Long Papers)*, pages 320–335, Dublin, Ireland. Association for Computational Linguistics.

Seth Ebner, Patrick Xia, Ryan Culkin, Kyle Rawlins, and Benjamin Van Durme. 2020. Multi-sentence argument linking. In *Proceedings of the 58th Annual Meeting of the Association for Computational Linguistics*, pages 8057–8077, Online. Association for Computational Linguistics.

Yanhe Fu, Yanan Cao, Qingyue Wang, and Yi Liu. 2024. TISE: A tripartite in-context selection method for event argument extraction. In *Proceedings of the 2024 Conference of the North American Chapter of the Association for Computational Linguistics: Human Language Technologies (Volume 1: Long Papers)*, pages 1801–1818, Mexico City, Mexico. Association for Computational Linguistics.

William Gantt, Shabnam Behzad, Hannah An, Yunmo Chen, Aaron White, Benjamin Van Durme, and Mahsa Yarmohammadi. 2024. MultiMUC: Multilingual template filling on MUC-4. In *Proceedings of the 18th Conference of the European Chapter of the Association for Computational Linguistics (Volume 1: Long Papers)*, pages 349–368, St. Julian's, Malta. Association for Computational Linguistics.

Jun Gao, Changlong Yu, Wei Wang, Huan Zhao, and Ruifeng Xu. 2022. Mask-then-fill: A flexible and effective data augmentation framework for event extraction. In *Findings of the Association for Computational Linguistics: EMNLP 2022*, pages 4537–4544, Abu Dhabi, United Arab Emirates. Association for Computational Linguistics.

Jun Gao, Huan Zhao, Changlong Yu, and Ruifeng Xu. 2023. Exploring the feasibility of chatgpt for event extraction. *Preprint*, arXiv:2303.03836.

Cuiyun Han, Jinchuan Zhang, Xinyu Li, Guojin Xu, Weihua Peng, and Zengfeng Zeng. 2022. DuEE-Fin: A large-scale dataset for document-level event extraction. In *Natural Language Processing and Chinese Computing*, pages 172–183, Cham. Springer International Publishing.

I-Hung Hsu, Kuan-Hao Huang, Elizabeth Boschee, Scott Miller, Prem Natarajan, Kai-Wei Chang, and Nanyun Peng. 2022. DEGREE: A data-efficient generation-based event extraction model. In *Proceedings of the 2022 Conference of the North American Chapter of the Association for Computational Linguistics: Human Language Technologies*, pages 1890–1908, Seattle, United States. Association for Computational Linguistics.

I-Hung Hsu, Zhiyu Xie, Kuan-Hao Huang, Prem Natarajan, and Nanyun Peng. 2023. AMPERE: AMR-aware prefix for generation-based event argument extraction model. In *Proceedings of the 61st Annual Meeting of the Association for Computational Linguistics (Volume 1: Long Papers)*, pages 10976–10993, Toronto, Canada. Association for Computational Linguistics.

Kuan-Hao Huang, I Hsu, Tanmay Parekh, Zhiyu Xie, Zixuan Zhang, Premkumar Natarajan, Kai-Wei Chang, Nanyun Peng, Heng Ji, et al. 2023. A reevaluation of event extraction: Past, present, and future challenges. *arXiv preprint arXiv:2311.09562*.

Kuan-Hao Huang, I-Hung Hsu, Prem Natarajan, Kai-Wei Chang, and Nanyun Peng. 2022. Multilingual generative language models for zero-shot cross-lingual event argument extraction. In *Proceedings of the 60th Annual Meeting of the Association for Computational Linguistics (Volume 1: Long Papers)*, pages 4633–4646, Dublin, Ireland. Association for Computational Linguistics.

Mike Lewis, Yinhan Liu, Naman Goyal, Marjan Ghazvininejad, Abdelrahman Mohamed, Omer Levy, Veselin Stoyanov, and Luke Zettlemoyer. 2020. BART: Denoising sequence-to-sequence pre-training for natural language generation, translation, and comprehension. In *Proceedings of the 58th Annual Meeting of the Association for Computational Linguistics*, pages 7871–7880, Online. Association for Computational Linguistics.

Fayuan Li, Weihua Peng, Yuguang Chen, Quan Wang, Lu Pan, Yajuan Lyu, and Yong Zhu. 2020a. Event extraction as multi-turn question answering. In *Findings of the Association for Computational Linguistics: EMNLP 2020*, pages 829–838, Online. Association for Computational Linguistics.

Jiangnan Li, Yice Zhang, Bin Liang, Kam-Fai Wong, and Ruifeng Xu. 2023. Set learning for generative information extraction. In *Proceedings of the 2023 Conference on Empirical Methods in Natural Language Processing*, pages 13043–13052, Singapore. Association for Computational Linguistics.

Qian Li, Jianxin Li, Jiawei Sheng, Shiyao Cui, Jia Wu, Yiming Hei, Hao Peng, Shu Guo, Lihong Wang, Amin Beheshti, et al. 2022. A survey on deep learning event extraction: Approaches and applications. *IEEE Transactions on Neural Networks and Learning Systems*.

Sha Li, Heng Ji, and Jiawei Han. 2021. Document-level event argument extraction by conditional generation. In *Proceedings of the 2021 Conference of the North American Chapter of the Association for Computational Linguistics: Human Language Technologies*, pages 894–908, Online. Association for Computational Linguistics.

Xinyu Li, Fayuan Li, Lu Pan, Yuguang Chen, Weihua Peng, Quan Wang, Yajuan Lyu, and Yong Zhu. 2020b. DuEE: A large-scale dataset for chinese event extraction in real-world scenarios. In *Natural Language Processing and Chinese Computing*, pages 534–545, Cham. Springer International Publishing.

Jiangwei Liu, Liangyu Min, and Xiaohong Huang. 2021. An overview of event extraction and its applications. *arXiv preprint arXiv:2111.03212*.

Xiao Liu, Heyan Huang, Ge Shi, and Bo Wang. 2022. Dynamic prefix-tuning for generative template-based event extraction. In *Proceedings of the 60th Annual*

Meeting of the Association for Computational Linguistics (Volume 1: Long Papers), pages 5216–5228, Dublin, Ireland. Association for Computational Linguistics.

Di Lu, Shihao Ran, Joel Tetreault, and Alejandro Jaimes. 2023. Event extraction as question generation and answering. In *Proceedings of the 61st Annual Meeting of the Association for Computational Linguistics (Volume 2: Short Papers)*, pages 1666–1688, Toronto, Canada. Association for Computational Linguistics.

Yaojie Lu, Hongyu Lin, Jin Xu, Xianpei Han, Jialong Tang, Annan Li, Le Sun, Meng Liao, and Shaoyi Chen. 2021. Text2Event: Controllable sequence-to-structure generation for end-to-end event extraction. In *Proceedings of the 59th Annual Meeting of the Association for Computational Linguistics and the 11th International Joint Conference on Natural Language Processing (Volume 1: Long Papers)*, pages 2795–2806, Online. Association for Computational Linguistics.

Yaojie Lu, Qing Liu, Dai Dai, Xinyan Xiao, Hongyu Lin, Xianpei Han, Le Sun, and Hua Wu. 2022. Unified structure generation for universal information extraction. In *Proceedings of the 60th Annual Meeting of the Association for Computational Linguistics (Volume 1: Long Papers)*, pages 5755–5772, Dublin, Ireland. Association for Computational Linguistics.

Qing Lyu, Hongming Zhang, Elior Sulem, and Dan Roth. 2021. Zero-shot event extraction via transfer learning: Challenges and insights. In *Proceedings of the 59th Annual Meeting of the Association for Computational Linguistics and the 11th International Joint Conference on Natural Language Processing (Volume 2: Short Papers)*, pages 322–332, Online. Association for Computational Linguistics.

Mingyu Derek Ma, Alexander Taylor, Wei Wang, and Nanyun Peng. 2023. DICE: Data-efficient clinical event extraction with generative models. In *Proceedings of the 61st Annual Meeting of the Association for Computational Linguistics (Volume 1: Long Papers)*, pages 15898–15917, Toronto, Canada. Association for Computational Linguistics.

Yubo Ma, Zehao Wang, Yixin Cao, Mukai Li, Meiqi Chen, Kun Wang, and Jing Shao. 2022. Prompt for extraction? PAIE: Prompting argument interaction for event argument extraction. In *Proceedings of the 60th Annual Meeting of the Association for Computational Linguistics (Volume 1: Long Papers)*, pages 6759–6774, Dublin, Ireland. Association for Computational Linguistics.

Helene Olsen, Étienne Simon, Erik Velldal, and Lilja Øvrelid. 2024. Socio-political events of conflict and unrest: A survey of available datasets. In *Proceedings of the 7th Workshop on Challenges and Applications of Automated Extraction of Socio-political Events from Text (CASE 2024)*, pages 40–53, St. Julians, Malta. Association for Computational Linguistics.

OpenAI. 2024. Gpt-4 technical report. *Preprint*, arXiv:2303.08774.

Giovanni Paolini, Ben Athiwaratkun, Jason Krone, Jie Ma, Alessandro Achille, RISHITA ANUBHAI, Cicero Nogueira dos Santos, Bing Xiang, and Stefano Soatto. 2021. Structured prediction as translation between augmented natural languages. In *International Conference on Learning Representations*.

Hao Peng, Xiaozhi Wang, Feng Yao, Kaisheng Zeng, Lei Hou, Juanzi Li, Zhiyuan Liu, and Weixing Shen. 2023. The devil is in the details: On the pitfalls of event extraction evaluation. In *Findings of the Association for Computational Linguistics: ACL 2023*, pages 9206–9227, Toronto, Canada. Association for Computational Linguistics.

Zheng Qi, Elior Sulem, Haoyu Wang, Xiaodong Yu, and Dan Roth. 2022. Capturing the content of a document through complex event identification. In *Proceedings of the 11th Joint Conference on Lexical and Computational Semantics*, pages 331–340, Seattle, Washington. Association for Computational Linguistics.

Colin Raffel, Noam Shazeer, Adam Roberts, Katherine Lee, Sharan Narang, Michael Matena, Yanqi Zhou, Wei Li, and Peter J. Liu. 2020. Exploring the limits of transfer learning with a unified text-to-text transformer. *Journal of Machine Learning Research*, 21(140):1–67.

Yubing Ren, Yanan Cao, Ping Guo, Fang Fang, Wei Ma, and Zheng Lin. 2023. Retrieve-and-sample: Document-level event argument extraction via hybrid retrieval augmentation. In *Proceedings of the 61st Annual Meeting of the Association for Computational Linguistics (Volume 1: Long Papers)*, pages 293–306, Toronto, Canada. Association for Computational Linguistics.

Taneeya Satyapanich, Francis Ferraro, and Tim Finin. 2020. CASIE: Extracting cybersecurity event information from text. *Proceedings of the AAAI Conference on Artificial Intelligence*, 34(05):8749–8757.

Abigail See, Peter J. Liu, and Christopher D. Manning. 2017. Get to the point: Summarization with pointer-generator networks. In *Proceedings of the 55th Annual Meeting of the Association for Computational Linguistics (Volume 1: Long Papers)*, pages 1073–1083, Vancouver, Canada. Association for Computational Linguistics.

Zhiyi Song, Ann Bies, Stephanie Strassel, Tom Riese, Justin Mott, Joe Ellis, Jonathan Wright, Seth Kulick, Neville Ryant, and Xiaoyi Ma. 2015. From light to rich ERE: Annotation of entities, relations, and events. In *Proceedings of the 3rd Workshop on EVENTS: Definition, Detection, Coreference, and Representation*, pages 89–98, Denver, Colorado. Association for Computational Linguistics.

Zhaoyue Sun, Jiazheng Li, Gabriele Pergola, Byron Wallace, Bino John, Nigel Greene, Joseph Kim, and

Yulan He. 2022. PHEE: A dataset for pharmacovigilance event extraction from text. In *Proceedings of the 2022 Conference on Empirical Methods in Natural Language Processing*, pages 5571–5587, Abu Dhabi, United Arab Emirates. Association for Computational Linguistics.

Beth M. Sundheim. 1992. Overview of the fourth Message Understanding Evaluation and Conference. In *Fourth Message Understanding Conference (MUC-4): Proceedings of a Conference Held in McLean, Virginia, June 16-18, 1992.*

Chenguang Wang, Xiao Liu, Zui Chen, Haoyun Hong, Jie Tang, and Dawn Song. 2022. DeepStruct: Pretraining of language models for structure prediction. In *Findings of the Association for Computational Linguistics: ACL 2022*, pages 803–823, Dublin, Ireland. Association for Computational Linguistics.

Xiao Wang, Weikang Zhou, Can Zu, Han Xia, Tianze Chen, Yuansen Zhang, Rui Zheng, Junjie Ye, Qi Zhang, Tao Gui, Jihua Kang, Jingsheng Yang, Siyuan Li, and Chunsai Du. 2023a. InstructUIE: Multi-task instruction tuning for unified information extraction. *Preprint*, arXiv:2304.08085.

Xiaozhi Wang, Hao Peng, Yong Guan, Kaisheng Zeng, Jianhui Chen, Lei Hou, Xu Han, Yankai Lin, Zhiyuan Liu, Ruobing Xie, Jie Zhou, and Juanzi Li. 2024. MAVEN-ARG: Completing the puzzle of all-in-one event understanding dataset with event argument annotation. In *Proceedings of the 62nd Annual Meeting of the Association for Computational Linguistics (Volume 1: Long Papers)*, pages 4072–4091, Bangkok, Thailand. Association for Computational Linguistics.

Xiaozhi Wang, Ziqi Wang, Xu Han, Wangyi Jiang, Rong Han, Zhiyuan Liu, Juanzi Li, Peng Li, Yankai Lin, and Jie Zhou. 2020. MAVEN: A Massive General Domain Event Detection Dataset. In *Proceedings of the 2020 Conference on Empirical Methods in Natural Language Processing (EMNLP)*, pages 1652–1671, Online. Association for Computational Linguistics.

Xingyao Wang, Sha Li, and Heng Ji. 2023b. Code4Struct: Code generation for few-shot event structure prediction. In *Proceedings of the 61st Annual Meeting of the Association for Computational Linguistics (Volume 1: Long Papers)*, pages 3640–3663, Toronto, Canada. Association for Computational Linguistics.

Xiang Wei, Xingyu Cui, Ning Cheng, Xiaobin Wang, Xin Zhang, Shen Huang, Pengjun Xie, Jinan Xu, Yufeng Chen, Meishan Zhang, Yong Jiang, and Wenjuan Han. 2024. Chatie: Zero-shot information extraction via chatting with chatgpt. *Preprint*, arXiv:2302.10205.

Tongtong Wu, Fatemeh Shiri, Jingqi Kang, Guilin Qi, Gholamreza Haffari, and Yuan-Fang Li. 2023. KC-GEE: knowledge-based conditioning for generative event extraction. *World Wide Web*, pages 1–17.

Wei Xiang and Bang Wang. 2019. A survey of event extraction from text. *IEEE Access*, 7:173111–173137.

Xinglin Xiao, Yijie Wang, Nan Xu, Yuqi Wang, Hanxuan Yang, Minzheng Wang, Yin Luo, Lei Wang, Wenji Mao, and Daniel Zeng. 2024. YAYI-UIE: A chat-enhanced instruction tuning framework for universal information extraction. *Preprint*, arXiv:2312.15548.

Derong Xu, Wei Chen, Wenjun Peng, Chao Zhang, Tong Xu, Xiangyu Zhao, Xian Wu, Yefeng Zheng, and Enhong Chen. 2023. Large language models for generative information extraction: A survey. *arXiv preprint arXiv:2312.17617*.

Aiyuan Yang, Bin Xiao, Bingning Wang, Borong Zhang, Ce Bian, Chao Yin, Chenxu Lv, Da Pan, Dian Wang, Dong Yan, Fan Yang, Fei Deng, Feng Wang, Feng Liu, Guangwei Ai, Guosheng Dong, Haizhou Zhao, Hang Xu, Haoze Sun, Hongda Zhang, Hui Liu, Jiaming Ji, Jian Xie, JunTao Dai, Kun Fang, Lei Su, Liang Song, Lifeng Liu, Liyun Ru, Luyao Ma, Mang Wang, Mickel Liu, MingAn Lin, Nuolan Nie, Peidong Guo, Ruiyang Sun, Tao Zhang, Tianpeng Li, Tianyu Li, Wei Cheng, Weipeng Chen, Xiangrong Zeng, Xiaochuan Wang, Xiaoxi Chen, Xin Men, Xin Yu, Xuehai Pan, Yanjun Shen, Yiding Wang, Yiyu Li, Youxin Jiang, Yuchen Gao, Yupeng Zhang, Zenan Zhou, and Zhiying Wu. 2023. Baichuan 2: Open large-scale language models. *Preprint*, arXiv:2309.10305.

Yunzhi Yao, Shengyu Mao, Ningyu Zhang, Xiang Chen, Shumin Deng, Xi Chen, and Huajun Chen. 2023. Schema-aware reference as prompt improves data-efficient knowledge graph construction. In *Proceedings of the 46th International ACM SIGIR Conference on Research and Development in Information Retrieval*, SIGIR '23, page 911–921, New York, NY, USA. Association for Computing Machinery.

Qi Zeng, Qiusi Zhan, and Heng Ji. 2022. EA^{2}E: Improving consistency with event awareness for document-level argument extraction. In *Findings of the Association for Computational Linguistics: NAACL 2022*, pages 2649–2655, Seattle, United States. Association for Computational Linguistics.

Model	Subtasks				Datasets					Backbone	Output Structure	Template in input	Special decoding
	ED	EAE	Joint	Multiple IE	ACE	CASIE	ERE	RAMS	WikiEvent				
TANL	✔	✔	✘	✔	✔	✘	✘	✘	✘	T5	Formal	✘	✘
Text2Event	✘	✘	✔	✘	✔	✘	✔	✘	✘	T5	Formal	✘	constrained
Set Learning	✘	✘	✔	✔	✔	✘	✘	✘	✘	T5	Formal	✘	constrained
KC-GEE	✘	✘	✔	✘	✔	✘	✘	✘	✔	T5	Formal	✘	constrained
Retrieve&Sample	✘	✔	✘	✘	✘	✘	✘	✔	✔	T5	Formal	✘	✘
UIE	✘	✘	✔	✔	✔	✔	✘	✘	✘	T5	Formal	✘	✘
DeepStruct	✔	✔	✘	✔	✔	✘	✘	✘	✘	GLM	Formal	✘	✘
InstructUIE	✔	✔	✔	✔	✔	✔	✘	✘	✘	T5	Formal	*	✘
YAYI-UIE	✔	✔	✔	✔	✔	✔	✘	✘	✘	Baichuan2	Formal	*	✘
LLM-EE	✔	✔	✘	✘	✘	✘	✘	✘	✘	Several	Formal	*	✘
GTT	✘	✘	✔	✘	✘	✘	✘	✘	✘	BERT	Formal	✘	pointer
DICE	✔	✔	✘	✘	✘	✘	✘	✘	✘	T5	Formal	✘	✘
X-GEAR	✘	✔	✘	✘	✔	✘	✔	✘	✘	BART∨T5	Formal	✔	pointer
BART-Gen	✘†	✔	✘	✘	✔	✘	✘	✔	✔	BART	Natural	✔	pointer
EA^{2}E	✘	✔	✘	✘	✔	✘	✘	✘	✔	BART	Natural	✔	pointer
Memory DocIE	✘	✔	✘	✘	✘	✘	✘	✘	✔	BART	Natural	✔	pointer
DEGREE	✔	✔	✔	✘	✔	✘	✔	✘	✘	BART	Natural	✔	✘
GTEE-DynPref	✔	✔	✔	✘	✔	✘	✔	✘	✘	BART	Natural	✔	✘
AMPERE	✘	✔	✘	✘	✔	✘	✔	✘	✘	BART	Natural	✔	pointer
QGA-EE	✘	✔	✘	✘	✔	✘	✘	✘	✘	BART∨T5	Iterative	✘	✘

Table 1: List of models we introduce alongside some of their properties. This is a slightly expanded table version of Figure 3. For the "Backbone" column, a BART ∨ T5 means that the model was trained with multiple configurations, some with BART and some with T5. For the "Template in input" column, a "*" means that there is an instruction on the nature of the output, but not the exact output template. †: The BART-Gen paper describe an event detection model, but it is not generative.

Author Index

Association for Computational Linguistics
209 N. Eighth Street
Stroudsburg, Pennsylvania 18360

CURRAN ASSOCIATES INC.
proceedings.com

ISBN 979-8-3313-0846-9